The Self-Promoting Musician

Musician

Strategies For Independent Music Success

by Peter Spellman

BERKLEE PRESS

Director: Dave Kusek

Managing Editor: Debbie Cavalier

Marketing Manager: Ola Frank

Senior Writer/Editor: Jonathan Feist

Contributing Editor: David Franz

Creative Consultation by Kristen Schilo,
   Gato & Maui Productions

Design by Lisa Vaughn,
   Two of Cups Design Studio

ISBN: 0-634-00644-4

1140 Boylston Street
Boston, MA 02215-3693 USA
(617) 747-2146

Visit Berklee Press Online at:
www.berkleepress.com

DISTRIBUTED BY

HAL•LEONARD®
CORPORATION
7777 W. BLUEMOUND RD. P.O. BOX 13819
MILWAUKEE, WISCONSIN 53213

Visit Hal Leonard Online at:
www.halleonard.com

Table of Contents

Acknowledgments **v**

Dedication **vi**

PART ONE: preparation

1. What's New About the New Music Business? **3**
2. Plan Your Work, Work Your Plan: Writing a Music Business Plan That Works **21**
3. Getting Ready to Do Business **37**
4. Empowering Resources for Self-Managed Musicians **47**
5. Have You Thought of Starting Your Own Record Label? **61**

PART TWO: going forward

6. How's Your Net Working? Increasing Your Contacts in the Music Industry **71**
7. Impressive Promo Kits **77**
8. Creative Publicity and Promotional Ideas for Musicians **87**
9. Finding Gigs in All the Right Places: Tapping the Sources of Lesser-Known Music Work **93**
10. Booking Club Gigs: Getting Your Foot in the Door without Getting It Slammed **103**
11. Live Deals: The Ins and Outs of Performance Contracts **109**
12. Twelve Things You Can Do to Get the Most Out of Every Gig **117**

PART THREE: rising up

13. Demo Diversity: Customizing Your Demos for Maximum Exposure **125**
14. Media Power: Creating a Music Publicity Plan That Works, Part 1 **131**
15. Media Power: Creating a Music Publicity Plan That Works, Part 2 **139**
16. Getting Played on College Radio **147**
17. Multimedia and Musicians: What It's About and How to Get Involved **161**
18. Using the Internet to Promote Your Music **179**

PART FOUR: staying fed

MUSICIANS' RESOURCE DIRECTORY: Customized for Music Performers &
Recording Artists, Music Composers & Songwriters, Music Industry Careerists,
Music Technology Careerists, and Music Educators & Therapists. Includes highly
rated books, magazines, organizations, and Web sites for each area. Updated
continually on-line! **211**

INDEX **244**

FIGURES & SIDEBARS

Figure 1.1   Anatomy of a Multinational Corporation......5

Figure 1.2   Inside a Record Label.................................6

Figure 1.3   Income Flow in the Recording Industry....19

Figure 2.1   Comparing Legal Structures for
Your Business...27

Figure 2.2   The Time/Money Marketing Concept...........31

Sidebar 3.1 Some Select SBA Publications 41

Figure 3.1   Business Letter Writing Tips.....................43

Figure 4.1   The Many Dimensions of Artist/
Band Management...49

Sidebar 4.1 Information Is Power 52

Figure 4.2   Seven Ways to Get the
Most Out of Your Day................................54

Figure 4.3   Be Your Own Best Manager 57

Sidebar 5.1 Create Strong Partnerships 67

Figure 6.1   Keep a Phone Contact Log.......................74

Figure 9.1   Booking Research Worksheet......................96

Figure 9.2   Performance Critique Worksheet.................99

Figure 11.1 Sample Performance Agreement...............113

Sidebar 11.1 When You Need a Music Lawyer..............114

Figure 14.1 Media Choices Compared..........................133

Figure 16.1 On the Radio Dial....................................148

Figure 16.2 How Radio Stations Are Organized...........151

Figure 16.3 Radio Formats 152

Figure 16.4 Radio Phone Log......................................154

Figure 16.5 DJ Response Card......................................156

Figure 17.1 Top Video Game Producers.......................163

Figure 17.2 Infomedia Convergence...............................165

Figure 17.3 Top Multimedia Producers 175

Figure 17.4 Top Software Game Publishers...................175

Figure 18.1 Our Technology Culture 181

Figure 18.2 Commerce by Computer..............................183

Figure 18.3 Web's World Widens..................................185

Figure 18.4 Cybermarketing 189

Sidebar 18.1 Netiquette 201

Sidebar 18.2 Getting Wired 204

ACKNOWLEDGMENTS

So many friends have had a hand in helping this work come into the world, but two stand out in particular. Thanks to Steven Kercher of Candescent Music Group for his creative ideas and initial editing of the manuscript. Thanks also to Robert Bloodworth, my "right (and often left)-hand man" at Berklee College of Music, for his ongoing support, encouragement and rich spirit.

A special thanks also goes out to The Mighty Charge and Friend Planet, two music groups with which I have performed, through which many of this book's lessons were learned. It is the inspiring example of musicians themselves (not always valued in a society that measures success by mutual fund performance) that has informed the writing of this book. Many thanks to musicians everywhere who have lived and taught the "independent" way.

I would also like to acknowledge the enthusiasm and support of Berklee Press as they shepherded this project along from rough manuscript to finished product. Special thanks to Senior Writer/Editor Jonathan "Eagle Eye" Feist for his patience and consummate copyediting skills.

Finally, I wish to thank my wife and family for their support and enthusiasm through the writing of this book and beyond. It is with great love and appreciation that this book is dedicated to them.

Peter Spellman
December, 1999

for linda—

earth to my dreams

PART ONE:
preparation

chapter

What's New About the New Music Business?

Five recording and distribution companies dominate the global music industry. Together, they manufacture and distribute over two hundred record labels, supplying music wholesalers and retailers with about 80% of the U.S. market. They are: Universal Music Group (UMG), Warner-Elektra-Atlantic (WEA), BMG Distribution, Sony Music Entertainment, and CEMA/UNI Distribution.

On the other side of the coin are over 2,500 "indie" labels, distributed by nearly 300 independent record distributors and accounting for most of the remaining 20% of recorded music sales (small by comparison, but still over $2 billion per year). These figures, of course, do not include the thousands of new releases by artists not affiliated with any distributor who record and release their own music.

In contrast to non-music industries, some of which have been in existence for hundreds of years, the record industry as recently as forty years ago was, by and large, a back room affair. In one short generation, it became a worldwide $40 billion industry, bigger than both the book publishing and motion picture industries. The music business grew so quickly, in fact, that no one has yet been able to figure out how to run the store. Joe Smith, former president-CEO of Capitol-EMI Music and industry veteran, confesses: "We created this business and made it up as we went along because we didn't understand all the things happening around us." He has also remarked, "Future planning in this business is where we're going to lunch Thursday."

But the business was changing, and in 1994, Smith decided to look into new opportunities. "I began to realize how administrative this job had become, so involved with numbers and logistics…I didn't want to do that for a long-term future."

Many have complained that the music industry is run by lawyers and accountants. The feeling is that the record business has become so concerned with the bottom line and with short-term profit that artists who once would have had time—three or four albums to develop a sound and a following—now have one, maybe two albums to "break" (start selling) before they lose their contracts. Some in the industry would prefer to treat music like other industries treat cars and refrigerators. But music cannot be treated as such. As the creative extensions of human spirit, music will always defy attempts at control. Often, just when the majors catch up with a "new" music trend, they find that that the market has shifted and music lovers have moved on to something else.

Short-Term Corporate Profits vs. Long-Term Music Careers

It's important to understand that music industry staff who are involved in acquiring, developing and marketing artists are not simply working for record companies. As Tony Powell, then-managing director of MCA Records remarked in 1992, "Record companies don't see themselves as record companies anymore. They see themselves as entertainment companies." Since the late 80s these companies have been explicitly defining themselves as "global" organizations (see Fig. 1.1 "Anatomy of a Multinational Corporation").

Record companies are concerned with developing global personalities exploitable across multiple media: recordings, videos, films, television, magazines, and books, and via advertising, product endorsement and sponsorship over a range of consumer merchandise. The quest is for entertainment icons whose sound and image can be inserted into the media and communication networks, which are enveloping the globe.

A look at the inner dynamics of record companies reveals some all-too-common human frailties that often result in artists feeling constrained in their careers. In the past, executives might sign artists without consideration of the opinions of other personnel within their company. However, as the costs of producing and marketing popular music have increased, and as record companies have been reorienting themselves towards entertainment rather than just music, other divisions within the corporations have begun exerting a greater influence over the type of artists that are acquired.

In addition to working with artists, all divisions of the record company (see Fig. 1.2 "Inside a Record Label") are attempting to represent themselves as an indispensable component of the recording industry. The day-to-day work of dealing predominantly with one specific medium—whether the music, the image in the video, the radio media, or the press—tends to result in different staff assessing the potential of artists in different ways and developing their own

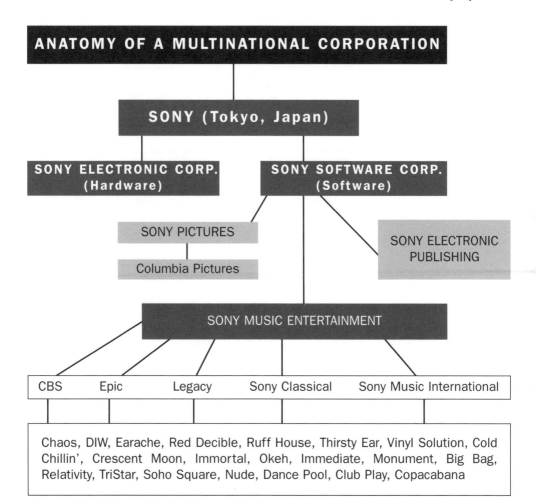

ANATOMY OF A MULTINATIONAL CORPORATION

SONY (Tokyo, Japan)

SONY ELECTRONIC CORP.
(Hardware)

SONY SOFTWARE CORP.
(Software)

SONY PICTURES

Columbia Pictures

SONY ELECTRONIC
PUBLISHING

SONY MUSIC ENTERTAINMENT

| CBS | Epic | Legacy | Sony Classical | Sony Music International |

Chaos, DIW, Earache, Red Decible, Ruff House, Thirsty Ear, Vinyl Solution, Cold Chillin', Crescent Moon, Immortal, Okeh, Immediate, Monument, Big Bag, Relativity, TriStar, Soho Square, Nude, Dance Pool, Club Play, Copacabana

Sony is a good example of a multinational entertainment corporation where music is just one "division" within the parent company. Sony Corporation is a $36 billion a year electronic software and hardware producer and manufacturer. Sony bought CBS Records in 1988 for $3.5 billion and the film division (Columbia and TriStar Pictures) in 1989 for $4.5 billion. Affiliates are CHAOS Records, Epic, Epic Associated, Epic Soundtrax, Sony 550 Music, Sony Wonder, TriStar Music Group, Sony Tree Music Publishing, Sony Pictures Entertainment, the TriStar movie studios, Columbia Records, and Robert de Niro's Tribeca movie and film production company. Sony Music also has has a joint venture partnership with other multinationals to sell its products through The Columbia House record club.

Prepared by MUSIC BUSINESS SOLUTIONS

Fig. 1.1

INSIDE A RECORD LABEL

STOCKHOLDERS OF LABEL'S PARENT COMPANY

Chairman and Board of Parent Company

President of Parent Company

Label President

Vice Presidents of

Business Affairs	Legal Affairs	A&R	Merchandising & Marketing	Manufacturing	Distribution	Finance	Internal Operations
MBAs OR LAWYERS WHO NEGOTIATE:	**IN-HOUSE LAWYERS, INCLUDING:**	**SEPARATE EXPERTS FOR EACH DEPT.:**	**PRODUCT MANAGERS WHO COORDINATE:**		**CPAs AND ASSISTANTS WHO CONTROL:**		
Artist Contracts	Copyright & Patent Law	Rock/Pop	In-house cover artists and graphic designers	Pressing Plants and Cassette Duplication	Direct Sales to Major Accounts, Chains, etc.	Purchasing	Buildings and Grounds
Publisher Mechanical Licenses & Rates	Interstate & international Licensing	Metal	LP, CD Mastering, etc	Printing of Jackets, Promo Materials, etc.	Shipping of Product	Royalty Payment, Artists & Publishing	Inter-Office Mail
AFM Phono Labor Agreement Revisions	Union Relations	Adult Contemporary	National Album and Single Promotions	Special Products for in-house use and outside clients	Receiving & Accounting & Returns	Accounting	Telephone & Data Systems
Video	Corporate Law	R&B/Dance	Field Promotion	Sub-contracting of excess requirements for Christmas & summer rush	Regional Distribution Centers, each with: Salesmen, Promo People, Warehousing, Delivery, Accounting, Collection	Inventory Control	Personnel
Production Contracts	Entertainment Law, All kinds; who write contracts for: Artist signings, Mechanical Licenses, Master Licenses, Video Prod.	Jazz	Radio Tracking			Tax Report Preparation	Secretaries & Receptionist
Foreign Licensing Deals		Easy Listening	Print & Media Advertising			Payables	Janitorial
		Classical	Coop-Advertising				Tape Library and Vaults
		Subsidiary or Associated labels					Restoration

6

Fig. 1.2

agendas and goals rather than working towards a shared overall vision.

Tensions and turf battles (especially between Artists and Repertoire [A&R] and Marketing) have thus become a "normal" part of the record company work climate. A major label president confided to me that when he assumed his post he was astonished to discover how little company departments actually communicated with each other on projects necessitating joint-action. One of his first acts was to call all staff members out of their offices into the hallway for an ad-hoc powwow just to dramatize his concern.

This incident highlights an ongoing problem for artists signed to major labels. With ten to thirty monthly releases, major labels and their respective departments cannot possibly get behind every single record. Each album may have a formal marketing plan but that plan can be cut short if another record scores a hit. Company resources are suddenly tipped in favor of the smoker and other releases will often get left in the lurch.

Further, interdepartmental rivalries and power plays lead to high job turnover. An artist's lead champion (often the one who initiated the signing) leaves the company for another and the artist is stuck—no longer a priority, yet tied to the record company for up to five more years. And it doesn't have to be someone leaving that changes the artist's destiny. It may also be the arrival of a new executive with a different agenda.

Many in the New England area are familiar with the band O-Positive, an award-winning act that filled rooms, pretested its product and had strong industry representation when it signed with Epic Records in 1989. Everything was going swimmingly. A generous recording and publishing advance enabled band members to quit their day jobs and focus on the task of recording their major label debut.

Once the record was completed, however, an upper level management purge occurred at Epic. Many of the familiar executives with whom the band was dealing were gone. In addition, there was a unilateral reassessment of the label's commitment to "baby bands." Video budgets were slashed across the board, tour support, independent radio promotion, and publicity were non-existent. The record was released with no support, and as a result, O-Positive's major label debut never had the chance to reach its audience.

A similar fate befell Lucinda Williams. Signed to RCA by Bob Buziak, she was wisely linked with record producer Peter Moore because he was sympathetic to her idiosyncratic blend of country, folk, and blues. However, Buziak left RCA and other staff had to be found to manage his acts. Williams was allocated a young executive who suggested she work with a "hit producer," thereby exhibiting a profound lack of knowledge and misunderstanding of her genre. Seeking to transform her into a straightforward Top 40 artist, he instead created a disillusioned artist. Fortunately, Williams' career received a second chance in the late '90s.

A lot of records are released in the hope and belief that they will succeed. However, there are occasions when staff know that a particular record is not going to make it, but are obliged to go through the motions anyway. This is done to maintain a relationship with an artist, lawyer, or manager, and is variously referred to as a "political signing," "grace and favor deal," "courtesy signing," or "public relations exercise." If a manager represents a successful act, for example, then that manager can often use the incentive of future access to that act to persuade companies to sign other artists.

Alternatively, major artists themselves may be able to get deals for their friends, with senior record company staff issuing contracts merely to keep an artist happy, rather than for any creative or commercial reasons. A marketing director at one of the labels confided that it was often easier to put out a record than fight with a manager who was important to the company.

A lot of the above goes far in explaining why nine out of ten newly signed artists never go on to record, much less release, a second record. This kind of mortality rate would sink almost any other industry but it's acceptable in music. Sort of gives a whole new meaning to the industry phrase "breaking an act," doesn't it? Perhaps it's time to dismantle the myth that a major recording deal is the ultimate Holy Grail of music career success.

Taking a New Approach

Artists seeking a major recording contract should seriously reconsider. It cannot be assumed that your record company will act in your best interest. Just the fact that musical artists are expected to foot the bill for the production of their music (just one of many "recoupments") should alert us to the horribly anti-artist bias prevalent in all major recording contracts. Do "signed" screenwriters, directors or actors have to pay for the production of their films? No, they don't. Do "signed" writers have to pay for the production of their books? Very rarely. The companies themselves assume this risk.

The incessant quest to repeat and clone "hits" is also ruining record companies. It's what I call the "all or nothing" investment strategy. Unless the act

comes screaming out of the starting blocks with a "hit" album, it will not survive past its first or second album. Running multinational record companies like
McDonald's franchises may be less stressful for the business affairs departments
of these labels. However, unlike hamburgers, homogenized music that looks and
sounds the same is ultimately doomed to failure.

Fortunately, with or without the bureaucratic corporate empires, music will
flourish simply because it doesn't need a megastructure. A number of trends
are encouraging this. While the dynamic nature of the industry resists full rational study, we can discern five broad characteristics, or "megatrends," that mark
the industry on the eve of the new millennium. As you read the following
pages, think of ways your music career can engage creatively with each broad
trend.

Increasing Demand for Music-Making

In 1967 the American record industry passed the billion dollar annual sales
mark for the first time. By 1973 annual sales had reached $2 billion, and by
1978 the industry had achieved sales of more than $4 billion. Music, by then,
had become the most popular form of entertainment.

Consider these current facts:

- Americans spend more money buying prerecorded music and videos than
  they do going to movies or attending sporting events.
- One out of five Americans plays a musical instrument. These musicians
  spend more than $5.6 billion a year on instruments, accessories, and sheet
  music.
- The annual sale of cassettes, CDs, records, and music videos, combined
  with their primary delivery medium, broadcasting, exceeds the GNP of
  over 80 countries in the UN.
- We own more CD and tape players than bathtubs, refrigerators and wash-
  ing machines.

Recorded music sales steadily increased from 1984 (after a brief slump
period) and have only begun leveling out over the past two years. According
to the Recording Industry Association of America's (RIAA) annual report,
recorded music sales for 1998 were $40.8 billion worldwide, of which America
had a 27% share (roughly $12 billion).

While rock and pop music account for the bulk of the music demand, let's not forget other "taste cultures." The American Symphony Orchestra League reports that there are more than 20,000 symphony concerts given every year. This particular audience now exceeds 24 million paying customers each season. Opera continues to attract its loyal audience, now being served by more than 300 professional and semiprofessional companies in the United States alone. Regarding classical music, the RIAA reports that sales figures for this repertoire now exceed those for jazz. This tremendous growth in music production and consumption is not unique to the United States. The rate of growth is even faster in some foreign countries, like Japan.

One of the fastest growing demands for music-making is now coming from visual media: television and film. With digital compression, cable channel selection will soon increase from 100 to over 300, and each new channel will require a certain amount of music. TV is already doing double-duty as a jukebox. And what about commercials? Have you noticed the increased use of "cutting edge" music and rhythms in this format?

It is interesting to note that only a small part of the time spent on musical consumption consists of that devoted to listening to tapes, CDs and albums bought in the stores by consumers, the traditional source of revenue for the music industry. An increasingly important objective of the music industry is that of acquiring a greater share of revenue from music that is "freely" consumed by people, as they listen to the radio, watch television, and so on.

The use of music in advertisements, motion pictures, and television series offers a domain in which considerable revenues are generated for the music industry. We are already seeing a pronounced shift of record company income from primary sources (selling records) to secondary sources (collection of publishing and performing rights). The old music business of selling packages of music to relatively passive consumers will remain a large business for quite some time. But a very different sort of music business is growing up alongside it.

Music demands are also coming from places traditionally uninvolved with music. As once disparate industries converge on the digital common, the need for audio creation, production, and performance talent increases. Industries as far-flung as book publishing, computers, and telecommunications are setting up music divisions and galvanizing new music career opportunities as a result.

THE LESSON?   Ask not where music is *sold*, but where music is *used*. When most of us consider the best places to grow a music career, we often think of the stage and the store; the stage is where you perform your music, the store is where you sell your music. These are where music has traditionally been sold. But what about the thousands of places where music is used?

Today, the uses of music have multiplied beyond our wildest dreams—not only in movies, shows, television, and jingles, but in computer video games, MIDI software, corporate and educational videos, background music services, audio books, even greeting cards! All of these uses are accomplished by a variety of licenses acquired and paid for by the user.

The best source for locating these opportunities is your own imagination. Where is music being used in your own environment? What possible outlets and inlets are waiting for you in your business, education and artistic communities? Brainstorm, make a list and start networking!

Music demand is greater now than it has ever been before, and this is great news for musicians.

Increasing Diversity of Music-Making

Music pundits love to ask the question: What's the "Next Big Thing" going to be? But I don't think this question is relevant any longer. The contemporary music scene amounts to a huge mobile-home park with dozens of self-contained trailers. The few musicians who have approached the "Next Big Thing" status—Pearl Jam, Green Day—don't even seem to want the mantle; they're suspicious of success and its accompanying responsibilities. Add it all up, and the very concept of one artist who can unite a large pop audience and help shape and define it (a la Elvis, The Beatles, or Bruce Springsteen) seems about as dead as the 45-rpm spindle. Next Big Thing? More like "Next Modest Thing That Might Appeal to a Portion of the Demographic."

Why? Because the music market is segmenting. This is most apparent in the ever-exploding variety of music styles and sub-styles. Statistics of recorded music sales since 1987 indicate, for example, that Rock's share of the pie has plunged from 65% to 29% in less than ten years. The slack has been taken up by rival genres like country, hip-hop, and the "others" category, which encompasses everything from ambient to zydeco. The 1990s have witnessed the number one slot in the Billboard album charts being held by artists as diverse as Metallica (heavy metal), Michael Jackson (pop), Garth Brooks (country), Nirvana (grunge), Aerosmith (rock), Snoop Doggy Dog (rap), and Ace of Base (Swedish pop).

Rapid segmentation spells trouble for the Big Five record companies, which must now work harder for a shrinking piece of the market. Segmentation does mean more markets, but they're smaller and harder to reach. Sony can't just keep selling more Mariah Carey albums; to compete globally it also has to figure out how to be a player in, say, the booming German market for "schlager" folk music. Of course, indies like Koch Germany and Fiesta, which specialize in schlager, are breaking open a lot of champagne these days.

THE LESSON: Find your niche. Discover an area of music that provides you with enough satisfaction for both your soul and your wallet, and then master it. When you focus on a niche, you can target your efforts more effectively.

This means matching your unique personality, values and skills to a particular music career path. Don't just position yourself as a bassist; become known as "a creative bassist specializing in funk, reggae, ska and salsa." In other words, own your territory. You need not fear missing opportunities by focusing. You can always add other dimensions to your path as you grow. The point is, the market has splintered into a thousand niches. Each music genre and each music instrument has its own media culture (magazines, radio shows, Web sites, newsgroups, etc.) that you can explore and use to promote your thing.

Increasing Professionalization of Music-Making

The music industry grew so rapidly in the 1960s (owing to rock's explosion), companies could not find enough qualified people to handle their affairs. The fast talkers and "snake oil peddlers" wormed their way into executive offices, and some still hide out there. But that was then, this is now.

Over the past twenty years or so, hucksters, gamblers, and amateurs have been replaced by responsible team players-educated musicians, trained managerial teams, degreed agents, and so on, who are paid not so much to take risks but to provide a fixed skill. The industry also became dominated by lawyers and accountants, and by the 1980s there was very little tension between musicians and "the business." Rock performers were more likely to complain about companies not exploiting them properly than to object to being "commercialized." Others, like those in the punk movement, avoided the industry altogether and developed their own DIY (do-it-yourself) network.

Professionalization has often been a bittersweet pill for musicians to swallow. The enthronement of lawyers and accountants often resulted in a general decline of creative direction in the larger record companies and a subsequent homogenization of pop music. Formulaic, least-common-denominator sounds began to dominate the airwaves and retail bins.

Artists in general tend to prefer a more casual approach to everything, including business. But like it or not, if you don't have your personal and business act together today, you'll find yourself with a lot of open weekends.

But this doesn't mean you can't use industry professionalization to your own advantage. Professionalization raises the expectations standard throughout the industry in terms of how business should be conducted. Professionalism means higher standards of presentation and communication, as well as greater attention to business and marketing strategy. Those with a handle on contemporary business practices will make more effective and efficient progress in the contemporary music world. Today's self-managed musician needs to understand the rules governing this game or risk being benched.

THE LESSON: Being "professional" means being punctual, calling when you're going to be late, following up, typing your letters on attractive stationery, watching the length of your breaks between sets, and dressing appropriately.

It also means seeking the education and training you need, and proceeding with strength. Many adult and continuing education courses are offered in basic computer training, business communications, and creative marketing. You can even take courses in overcoming shyness, networking, and developing your telephone chops. The sooner you acquire the tools and knowledge you need, the sooner you will make the progress you crave in your music career. See chapters two and three for numerous other ways you can develop business professionalism.

Miniaturization of Music-Making

First came the cumbersome gramophone, then the long-playing record, next came tape players/recorders, then CDs, briefly DAT, then DCC (digital compact cassettes) and the MD (mini-disc), and now MP-3 players no bigger than a pack of cigarettes. Everything has become smaller. Think, too, of performance—from the big bands of the thirties and forties, to the seven-piece fusion groups of the sixties, to trios like The Police, and now soloists with synthesizers—everything has become smaller. There are still exceptions, but generally there has been a slow but steady miniaturization of music-making.

Smallness has also become a plus for companies that produce music. As music technology becomes more accessible we are seeing a proliferation of great music from places way outside the Los Angeles/New York/Nashville nexus. Increasingly, independent production companies have emerged as the seedbeds for new talent. The "indies" are now more important than ever. Indie market share is growing. They're the ones breaking new acts, developing market niches and regionally pretesting their artists.

The major record companies, on the other hand, are optimized for largeness. Today, they tend to act more like film distributors than production houses. They have the resources and capital to take new music to the masses, but little ability to create such music themselves. In other words, they are ponderous giants with little agility. Distribution is the only key holding indies back from becoming truly "independent." But it appears likely that in the near future, music distribution will have its equivalent to desktop publishing and transmission.

Technology has radically changed the relationship between creator, producer, distributor, retailer, and consumer. Within a short period of time, the music industry has transformed itself into an operation that makes use of, and relies heavily on emerging new technologies. At a grassroots level, this process began where music is created—in the recording studio, where engineers found themselves parting from analog and moving onto digital transmission.

Digital tools and resources today are vast, plentiful and increasingly more affordable: desktop multitrack recorders, MIDI, digital samplers, keyboard workstations, personal computers and the World Wide Web are transforming how we create, perform, produce, market, and distribute our music. Technology has been the central force behind the evolution of popular music, and each new development has allowed the emergence of a "new sound." Yet, it does not stop here.

As digital recording formats fall in price, it is possible for anyone with a personal computer and a recordable CD to record, master, and manufacture CDs of their own music (or that of others) individually, or in quantity, for a reasonable price. With computer graphic software, all CD tray inserts and other artwork can be produced as well. Recording studio, mastering facility, pressing plant and art department all on a desktop. The home studio becomes the home record company. Miniaturization again.

THE LESSON: The implications of these developments for musicians are nothing short of revolutionary. Technology has given young musical entrepreneurs a way to end-run the established powers. Street-level music technologies (synths, samplers, tape decks, turntables) have spawned whole new musical genres such as rap, industrial, and the many flavors of techno.

Using much-improved digital home recording equipment and independent studios, it's now possible to produce a quality album for as little as $2,000—about a hundredth of what it could cost to record at high overhead Sony or Time Warner. With a $1,299 iMac and a few hundred dollars, worth of software, an artist will be able to record, mix and master their album, then make it available on their Web site to fans throughout the world. Miniaturization of music technology is enabling musicians to have, once again, complete control over the creative processes of production and promotion.

Sensualization of Music-Making

By "sensualization" I don't just mean eroticization (though this is certainly part of it), but the growing involvement of other senses in music production and consumption beyond the auditory. Music-making is becoming increasingly multimedia and, therefore, multi-sensory. As already mentioned, record companies are repositioning themselves as entertainment companies. The new goal of these companies is to exploit their artist/stars on a global scale and create "synergies" (i.e., powerful alliances) across other "divisions" within the parent corporation. Ideally, they want stars who can sing a song, star in a video, perform on stage, act in a movie, write a book, schmooze with TV culture, and if at all possible, develop clothing, perfume and food product lines as well.

Here's a trick question: Want to take a guess at which is the largest music broadcasting station in the world? Ironically, it's a television station! MTV was born August 1, 1981, the brainchild of Warner Communications. By 1998, it was reaching a potential audience of more than 100 million viewers in 70 countries, injecting a lethargic record industry with a fiscal shot in the arm. Music Television has influenced not only the music business, but also film, advertising, television, and virtually all aspects of youth culture, leaving the *Washington Post* to call it "perhaps the most influential single cultural product of the decade." Whoa!

So, music video is here to stay. Visuals are now a necessary accompaniment to the music from the major label's perspective, and there's no doubt

15

about video's power to create success. Janet Jackson, Paula Abdul, Milli Vanilli, and Bobby Brown were all wallowing in obscurity before MTV exposure sent their records to multi-platinum status. Of course, the ultimate example of a multimedia music career is Madonna. After inking a $60 million deal with Warner Brothers, the music diva's cultural repertoire rapidly expanded to include print, film, fashion, music, and most of all, her music videos. As mini-events that artfully combine her music and persona, Madonna's more than 75 music videos have contributed largely to her success as multimedia star.

Music video, however, is really just the tip of a huge iceberg that is destined to completely transform the experience of music-making. Amazing, almost science-fictionlike developments are changing the basis of our interactions with creative technology, on a fundamental level. Computers equipped with three-dimensional sound and visuals can now immerse the user in an artificial (i. e., virtual) reality, where fantasy and magic replace the accepted rules of nature. At the same time, interactive media (CD-I, etc.) are bringing exciting new forms of entertainment, education and creativity to life. These capabilities are revolutionizing our ideas about computers and music, irreversibly transforming the process of artistic and musical creation, and providing new ways to distribute and present multimedia productions. The first crop of virtual reality and interactive music products are in the market. With them, we are able to create software-based instruments and controllers that are free from the constraints of physical law.

But virtual reality can't free us from the constraints of our own imagination and creativity. In the end, the music still has to come from us. The point is, however, to become aware of this trend and not to be caught with your head in the sand. The new technologies present tremendous opportunities for an unprecedented "sensualization" of musical expression.

THE LESSON: It's a 'multimedia' world and creative alliances that cross industries are the key to survival. I had the gratifying experience of seeing what this means while working on a multimedia project this past year.

My partner and I (collectively known as Friend Planet) became involved in scoring a video game designed to educate diabetic kids about self-care. It turns out that a large Boston hospital has a special division that develops multimedia products for chronically ill children. There we were—musicians collaborating with physicians, computer animators, programmers and interface designers. Unusual and highly satisfying. Multi-media. Multi-sensual.

Globalization of Music-Making

Ever since the inception of Armed Forces Radio during WWII, American pop-ular music has been penetrating every nook and cranny of the planet. As of 1999, one of every four people on the planet is able to watch MTV. Its owner, Viacom Corp., is predicting that the cable channel will bring in more money internationally within eight years than it makes domestically. A basic charac-teristic of the international music industry has been its domination by American interests—not only in terms of product and flow, but also in its legal, political, and economic practices. Simultaneously, the U.S. share of recorded music sales has dropped to 27%, from over 60% just thirty years ago.

Other countries are asserting their own sounds, a trend reflected by the structures of major record company ownership. CBS is now part of the Japanese Sony empire; RCA has been absorbed by Bertlesman Group (BMG), a German-based company whose central interests are publishing and distrib-uting books and magazines. As the other three "majors" (Thorn-EMI and UMG) are based in Great Britain and Canada respectively, WEA (Warner/Elektra/Atlantic) is the only American major label left.

Most of these mergers and acquisitions took place during the 1980s. The domination of the "West over the Rest" in the distribution of internationalized popular music is still, however, inarguable. The purchase of CBS Records by a Japanese company has not altered the Anglo-American content of interna-tionalized music. Sony bought CBS primarily to acquire its popular music repertoire. However, the direction of profit flow will almost certainly be affect-ed. Many people have, understandably, expressed concern about the largely unidirectional flow of musical product around the world, fearing it will adversely affect cultural diversity.

While the globalization of the music industry appears at first glance to spell world cultural homogenization, the reality shows a different picture. What we see in almost every country are local musicians who are producing new com-binations of musical elements and adding to global cultural diversity. They are not all sounding alike. In fact, within and among countries, there is an amazing diversity of music as creative musicians experiment with new forms and sounds. From Bulgaria to Boston, Zaire to Martinique and New York to Paris, pop is going global. As never before, exotic imports and weird new hybrids are flourishing: Polish reggae, Moroccan flamenco, even Cambodian heavy metal are on the rise.

Additionally, peripheral musicians are becoming indirectly acquainted with each other's music through small, self-production recording and distribution processes that do not depend upon the mediation of the core industry. The result of these interactions is a new eclectic approach to music-making and marketing.

In observation of this new eclecticism, the core industry itself has begun to look to all cultures for potential raw materials and consequently its former rock 'n' roll center has splintered into many subcategory fragments. Music has become increasingly experimental and fragmented while at the same time its once diverse and exotic elements are becoming more widely familiar, more accepted, and more predictable. The richness of world-cultural music and its arrival on these shores is perhaps one of the most refreshing trends in the music industry today, and this movement is expected to continue.

THE LESSON: A shrinking planet combined with far-reaching communications technologies allows today's artists to mount a global presence. Internet-based music services are springing up like mushrooms in a moist meadow, offering unsigned bands the opportunity to hawk their wares to an increasingly wired global audience.

Even traditional "lo-fi" international touring is more a possibility today than ever before. As already noted, the world's soundtrack for the last forty years has been American popular music—primarily rock 'n' roll and blues, but other styles as well. American pop has become our passport. The world wants to hear American pop sung in English by native speakers. In Tahiti, for example, as in many parts of the world, tourism plays a major part in the local economy and the majority of tourists are French and English-speaking; as a result, a great market has developed for American pop performed in English. I know an American singer from Massachusetts who is currently in Thailand fronting an all-Thai blues band and earning upwards of $3,000 per week! The whole world is indeed your stage.

Increasing demand, diversity, professionalization, miniaturization, sensualization, and globalization of music-making: six huge currents flowing through the new music industry. Of course, there are many other smaller trends within each of these "megatrends" we could examine as well—for example, some of the controversies surrounding copyright vis-a-vis the Internet, or the much bal-lyhooed censorship rifts that occasionally rock the boat.

This first chapter painted, in broad brushstrokes, a big-picture view of the

INCOME FLOW IN THE RECORDING INDUSTRY

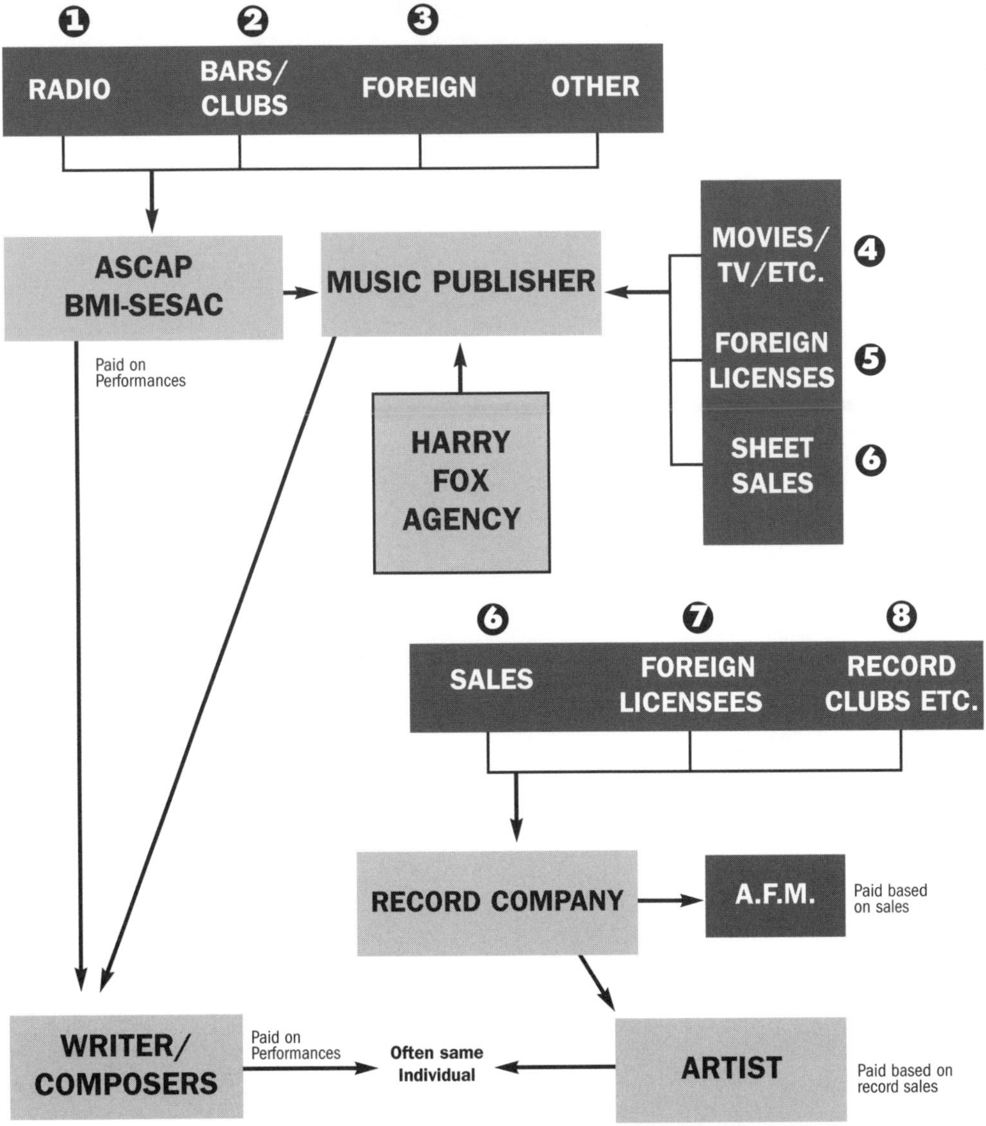

1. Paid on contractural amount based on percentages.
2. Paid on contractural amount based on usage, etc.
3. Paid on usage of songs.
4. Paid on negotiated amount per use.
5. Paid on contractural amount per use.
6. Based on sales of actual units.
7. Based on percentage of sales of product.
8. Based on percentage of sales of product.

Fig. 1.3

industry for the music community to consider. No one starts a business or launches a career in an industry without first understanding that industry—its strengths, its weaknesses and its overall direction. Only by understanding the context can you know your place within it and plan the smartest path possible for the achievement of your goals. The following chapters will help you flesh out a smart music career path in light of these trends. Forward!

Further Resources

Resources are extensive for current industry happenings and trends. See the Resource Guide at end of book under "Industry Careerists" section.

2

Plan Your Work, Work Your Plan: Writing a Music Business Plan That Works

Scenario 1: A talented band wants a record deal but their gig schedule is erratic and members' day jobs keep sucking their energies so there's not much left for anything else. **Scenario 2:** A terrific songwriter keeps churning out tunes weekly but they just sit in her notebook while she dreams of someday recording them. **Scenario 3:** A singer and producer team up and record two cuts for release but then realize all the cash has gone to recording and manufacturing with none left for promotion and marketing. **Scenario 4:** A music school graduate with great promise sits in his insurance job cubicle and wonders, "What went wrong?"

Sound familiar? After fifteen years of working in artist development, I've become painfully aware of a tremendous amount of musically gifted talent being squandered. Some musicians progress in fits and starts—one step forward, two back; two steps forward, one back...and so on. Others are just spinning their wheels, stalled. Still others are going in circles. A few, perhaps the most tragic, are spinning their wheels and going in circles.

What accounts for all this misguided effort? It could be many things: a *lack* of talent, drug abuse, laziness, etc. But, more often than not, musicians tend to get nowhere because of the absence of a map. A map is a plan that points to your destination and lays out the best routes to get there. Maps give us the "bird's eye view," the lay of the land, so to speak, so that our journey toward our destination is discernible and deliberate, rather than haphazard and blind. Singer-songwriter Kelly Pardekooper of Iowa City put it this way: "The bottom line for me is that until I had a plan written down in black and white, I was just swimming in the dark, I had no anchor for my boat, no Felix for my Oscar."

A good music business plan is the map to the fulfillment of your goals. Whether you're a band, soloist, production house or some other business, a plan can turn foggy notions into operational strategies, hunches into actions, dreams into reality.

21

Mapping Out Your Music Destinations

Dreams. This is where it all begins isn't it? For this reason I like to think of one's business plan as a "vision/mission." It starts with vision. Before your first gig, you envisioned yourself playing it. Remember? Vision precedes mission and fuels it with the necessary energy to go the distance. Mission implements vision and provides the vehicle that moves you towards your goal. Together they're unstoppable!

"Success" can be defined as the progressive realization of a worthwhile goal. If you are doing the things that are moving you toward the attainment of your goal today, then you are "successful," even if you are not there yet. It's the goal that starts the whole journey. An illuminating study on goal setting sponsored by the Ford Foundation found that:

- 23% of the population has no idea what they want from life, and as a result, they don't have much;
- 67% of the population have a general idea of what they want, but they don't have any plans for how to get it;
- Only 10% of the population has specific, well-defined goals, but even then, seven out of the ten of those people reach their goals only half the time;
- The top 3%, however, achieved their goals 89% of the time—an .890 batting average!

What accounts for the dramatic difference between that top 3% and the others? Are you ready? The top 3% *wrote down their goals*. Are you laughing yet? It can't be that simple! Or can it? Dreams and wishes are not goals until they are written as specific end results on paper. In some very real sense, writing them down materializes them. Goals have been described as "dreams with a deadline." Written, specific goals provide direction and focus to our activities. They become a road map to follow. And the mind tends to follow what's in front of it.

So what is your dream-goal? Is it to be the most-in-demand session player on the East coast? To be the next Goo Goo Dolls? To get your song cast with a multiplatinum-selling recording artist? To start a company that creates soundtracks for video games and commercials? Or is it to simply earn extra income playing music while holding down a successful non-music day job? Each one of these requires a specific map.

Are you even aware of your options? Music careers today are being rewritten as traditionally separate industries converge and spawn new opportunities for those familiar with audio in its manifold expressions. For example, did you know that book publishers are establishing music divisions as they "repurpose" their titles onto CD-ROMS and other multimedia formats? Think about where music is *used* today and an explosion of possible paths will present themselves.

Knowing your options and establishing clear goals is your first step. In the entrepreneurship courses I teach, one of the early assignments is for students to write their own obituaries. While on the surface morbid, it forces people to consider seriously what they want to be remembered for at the close of their earthly lives. Try it. All of the achievements and accomplishments revealed in this exercise are translatable into specific goals from which you can work backwards to the present.

The Musician and Business

And speaking of entrepreneurship, unlike the medical doctor and investment banker, musicians are self-contained business entities with all the responsibilities and obligations which are part of all business activity. Since most musical work falls into a "do-it-yourself" approach, it's important to understand that the "it" you will be doing, for the most part, is business. Whether it's booking a gig, negotiating a contract or organizing a promotion plan for your CD, the fact is you are exercising a variety of skills to grow a business, You Inc.

The trick is figuring out what you're good at and then translating those skills into "profit-centers" or revenue streams. Most musicians wear a number of different "hats." In any one week you may wear a performer's hat, an educator's hat, an agent's hat, an arranger's hat, and a songwriter's hat. Sometimes you will wear all these hats in a single day! Each "hat" is a potential revenue stream and activity center that can be strategically managed to expand your market audience. And each stream you choose to develop requires it own smaller plan within your larger plan.

Of course, the challenges of this loom large. You probably went into music because you didn't necessarily want to do business. Perhaps you watched your parents or relatives chafe under the constraints of business jobs. Maybe you cling to an anti-materialism that scorns and fears the pursuit of the almighty dollar, and that casts "art" and "commerce" as hopeless opposites. We can add to this the fact that few of us ever received real-world strategies for developing successful careers from our schools and homes.

But whatever the poison, the effect had kept many musicians ignorant of how to go about creating success for themselves in the world. This is often the reason for all that erratic progress, those fits and starts, in musicians' lives. Even when the goals are clear, the best paths to those goals remain a mystery.

In addition, creating your own personal music career map sometimes means clearing out previous experiences that may be holding you back. I call this clearing process "emotional bushwhacking." All of us carry around excess baggage and psychic trash that burdens our journey. This stuff has the effect of weighing us down and blurring our sight. Someone once said we don't see things as *they* are, we see things as *we* are. The world is mediated to us through a lens created over the years of our lives, through our family experiences, our schooling, and the choices (both good and bad) we've made.

You'll need all the resources and energy you can gather for your career journey. The key is in understanding yourself enough to become aware of those things which tend to derail your efforts and short-circuit your progress. Perhaps the most honest indicator of our emotional fitness is our relationships. You'd do well to look at these closely. Why? Because the music business is one of the most relationship-driven businesses on the planet. Your ongoing success will be determined, largely, by the quality and quantity of the relationships you build over time. Clearing out the emotional weeds that choke our actions and attitudes is an extremely important ingredient of the journey to your goals.

It takes great courage to look these things square in the eye, and many of us will need help sorting it all out. Fortunately, there are people who specialize in helping humans become emotionally fit. Seek a referral from friends or from your school for a counselor who specializes in personal development. Many have "sliding scales" and will adjust charges based on your ability to pay.

How to Structure a Music Business Plan

With these foundations laid, it's time to get down to the plan. A music business/career plan will have six major components. They are:

I.   A summary statement
II.   A solid description of your business/career path
III. A marketing plan
IV. An operations plan
V.   A project timeline
VI. Financial information

We will look at each in turn. You may want to make a rough outline for your own plan as you read this chapter. Don't be surprised, however, if the complete plan ends up forty pages long! That's about right.

Would you like some free help drafting your plan? Then contact your local SBDC (Small Business Development Center). This is a federal program sponsored by the SBA (Small Business Administration) designed to provide small business owners with counsel and resources. These centers work out of colleges and universities, and offer *free* small business counseling and training, usually through another program called SCORE (The Service Corps of Retired Executives). Further info on both SBDCs and SCORE can be found at the end of this chapter, and both are discussed in more detail in chapter 3.

Let's first get an overall sense of where we're going by fleshing out a complete outline of a typical business plan:

I. SUMMARY STATEMENT
II. DESCRIPTION OF YOUR BUSINESS OR PROJECT
    A. History and Background Information
    B. Management Description
    C. Business Structure
III. MARKETING PLAN
    A. Your Market's Description
        1. General Market Description
        2. Specific Market Description
        3. Competition Profiles
    B. Your Strategic Marketing Plan
        1. Positioning
        2. Marketing Mix
        3. Pricing Philosophy
        4. Method of Sales/Distribution
        5. Customer Service Policy
IV. OPERATIONS PLAN
    A. Facilities and Equipment
    B. Plans for Growth and Expansion
    C. Risks
V. PROJECT TIME LINE

VI. FINANCIAL INFORMATION
   A. Financing Required
   B. Financial Projections

I. SUMMARY STATEMENT. Here you want to answer the following questions as succinctly as possible: Who are you? What will you do (goals)? Why will the business be successful? How will it be financed? When do you think it will turn a profit? (Remember, a 'profit' is not how much money you *make*, but how much you *keep*). Be ruthlessly realistic!

It is also in the summary statement that you list the products or services being offered (e.g., CDs, tapes, performances, etc.) as well as the names and positions of all personnel involved. The summary should close with mention of anything that differentiates your project from all other similar ones. Try to keep your summary statement to fewer than 200 words.

II. DESCRIPTION OF YOUR BUSINESS OR PROJECT
This section begins to flesh out the summarization above.

A.   Begin first with the *history* and *background* of your project. This provides the overall context in which to view your current work. List all data that pertains to the various facets of your present business. Don't pad it with your whole life story; just include the pertinent highlights that have brought you to the present moment. An inventory of your general and unique skills would also be appropriate here.

B.   A *management description* should follow next. How is your business project organized? What kinds of procedures are in place to insure your business is both effective and efficient? What does the management leadership look like (its style and communication chain)? How are decisions made and facilitated? What kind additional human resources are needed to ensure smooth operation and growth?

C.   Decide on the business structure you will use (i.e., sole proprietorship, partnership, corporation, etc.). This is one of the first questions the start-up businessperson should ask. The answer to this question has many legal and tax implications, and varies greatly from state to state (see Fig. 2.1

COMPARING LEGAL STRUCTURES FOR YOUR BUSINESS
The chart below compares the advantages (+) and the disadvantages (-) of each of the five legal structures available to entrepreneurs

SOLE PROPRIETORSHIPS

+ Controlled by owner
+ All profits to owner
+ Little regulation
+ Easy to start and maintain retirement
+ Earnings taxed at personal level

- Personal liability for business debts
- Limited resources
- Likelihood of no continuity at or death

GENERAL PARTNERSHIPS

+ Joint ownership and responsibility
+ Access to more money and skills
+ Earnings taxed at personal level
+ Limited regulation and easy to start

- Conflict of authority
- Partners liable for actions of others
- Profits divided
- Possible end of business at retirement or death of one partner

LIMITED PARTNERSHIPS

+ General partner(s) runs business
+ Limited (silent) partners have no business liability beyond invested money
+ Profits divided as per partnership agreement
+ Earnings taxed at personal level

- Limited partners have no say in the business
- General partners have personal liability for business debts
- More regulations than for general partnerships

SUBCHAPTER S CORPORATIONS

+ Limited personal liability
+ Legal entity with transferrable ownership
+ Earnings taxed at personal level

- Closely regulated by state and IRS
- Costly to form and maintain
- Restricted to 10 or fewer stockholders

STANDARD OR C CORPORATIONS

+ Limited personal liability
+ Legal entity with transferrable ownership
+ Employee benefits deductible
+ Perceived status for raising funds

- Closely regulated by state and IRS
- Costly to form and maintain
- Potential double taxation on personal and corporate income

Fig. 2.1

"Comparing Legal Structures for Your Business"). Again, seek the advice of your small business advisor at your local SBDC office for your own state's or town's specific requirements.

III. MARKETING PLAN

Now we are getting into the essence of what about you is unique. Marketing must eventuate in selling, and it is an absolute truth that unless a start-up business can sell its offering, it will not survive. Getting orders—selling your compositions, recordings or performances to paying customers—is of crucial importance to your new business.

To compete successfully in the music business, then, you must follow the same strategy that every successful businessperson uses. This strategy includes:

- Developing a product—in this case, your music service or product;
- Locating clients for your product—doing market research;
- Bringing your product to the marketplace—using sales technique to convince potential clients to buy your music service or product.

"Marketing" is often equated with "selling" or "advertising," but it's really much broader. I like to think of marketing as essentially *communication*. This gets to the core of what marketing is all about. So a definition of marketing in this context might be "communicating so effectively with your market audience that it will want to know more about you."

A. YOUR MARKET'S DESCRIPTION. The first thing you need is information about your market in order to position your offering correctly and find your own unique niche within it. This is called market research and, like all of your planning, should be viewed as an ongoing *process*. You will need both general and specific information about your market.

1. **General Market Description.** The general markets for musicians are the music industry and music-loving consumers. Without a general understanding about this larger market context you will have a difficult time trying to find your way within it. It is helpful, therefore, for today's musician to have a grasp of such things as record company structures, music publishing, recording contracts, distribution, and music media, and how all of these work together to bring music to people. You can learn about the

industry by talking with industry people, taking courses and reading books and trade magazines. You'll find numerous sources for learning about the industry in the Resource Guide at the back of this book.

2. **Specific Market Description.** Here you will want to ask: Into which part of this larger market do I fit? In other words, who are *my* customers? What is their general age, their gender, professions, lifestyle and interests? What books and magazines do they read? To which radio stations do they listen? Which Web sites and on-line discussion groups do they frequent? This information will prove crucial to the development of your marketing strategy.

3. **Competition Profiles**. In addition to your customers, you'll also want to describe your competition. Be as specific as you can be. Gather information on three or four successful competitors, assess the relative strengths and weaknesses of each, and compare your product or service with similar ones in terms of price, promotion, distribution, and customer satisfaction.

B. **YOUR STRATEGIC MARKETING PLAN.** Now that you've gathered information on both your general and specific market-audience, you're ready to develop your marketing plan or strategy. This too can be broken down into several component parts.

I. **Positioning.** This is related to finding your market niche. No matter which products or services you provide, you can carve out a niche for them based on your experience, skills, and interests and then build up that niche as you work to serve it. Ask yourself questions like: What do I do best? Who needs that the most? Where can I provide that product or service that will give me a chance to expand what I do to utilize my other interests? And, perhaps most importantly, what do I have to offer that is special or unique? The answers to these questions will help you "position" yourself most effectively to promote what you're selling.

The idea here is to position yourself in peoples' minds. It's this internal positioning that you're after so that when people need what you have, they think of you first.

2. **Marketing Mix.** The particular combination of marketing methods you choose for your marketing campaign is referred to as your "marketing mix." Methods can include news releases, sponsorships, networking, publicity flyers, contests and giveaways, classified ads, trade shows, radio spots, cable TV programs, Web sites, charitable donations and hundreds more.

   When making your selection, keep in mind this fundamental rule of successful marketing: The measure of a successful marketing campaign is the extent to which it reaches at the lowest possible cost the greatest number of people who are likely to buy your product or service. Generally speaking, the more of your time a marketing activity requires, the less money it costs you, and vice versa. For example, networking costs almost nothing in money but plenty in time. On the other hand, advertising in a city newspaper costs a bundle while requiring little in time (see Fig. 2.2 "The Time/Money Marketing Concept").

3. **Pricing Philosophy.** How much you charge for your product or service will depend on many variables. Here is where your research about your competitors especially comes in handy. Undercutting your competition is one common way to gain market share. But there is another approach. Research has shown that buyers, when making purchase decisions, select what they consider to be the best value—all things considered. Price, therefore, is only one part of the purchase decision process. If you want to increase your customers' perceived value of your product, you can do so by either increasing the benefits or decreasing the price. It is almost always preferable to work on the benefits (i.e. values), tangible and intangible, rational and emotional, large and small, that will make it possible to sell at a higher price.

4. **Method of Sales/Distribution.** This is related to your marketing mix and details the methods you will employ in implementing the various parts of your mix. For a musician, one method might be the use of a booking agent. Another might be a record distributor, a mail order catalog or a Web site. Perhaps all four.

5. **Customer Service Policy.** When considering customer service, it is always useful to consider why you, yourself, continue to frequent certain

THE TIME/MONEY MARKETING CONCEPT

Every marketing effort takes a certain amount of time and money. Networking is a high-time, low-money marketing strategy, whereas advertising is a low-time, high-cost marketing strategy. You need to decide where those precious few dollars will go as you promote your music.

Fig. 2.2

businesses. More than price, more than product quality, you will often return again and again to these businesses because you feel taken care of. The people of those businesses go the all-important extra mile to make you feel special. They anticipate your needs and provide for them in the various ways they deal with you.

See if you can incorporate elements of this customer service policy into your own. Write down your philosophy, and then list all applications you can imagine related to your business. How can you go the "extra mile" for your clients? Find ways of distinguishing yourself from your competitors in this area and you will insure a faithful clientele for years to come.

IV. OPERATIONS PLAN.

This has to do with the overall running of your business, as well as the physical and logistical manufacturing of your product or service. It typically includes three parts:

A. **FACILITIES AND EQUIPMENT** encompasses such things as your rehearsal space, office space, studio, the manufacturers you will use for your CDs and tapes, your instruments, sound and light equipment and vehicles you use to haul it all around. A brief note on equipment insurance should also be included here. Investors like to see the founders of a company have a cash investment in the business in addition to "sweat equity," so equipment should be viewed as capital you can leverage.

B. **PLANS FOR GROWTH AND EXPANSION** is where you project your business goals three to five years into the future: What will you need when you progress from local to regional success? Regional to national? National to international? On the other hand, your goal may be to remain at a modest size in one geographic area.

Perhaps you'll want to develop sub-companies within your primary company. Maybe a publishing wing, or a video branch, or perhaps a jingle production studio. Think it through as carefully and completely as possible.

C. **RISKS** is another very important part of the plan. Not only does it show you're being open and honest with your financing source, but it forces you to consider and assess alternative strategies in the event your original assumptions do not materialize.

V. PROJECT TIME LINE.

This projects the schedule for your goals, both short-range (e.g., obtaining radio airplay, booking high-profile gigs, selling 1000 CDs, procuring management, etc.) and long-range (e.g., signing a recording contract, having your song performed by a mega-star, generating $25,000 per year in royalty residuals, etc.). Think through the essential steps needed for the attainment of each goal to the best of your ability.

VI. FINANCIAL INFORMATION.

No matter how wonderful your plan is, it isn't going anywhere without capital investment, whether it's yours or someone else's. This final section of your plan should be broken down into three subsections: required financing, current financial statements, and a three-year financial forecast. Needless to say, this is the part of the plan potential investors and lenders will concentrate on the most. So the following is written primarily with investors in mind.

A. **FINANCING REQUIRED.** While your first thought may be to ask for cash exclusively, there may be other resources that would help you even more. Perhaps what you really need is some people assistance, or a touring van, or a new computer. These can sometimes be provided more easily than cash.

Whatever you decide you need, make sure it's based on a hard-headed and realistic assessment of the true costs of achieving your goals. A basic rule of thumb in estimating costs is to add 15% onto whatever figure you come up with. This covers all those additional "hidden" and unexpected expenses that inevitably accrue.

B. **FINANCIAL PROJECTIONS.** Financial projections are a key part of a business plan. They provide the reader with an idea of where you think the business is going. Perhaps more importantly, they tell a lot about your intrinsic good sense and understanding of the difficulties your company faces.

Often, financial projections are optimistic to an outlandish extent. They are usually prefaced with words like, "Our conservative forecast is..." Do not use the word "conservative" when describing your forecast. Be careful also not to use the "hockey stick" approach to forecasting—that is, little growth in sales and earnings for the first couple of years followed by a sudden rapid upward surge in sales and totally unrealistic profit margins. Excessively optimistic projections ruin your credibility as a responsible businessperson.

Include monthly cash flow projections, and quarterly or annual order projections (e.g., for studio time, CD manufacturing, etc.), profit and loss projections, and capital expenditure projections (see your accountant for explanations of the above terms). In making financial projections it is usually a good idea to include "best guess," "high side," and "low side" numbers. Sensible investors want to know what returns they can expect and especially how they will achieve liquidity. Tell them. Again, include alternative strategies and "fallback" plans.

Don't worry if you feel a bit overwhelmed by the avalanche of detail your business plan requires. Who wouldn't? Give yourself time. It's helpful to set yourself a goal for completing the first draft of your plan—say three months from now.

Begin with one section at a time and meet periodically with your small business advisor to review your plan's development. He will be able to discern blind spots as well as affirm the plan's overall direction. If you're thinking of foregoing the effort altogether and just "winging" it, just remember that no planning inevitably leads to wasted time, money and energy—all three of which are generally in short supply. The book and software resources at the end of this chapter will take some of the pain out of the process.

Remember too that the musicians you currently respect rose to their success with strategic planning and a keen sense of what "doing business" really means. Furthermore, today we are seeing the smarter bands being brought home because they know the inner workings of the music business and how to best organize their limited resources in order to penetrate it. How about you? Are you planning for success?

Further Resoruces

BOOKS

Pinson, Linda and Jerry Jinnett. *Anatomy of a Business Plan: A Step-By-Step Guide to Starting Smart, Building the Business and Securing Your Company's Future,* Third Edition. Denver: Upstart Publishing, 1996.

Bangs, David H. *Smart Steps to Smart Choices: Testing Your Business Idea.* Denver: Upstart Publishing, 1995.

McLaughlin, Harold J. *The Entrepreneur's Guide to Building a Better Business Plan: A Step-By-Step Approach.* New York: John Wiley and Sons, 1992.

Arkebauer, James B. *The McGraw-Hill Guide to Writing a High-Impact Business Plan: A Proven Blueprint for First-Time Entrepreneurs.* New York: McGraw-Hill, 1996.

Cohen, William A. *Model Business Plans for Product Businesses.* New York: John Wiley and Sons, 1995.

Model Business Plans for Service Businesses. New York: John Wiley and Sons, 1995.

SOFTWARE

Biz PlanBuilder. JIAN, Mountain View, CA. The program is organized around an elaborate template. As you answer an extensive series of questions, it creates an impressive document of more than 20 pages with headlines, chapters, introductions, and most of the pertinent information a bank requires to give you a loan or a line of credit.

ON-LINE RESOURCES

Service Corps of Retires Executives (SCORE). http://www.score.org/. A non-profit association dedicated to entrepreneur education and the formation, growth and success of small business nationwide.

Small Business Development Centers (SBDCs). http://www.sba.gov/gopher/Local-Information/Small-Business-Development-Centers. A complete on-line directory of SBDCs nationwide. SBDCs offer free one-stop assistance to small businesses by providing a wide variety of information and guidance in central and easily accessible branch locations.

The Moneyhunter Home Page. http://www.moneyhunter.com/.

Business Plan templates can be found on-line at:

http://www.panamglobal.com/busplanTemplet97.html
http://www.sbaonline.sba.gov/starting/businessplan.html

3

Getting Ready to Do Business

Today's economy has little room for those who cannot read, write, compute, frame and solve problems, use technology, manage resources, work in teams, and continue to learn on the job. While it may be clear that you need good business and management chops in the new music business, it's sometimes hard to know how to get them. Plus, business-related questions come fast and furious to the start-up: Do I *trademark* my band or business name now or wait? Do I need equipment *insurance* and, if so, where can I find some fair deals? What about *taxes*? Do I have to pay quarterly or yearly as a self-employed musician? Do I need a special *license* to perform the work of a booking agent or artist manager? These and other questions are part and parcel of "doing business." And a lot of business success lies in having the right and timely answers to those questions.

Fortunately, it's a great climate for those needing business information. Today, career- and business-planning information is hyper-abundant and readily available, if you know where to look. The "small office, home office" (SOHO) trend has hatched an entire industry focused on entrepreneurs and what they need. Books, magazines, software, Web sites, cable TV and radio shows designed for micro-businesses are popping up everywhere.

But besides *information* you'll also need *guidelines* for the ever-growing variety of business demands that you will face: What's the best office setup for my needs? How do I hire help and where do I find it? What's the most effective use of my time? How much should I spend on promoting my music service or product? Where can I find the answers to these questions without having to enroll in an MBA program?

To start, check out the Small Business Administration.

Getting to Know the SBA

The United States Small Business Administration (SBA) is one of those quiet government programs in which pearls lie hidden. This is about the best return on your taxes you'll ever get, so listen up.

Congress created the SBA in 1953 to encourage the formation of new enterprises and to nurture their growth. It exists to serve small businesses by providing information and financial backing and speaking on their behalf in the corridors of Capital Hill.

The SBA's mandate is very broad. The agency's definition of "small business"—service companies and retailers with annual revenues of $3.5 million or less, manufacturers with fewer than 500 employees, wholesalers employing fewer than 100 workers—embraces over 98 percent of the companies in the United States.

The SBA's staff is 4,000 nationwide, organized in 110 offices. So taking advantage of the SBA requires learning what it's equipped to offer, and then learning how to tap into its abundant resources.

SBDCs (Small Business Development Centers)

When I was starting my consulting company (Music Business Solutions) in 1992, I contacted an SBA program called the Small Business Development Center (SBDC) in Salem, Massachusetts. SBDCs operate out of about 650 colleges across the country providing management training and other start-up assistance to emerging businesses.

I was matched with a small business adviser who reviewed my business plan, provided me with my first computer training and offered suggestions and ideas galore for making Music Business Solutions a success.

Though untutored in the music business, my adviser was very experienced in the ways of general business management and marketing. Together, we forged a plan to launch and grow my business. In addition, he demystified the computer for me and introduced me to a whole new world of software resources I never knew existed.

To find the SBDC nearest you contact your local SBA office. You can find their number in the U.S. Government section of your phone book. You can also find a list of all SBDCs in the U.S. at: http://www.sba.gov/gopher/Local-Information/Small-Business-Development-Centers/.

SCORE (The Service Corps of Retired Executives)

If you don't live near a college with an SBDC, you generally won't be able to take advantage of their services. That's where the Service Corps of Retired Executives (SCORE) comes in. SCORE complements the work of SBDCs. In fact, many SCORE representatives work out of SBDCs. Some 12,000 volunteers are available to consult, without charge, on topics ranging from writing a business plan to exporting your product. "Their advice is geared to early-stage businesses," says Mark Quinn, acting district SBA director in San Francisco. "Lots of people seeking advice are individual proprietorships—very, very small."

Managerial deficiencies are the reason for nine out of ten business failures. Through in-depth counseling, SCORE volunteers help business owners and managers identify basic management problems, determine their problems' causes, and help them become better managers. SCORE also offers "pre-business" workshops nationwide to current and prospective small business entrepreneurs, covering a vast range of pertinent topics.

Almost any small independent business not dominant in its field can get help from SCORE. The approach is confidential and personal. Clients don't even need to have a business; consultation and counseling *before* a business start-up takes off is an important part of the service too. Some will even provide training in computer programs and bookkeeping, as well as some much-needed handholding through the process of writing a formal business plan. For those serious about growing their business, this will be the best return on your taxes you'll ever get. And you can now even get counseling via e-mail. To locate the SCORE office nearest you, call (202) 205-6762 or see the SCORE Web site at http://www.score.org/.

SBIs (Small Business Institutes)

Another relatively unknown SBA program is the Small Business Institute (SBI) which gives small business owners an opportunity to receive intensive management counseling from qualified college-level business students working under expert faculty guidance. Government funding for SBIs was discontinued in 1996, but over 90% of established SBIs continue to operate.

Students meet frequently over the course of the full university term (or more) with the small business owner to identify and solve specific management problems. Business clients get a detailed report on the steps they need to take to improve their operation.

While this resource can end up being heavy on the theoretical and light on the practical, it's still free feedback from people who understand the logistics of doing business in the '90s. All small business owners/managers are eligible to participate. SBI often overlaps with both the SCORE and SBDC programs.

For additional information about the nearest SBI services, contact the Small Business Institute Directors Association (see Resources at end of the chapter).

SBA Publications

Small businesses can benefit from the SBA's numerous publications and video tapes, which are produced by local offices as well as through the Washington headquarters.

Though they are sometimes elementary, these publications do cover a vast array of topics, from the ABCs of borrowing or leasing office equipment to selling by mail order to computer security.

Many of these pamphlets are free. Others carry charges ranging from 50 cents to a few dollars. Unfortunately, you often must work to get the pamphlet mailed to you. I've heard of it taking as many as three attempts to secure a single SBA publication.

The agency operates a toll-free Small Business Administration Answering Desk in Washington, D.C. (800-827-5722), but dialing it can sometimes land you in a voice-mail jungle. Calling the SBA office in your region is probably a better bet. Again, check your phonebook under U.S. Government.

What good are SBA programs? It depends on what you need, what you already know, and how hard you're willing to work. Some business people come expecting the SBA to help them out of a deep hole. But much of the SBA's best help is for people with little or no business experience.

Musicians and music-related businesses requiring guidelines on starting and developing a successful enterprise should make the SBA their first step on the business trail. It won't necessarily provide you with music industry insights, but insofar as you're a business, it could help you immensely.

SOME SELECT SBA PUBLICATIONS

ORDER FROM: The Small Business Administration,
409 Third Street, SW, Washington, DC 20416
Ph: 202-205-6744, Fax: 202-205-7064
Web site: http://www.sbaonline.sba.gov

EB02	Marketing Strategies for Growing Businesses
EB06	Strategic Planning for Growing Businesses
FM01	ABC's of Borrowing
FM08	Budgeting in a Small Service Firm
FM10	Record Keeping in a Small Business
MP06	Planning & Goal Setting for Small Business
MP14	How to Get Started with a Small Business Computer
MP15	Business Plan for Home-Based Businesses
MT08	Researching Your Market
MT09	Selling By Mail Order

Alternative Approaches

Business advice may also come from unusual places. Boston band Two Ton Shoe realized early on that they'd move their project along faster with an organized plan. To help the process, they posted announcements at the Harvard Business School saying they were looking for management consulting for launching their own record label. This resulted in them teaming up with a trio of HBS students who succeeded in getting class credit for developing an independent study project with the band as the focus. This was similar to a typical SBI project but a little less formal.

The students spent their spring semester working with the act to develop a comprehensive business plan, including a section on industry trends and local factors. "Needless to say, this was a big bonus for us, and free!," says Two Ton Shoe guitarist Jake Shapiro. He continues, "Two years down the road, we've maintained relationships with the HBS grads and it's quite possible that we will form a management team with one or more of them as our label and band grow."

41

Assessing Your Business Readiness

In general, musicians (and other artists too) have traditionally struggled with the world of business. Here are some guidelines for pulling your business life together.

First, become acquainted with how business, and specifically, the music business, works. What makes business tick? Read books and magazines but be sure to also meet people working in the biz. Internships, apprenticeships and informational interviewing are all viable ways to obtain this "experiential intelligence."

Second, scrutinize your current ways of managing your career/business. What's working? What's not? Why? A few minor adjustments to the ways you organize your time, money and energy can pay you back a hundred-fold. Do you feel like you're spinning your wheels? Then you probably need some goal clarification. Is money always in short supply? Then you can probably use some financial planning know-how. Is your music product not getting the necessary exposure it deserves? A critical look at your marketing and promotion strategy might pay off.

Third, know your resources. As a citizen in the New Economy, knowledge is a key asset, and never has there been available such a wide range of information and knowledge as there is today—most of it free for the taking. Specialized publications, Web sites, organizations, seminars—even your state and local governments—offer world-tested information designed to build your successful career and business. Tap these and grow! The following chapter will look at some of these, as well as at some tools to help you manage your career and business affairs more effectively.

Further Resources

BOOKS

The Entrepreneur Magazine Small Business Advisor. Edited by the Staff of Entrepreneur Magazine. New York: John Wiley and Sons, 1997. Sort of like having a team of top business consultants on call 24 hours a day, but a whole lot cheaper. Covers all relevant topics to help you start, manage and grow a successful small business. Chapters include listings of trade associations, periodicals, on-line services, software, government agencies, and other valuable sources of business assistance and information.

BUSINESS LETTER WRITING TIPS

WRITING TIPS

- Get to the Big Idea quickly
- Write to a name or a job title not a company
- Use a conversational style
- Be brief, keeping letters to one page
- Emphasize the positive

- Use colorful nouns and active verbs
- Use short words, sentences, and paragraphs
- Sign off with neutral phrases like 'Sincerely' or 'Yours Truly'

THE LETTER-PERFECT LOOK

An impressive letter package provides instant credibility, makes readers easily receptive to your message, and can elicit important goodwill.

Create a "look" for your letters:

- Create a company logo and use it
- Buy matching letterhead & stationery if possible

- Avoid "cute" designs and colors
- Use an inkjet or laser printer
- Place addresses correctly

Have no errors in the letter:

- Always spell names correctly!
- Always use a spell checker
- Use a grammar checker or have someone proofread for grammatical errors

- Demand typo-free letters (just one can sink you)

Make the letter easy to read:

- Use lots of white space, with a one-inch margin on all sides
- Keep paragraphs short

- Keep letters short; people are busy!

For further insight see *The Complete Book of Contemporary Business Letters*, ed. by Stephen P. Elliott (Round Lake Publishing, 1993)

Fig. 3.1

Halloran, Mark, et al. *The Musician's Business & Legal Guide.* Second Edition. Upper Saddle River, NJ: Prentice-Hall, 1996. All the nitty-gritties are covered: legal implications of group breakups, setting up money deals, music licensing, performance contracts, music unions, management and agent agreements, the varieties of recording deals, sampling, copyright and more. The cool feature of this book is the way the authors dissect contracts and interpret "legalese" in lucid commentaries inserted throughout the running text of the document.

Stim, Richard. *Music Law: How to Run Your Band's Business.* Berkeley, CA: Nolo Press, 1998. Chock full of practical and timely information, including drafting partnership agreements, touring on a budget, using and licensing samples, dealing with taxes, and much more.

Edwards, Paul and Sarah Edwards. *Teaming Up: The Small Business Guide to Collaborating with Others to Boost Your Earnings and Expand Your Horizons.* New York: J. P. Tarcher/Putnam, 1997. In clear and effective language, the authors guide the entrepreneur through the whole process of deciding whether or not to team up, scoping out possible collaborators, the varieties of teaming up (from networking to joint ventures), the psychological challenges of collaborating, how to avoid legal pitfalls, and how to deal with "business breakups."

————. *Working From Home and The Secrets of Self-Employment.* New York: J. P. Tarcher, 1996. The Edwards are considered the micro-business gurus. Their books are wonderfully resourceful.

Wacholtz, Larry. *Star Tracks: Principles for Success in the Music and Entertainment Business.* Nashville: Thumbs Up Publishing, 1996. A blow-by-blow of how the major label recording industry works today. After a brief summary of industry components (players, publishers, producers, labels, managers, etc.), Wacholtz launches into topics ranging from copyrights to music business economics, the songwriting craft to creating a successful music business career.

The Wall Street Journal Almanac. Edited by the Staff of the Wall Street Journal. Ballantine Books, 1999. The newspaper has combined its most instructive facts, figures and long-range interpretations to produce an authoritative resource on a variety of topics that should prove useful to anyone interested in business, finance and culture. The almanac focuses on media and entertainment, politics, technology, and sports, along with top news stories of the year, to paint a revealing picture of trends and issues.

PERIODICALS
Wall Street Journal (daily).

USA Today (daily). Good for trends and leads.

Home Office Computing (monthly). Helping small businesses use technology for greater productivity.

Fast Company (bimonthly). Chronicles stories of emerging companies in the new economy.

Inc. Magazine (monthly). Small-business oriented.

ORGANIZATIONS
Small Business Institute Directors Association (SBIDA), 609-895-5522; http://www.cba.uc.edu/cbainfo/SBIDA/welcome.htm/.

On-Line Resources

GENERAL BUSINESS
smallbizNet, http://www.lowe.org/. A Web site offering a wide range of resources and an article delivery service is the Edward Lowe Foundation's smallbizNet. Edward Lowe was an entrepreneur who "brought the American house cat in from the cold—from out of the barn and the alleyways—and turned it into the most popular pet in the United States. He did this by inventing a product called Kitty Litter." The Edward Lowe Foundation (1-800-357-LOWE) is an organization committed to championing "the entrepreneurial spirit by providing information, research, and education experiences that support small business people and the free enterprise system."

Entrepreneurial Edge Online, http://www.edgeonline.com/. Created through a partnership between ELF and the publishers of Entrepreneurial Edge magazine. This site contains a digital version of the magazine, archives of past issues, and interactive forums. It also features "Business Builders," a collection of 48 "self-paced training modules" that walk entrepreneurs through the "step-by-step procedures of marketing, managing, promoting and growing their business."

Idea Café, http://www.ideacafe.com/. There's always something on the back burner (on the front burner too, for that matter) at the Idea Café. This gathering place of "success tips for entrepreneurs by entrepreneurs" sports colorful, upbeat graphics and a selection of articles covering topics from Idea Café.

Small Business Advancement National Center, http://www.sbaer.uca.edu/. This excellent site originates from the University of Central Arkansas and offers the results of small business studies and details on upcoming conferences. You also can find bulletins, publications, databases, and news from organizations such as the Small Business Institute and the International Council for Small Business. A unique feature is a link to send business-related e-mail to congressional leaders. And don't forget to read the Small Business Tip of the Week.

MUSIC BUSINESS
IndieCentre, http://www.csd.net/~muji/indiecentre.html.

Indie Music Resources, http://kathoderay.org/music.

International Entertainment, Multimedia & Intellectual Property Law & Business Network, http://www.laig.com/law/intnet.

Hollywood Law Cybercenter, http://www.hollywoodnetwork.com/Law.

Guitar Nine—Label Resources, http://www.guitar9.com/labelres.html?dest=labelprofit.html.

Deterrent DIY Tour Manual, http://www.islandnet.com/~moron/deterrent/tour_gd.html.

GAJOOB Magazine's DIY Recording Artist, http://www.utw.com/~gajoob.

Music Business Solutions (Peter Spellman), http://www.mbsolutions.com/.

Outer Sound: A Community for Independents in Music, http://www.outersound.com/basic/frame.htm.

4

Empowering Resources for
Self-Managed Musicians

According to the Small Business Administration (SBA), the number one reason for small business failures in the United States is a lack of effective management. Eight out of ten new businesses fail each year due to management incompetence, *not* a lack of business.

The same can be said about bands and other independent music projects. Musicians come together, decide to form a band, woodshed for months in basements and garages, land their first gig, perform it and go back to the basement.

A few months later they land their second gig and then, in another couple of months, a third. In between gigs, they're practicing, practicing, practicing. Some start to feel stir-crazy. Soon, a band member gets discouraged and quits. It takes three months to find a replacement and the cycle begins again. One step forward, two back. Sound familiar?

Now some musicians might not mind this. They're content to play when they feel like it and don't entertain goals beyond the garage. But for those trying to take their music out there for others to hear and support, they had better heed the SBA's findings: *Most businesses fail* because of lack of effective management.

This is both good news and bad news for musicians. The bad news is that top-notch managers are extremely hard to find. An effective artist manager is reluctant to take on unproven talent. Yet how can talent prove itself without good management? It's a classic "Catch 22."

The good news is that you can learn how to *manage your own career.* Daunting, you say? Perhaps at first, but what's the alternative? Staring at those same four walls months at a time, or worse, letting disillusionment sap every last vestige of musical inspiration from your soul? It happens.

Self-management need not be daunting. In fact, most bands are already managing themselves to a greater or lesser degree. With a few basic skills and a working knowledge of some powerful resources, you can raise your music project to the next level of success (see Fig.4.1 "The Many Dimensions of Artist/Band Management"). Effective management begins with *you*.

Requisite Skills for Successful Self and Project Management

What are the required skills for effective career and business management?

1. ORGANIZATION. Numero uno is organization. Management and organization are closely linked. Music management involves continual organization of people, equipment, time, information, and long and short-range goals. Organization is the foundation on which all successful management rests.

Organization is closely related to *planning*. Plans are like maps helping you get to your destination quicker and to avoid dead-ends in the process (see chapter 2). To be an effective planner, you need: a knowledge of how your business works, an understanding of the marketplace, an awareness of the specific tasks needed to complete your goal, information about external conditions that may effect your business, an understanding of what obstacles you are likely to encounter, a knowledge of how fast you work, a familiarity with people and services you may require, and a knowledge of how to go about getting the information you lack.

You're going to invest some time gathering the information that will turn you into an effective planner, but it is an investment that pays high dividends. Time efficiency expert Robert Moskowitz calls planning "the mechanism that lets you get out of the crush and constant flow of events...Good planning puts you in the driver's seat instead of under the rear wheels."

2. OVERSIGHT. This means keeping the *whole* project in full view. A contemporary music project has many dimensions and the self-managed musician endeavors to keep an eye on every one of them simultaneously (see Fig. 4.1).

- *Musicianship:* writing, rehearsing and repertoire;
- *Business:* licenses, legalities, taxes and accounting;
- *Recording:* studio research, choice of producer, engineer and masterer, and manufacturer;
- *Performance:* booking, stage show, sound and lights, touring;
- *Promotion and marketing:* publicity, radio, reviews, distribution, merchandising and video.

THE MANY DIMENSIONS OF ARTIST / BAND MANAGEMENT

BUSINESS
- Planning
- Office setup
- Resource management
- Networking
- Publishing

THE MUSIC
- Repertoire
- Rehearsals
- Writing
- Gear

LEGALITIES
- Licenses
- Contracts
- Insurance
- Taxes
- Trademarks

THE SELF-MANAGED BAND/ARTIST

PROMOTION/ MARKETING
- Planning
- Media/publicity
- Distribution
- Merchandising
- Video

PERFORMANCE
- Stage show
- Booking
- Touring
- Sound and lights

RECORDING
- Studio research
- Pre-production
- Production
- Manufacturing
- Record labels

Music Business Solutions

Fig. 4.1

Being organized helps to facilitate the oversight of this multidimensional project so that no single area is neglected in the overall progress of your business. Keeping a handle on each of these dimensions and learning to balance them is the key to success. Using a year-at-a-glance calendar helps to both organize your time and provide that "bird's eye" view of your progress toward your goals.

3. COMMUNICATION. The self-managed musician is in constant communication with a myriad of people in an effort to promote his or her music project. Management communications take many forms: letters, phone calls, e-mails, flyers, business cards, promotion kits, etc.

Effective management communication means grammatically correct writing, articulate speaking and creative use of graphic design. This word brigade represents you and your music to the world. The saying, "You never get a second chance to make a first impression" is particularly apt in the music business. A misspelled word or smudged Xerox can banish your project to the bottom of the pile in an industry driven by state-of-the-art communications. High-quality communications insures a hearing and ranks you with the winners.

Well-managed communication also happens in-house in the form of planning meetings among group and support team members. Don't ever assume everyone in your band or on your team knows what you're thinking. *Tell them* your ideas and plans, and welcome feedback. Many bands have split because of a series of communication breakdowns.

4. CONTACTS. Successful music management depends on contacts and other support resources. "Networking" is where communications and contacts overlap. It's the process of building strategic alliances with those who can help further your career. And, after the music, *nothing* is more important than who you know in the music industry.

Making music-industry contacts assumes, of course, a certain level of interpersonal and relationship-building skills. In my work with artists over the years, I have noticed that, as a group, they tend to be of a more solitary and contemplative nature. And this is appropriate in light of the work they do.

But too much isolation can lead to difficulty in forming friendships, intimate relationships, and social contacts. As a result, artists often find themselves painfully unprepared for the ways of the world. This is a key reason, I believe, why artists have such a hard time with the *business* of music. Doing business, making contacts, and networking all involve a high level of social interaction. The successful self-managed artist will learn to strike a balance between art and business, creativity and commerce, isolation and interaction.

Organization, oversight, communications, and contact building are the four primary skills needed to successfully manage your band or music career. How do you measure up? If you're a solo artist without a manager, you'll need to develop these skills on your own. In a band, the managerial responsibilities can be shared among all the members and *they should* be. One member might be good on the phone, another with computer work, still another with schmoozing.

Sit down with the above list of required skills and together assess what you can and cannot handle in-house. The places you find "gaps" can be filled by using outside help.

Tools to Help You Manage More Efficiently and Effectively

Now that you understand the skills needed, you can explore some empowering resources that will make the implementation of these skills smoother.

COMPUTER TECHNOLOGY

Technology is a houseguest that has taken up residence in our lives unbidden. We have the options of welcoming this guest warmly or giving him the cold shoulder. But it doesn't matter, because the guest is here to stay. The attainment of techno-wisdom requires that each of us walk a personal tightrope between what the market offers and what is best for us.

The past twenty years have seen a virtual revolution in tech products and services for business and project management. The most important one has been the popularization of the personal computer (PC). Only 20 years ago, there were 50,000 computers in the world; now that many are being installed daily.

No longer are computers the domain for tech-heads alone. With user-friendly interfaces and icon-driven commands, computer technology has come within reach of even the most terrified technophobe. You may already feel like an octopus juggling rehearsals, songwriting, family and your day job, but dedicate one arm to the computer and you will shorten your workday, cut your costs, and, in the end, improve your profits.

A computer can track all your contacts (name, address, phone, fax, plus a log of all your conversations with that contact); store and print mailing labels; assist you in developing both your business and publicity plans; design killer flyers, postcards and other promotional materials; organize your accounting and tax preparation; and with a modem (telephone/computer connector), open a vast sea of music industry information and contacts on the Internet and beyond.

The big news in hardware today is that you'll get more computer for less money. What's more, multimedia, the latest innovation to win top billing at computer outlets, is going mainstream. This technology gives computers the

sidebar: 4.1

INFORMATION IS POWER

INTRODUCTION Remember that the primary purpose of a filing system is retrieval, not storage. If you won't use a piece of information again, there is no reason to file it. But if you will need it you'll have to have a way to find it. So your filing system should be designed to help you find information, not just provide you with a place to keep it.

To work effectively, any filing system should group the many types of information you use into clear and simple categories that correspond to the various aspects of your work. Also, it should be easy to weed out and keep current. Here are several kinds of files to help you manage your information:

❶ Project Files
• Create a separate file for every major project you're working on.
• File your Project files in alphabetical order.
• On the inside cover of each file, record the pertinent information related to that project—the names, addresses, and telephone numbers of contact people, your deadlines, meeting dates, work schedules, etc.
• If the papers related to a project outgrow one file folder, separate them into additional folders and place them in an accordion file labeled with the name of the project.

❷ Client or Customer Files
• If you provide a service, create a file for each of your clients or customers. As with project files, use the inside cover to record pertinent information you want to have readily available.

❸ Subject Files
• Create a file to keep information on subjects of interest to you. For example, "Sponsors," "New Guitar Gear," "Industry Trends," etc.

④ An Upcoming File
- Use a file folder labeled "Upcoming" to keep announcements, confirmation letters, convention programs you plan to attend, and so forth.
- Before you file anything, mark the date of the event in the right-hand corner of the first page with a bright-colored marker. File the material in chronological order, with the nearest event at the front of the file.

⑤ Business Card Files
- Rolodex filing system. I use one of these but also put the most important numbers in a telephone directory. And I also have full records in my computer database.

⑥ Tips for organizing your computer files
- Create directories and/or disks with the same names as your paper files.
- Back up the contents of your hard disk on floppy disks or use a Zip drive.
- Erase unnecessary backup files daily and purge inactive files monthly
- Use a utility that enables you to find your files.

⑦ Filing Rules of Thumb
- File each folder, card, or record in one and only one designated place.
- File material immediately. Don't create "file piles."
- Put the most recent materials in the front of the file.
- Don't overstuff files.
- Label all file folders.
- Separate "active" files from "storage" files.

ability to provide music, realistic human-voice narration, snippets of colorful full-motion video, and animation—a real plus for musicians looking for an inexpensive route to video production.

New technology blossoms and becomes extinct at about the same rate weeds grow in your garden. This is why you need to carefully assess your needs before making any major hardware or software purchase.

- Assess what you hope to do with your computer hardware and software.
- Create a list of computer components and types of software you wish to purchase.

SEVEN WAYS TO GET THE MOST OUT OF YOUR DAY

❶ KEEP YOUR TARGETS IN SIGHT AT ALL TIMES.

Post your goals in a prominent place where you can refer to them for direction, inspiration, and motivation. This could be hanging on a wall near you desk, in your personal organizer or calendar, or in a handy folder. Remember: out of sight, out of mind. The mind goes toward what's in front of it. To keep your business on track, keep goals always in sight and on your mind.

❷ PLAN YOUR WORK, WORK YOUR PLAN.

Chart your goals and work backward in time to create smaller project tasks, so that all aspects of your work build on each other. Define specific annual goals, with monthly and weekly tasks that enable you to reach them. Once your plan is on paper, refer to it regularly to keep your energies focused and as a record of your accomplishments. When making your daily To-Do list, be realistic and target only 6 to 10 items you'd like to accomplish. If the list is too long, you'll become demoralized and feel that you're never getting ahead.

❸ KNOW YOUR INTERNAL BIOLOGICAL CLOCK.

Be aware of which activities work better for you at different times of the day. Are you someone who springs out of bed each morning singing? Or do you really start rolling in mid-afternoon? Whatever your personal bio-clock dictates, try to match important tasks to periods when you're most alert. One of the main attractions to the entrepreneurial life is the liberty to design your day. Use this freedom to optimize your productivity by staying in touch with your physical and mental states.

❹ "BANK" TIME FOR DIFFERENT ACTIVITIES.

Individuals can be significantly more productive if they group similar activities into time segments. For example, many solo entrepreneurs avoid telephone interruptions by having a machine, voice mail, or a service pick up their calls during certain hours. They "bank" return phone calls for a specific time of the day and make all calls then.

❺ END THE DAY WITH REVIEW AND PLANNING.

Take a few minutes at the end of each day to review what you've accomplished and what remains to become part of tomorrow's list. You may want to adopt the habit shared by many entrepreneurs of planning tomorrow's activities—and creating a detailed To-Do list—at the end of the day. Using this technique you don't have to think about what needs to be done when you hit the office fresh in the morning; it's there on paper right in front of you. An added bonus is that you can walk away from the office at night knowing that you're prepared to make tomorrow a productive day. Some even say that putting plans on paper the night before allows your subconscious mind to do some problem solving while you're sleeping.

❻ REFINE, DON'T REINVENT.

Once you find a time management system that fits you, use it faithfully and continually refine it to suit your changing needs and interests. Resist the temptation to jump on the latest bandwagon or to adopt a new system every year. Ironically, it takes a lot of time to master a time management system—and you don't want to be spending valuable time always trying to get organized. A simple system can serve you well for many years.

❼ GIVE YOURSELF CREDIT.

No independent entrepreneur can hit peak productivity 100% of the time. As seasoned entrepreneurs can attest, some days seem to evaporate and leave little progress to show. Accept this as a natural condition, and don't be hard on yourself. Focus instead on the achievement of the day, and trust that you're working better—and smarter—all the time.

Fig. 4.2

- Understand the computer jargon that goes hand-in-hand with buying computer hardware and software.

A good way to become acquainted with a computer is to ask a friend who already owns one to show you around the electronic landscape. There are also numerous introductory courses offered through adult and continuing education programs in your area. You can sometimes access free computer training at your local Small Business Development Center (see chapter 2). If you hate computer books but want to tackle the basics in a hurry, read *Computers Simplified* by Richard Maran and Eric Feistmant (see Further Resources at end of chapter).

It used to be that you had to spend vast sums of money for all the software programs you would need to perform the above-mentioned functions. No longer. Today you can purchase "integrated" software packages which include impressive word processing, drawing, painting, communications, database, spreadsheet, presentation and contact management programs—all linked with buttons that automate common tasks, and often "bundled" with your computer in one box. Examples of such integrated programs include AppleWorks (formerly ClarisWorks) and Microsoft Works. They are both highly rated and affordable.

Computer Peripherals

To get the most out of your computer you'll want to add a number of plug-in "peripherals" or components. These would include, first, *a printer.* There are a number of printer types out there but if you want to project a professional image, a *laser* printer is increasingly the printer of choice.

Offering print quality that approaches professional typesetting along with a wide choice of fonts and type sizes and the ability to reproduce graphics and half-tones, a laser printer turns an ordinary PC into a self-contained publishing house. Current laser printers offer twice the resolution of the original models, and most sell affordably in the $300 to $800 price range. Add another $1500 for color laser. You may also want to have a dot matrix printer around for "draft" quality output. Prices on these have also come down, and $100 or so will fetch you an excellent-quality dot-matrix model.

Another great small-business technology resource is the *facsimile* machine (or "fax"). The fax is a high-speed, low-cost replacement for services such as the U.S. Postal Service and Federal Express. For the cost of a phone call, you can instantly send and receive documents over your telephone lines. This is a great tool for keeping the industry informed of your band's activities and working out contract drafts, whether for a performance or a record deal.

You can purchase a separate fax machine that produces hard copy for around $200. Or, you can cut out the paper entirely and use a *fax-modem*, which turns your computer into a send/receive fax machine. There are also some newly available multifunctional units that can scan, copy, and print as well as fax. They're currently priced in the $350–500 range.

A final peripheral, briefly introduced above, is the *modem*. A modem (MOdulator/DEModulator) can connect your computer with global electronic networks, government databases, and libraries full of business and background information via your telephone line. Most home computers come with an internal modem. External modems are also available (including cable modems), and may offer greater flexibility if you have special telecommunications needs or plan to upgrade to a better modem in the future. Expect to pay more for these.

Other Management Resources

Successful management requires speedy and efficient communication. Since your customers will probably first get to know you and your business over the *telephone*, here are some tips for developing a phone system that renders you reachable and responsive.

Try multi-feature phones and phone services. The growing number of custom-calling services now being provided by phone companies allow even the most humble handsets to perform functions once limited to expensive corporate installations. Ask your phone company about these. Features like hold, redial and caller ID cut costs in time and aggravation.

For a self-managed musician trying to cover all the bases, an *answering machine* is also essential. Record a greeting that is both creative and professional, and be sure to purchase a machine that allows a caller to talk as long as they like. If your machine has a limited recording capacity, then tell the caller this in your message. There is nothing worse than being cut off mid-sentence while trying to leave a message.

Once you've decided on your telephone system, stick with it so people aren't confused by constantly changing numbers or voice-mail procedures. Also, be sure to list your fax and voice numbers on business cards, stationery,

BE YOUR OWN BEST MANAGER

- Identify your values and operate from them
- Clarify your purpose, priorities and goals
- Design and implement an effective business plan
- Create strategic plans of action
- Learn to work smarter—not harder
- Track important components
- Eliminate time wasters
- Plan your days
- Set a schedule and keep it
- Get feedback from colleagues and experts
- Collect information: quotes, articles, statistics
- Keep your workspace organized
- Enhance your telephone skills
- Follow through with customers and clients
- Market your business consistently
- Join at least one professional association
- Develop powerful networking abilities
- Keep accurate records
- Be a calculated risk-taker
- Be willing to move on
- Make sure your needs are being met
- Exercise regularly
- Create a support system
- Continue your education
- Get out of the house/office every day!
- Remember we're all human and make mistakes
- Keep things in perspective
- Take responsibility for yourself
- Choose appropriate advisors
- If there are tasks you hate—delegate (or subcontract)
- Respect your mind's and body's cycles
- Balance your personal and professional life
- Acknowledge your accomplishments every day

Fig. 4.3

flyers and tapes. Be cautious, however. Fax-machine owners are increasingly being deluged by junk fax-mail.

To complete your self-management workspace, you will want to stock up on necessary office supplies and keep them on hand. Visit discount stores like Staples or Office Depot for the best prices on calendars, stationery, envelopes, stick-on labels, packing tape, mailers, paper clips, notepads, and hole punches. They can also supply more specialized products like light tables and postage meters.

The self-managed musician will be spending a good portion of time at a desk so when it comes to office furniture, think *ergonomics*. Ergonomics is the science of comfort and convenience, or fit and function. Poor ergonomics can cause cumulative trauma disorders (CTDs), which include such common ailments as tennis elbow and writer's cramp. Ergonomics has as much to do with habits as it does with equipment. Since CTDs arise from repetition, try to avoid getting into a rut. Vary your activities.

Lighting is another issue we tend to take for granted. Light completely surrounds you, and it can affect your vision, mood, and overall productivity. Use a combination of sources to create an even light throughout your workspace. Lights aimed strategically to reflect off ceilings or walls will illuminate the space in a diffused, general way. Pay careful attention to *task lighting*, or light directly aimed at your work. Insufficient lighting on the spot where you read or do other detailed work is a sure cause of eyestrain, headaches and general irritability. For a chock-full-of-info primer on creating a healthy and efficient workspace see *Office Access* (1993, HarperCollins).

Successful self-management creatively combines internal skills with external tools. Fortunately, today's independent musician has access to the resources that can elevate his or her project to a level where that success is within reach.

Further Resources

BOOKS

Maran, Richard and Eric Feistmant. *Computers Simplified*. Regents/Prentice-Hall, 1999.

Shine, Gary L. *How to Avoid 101 Small Business Mistakes, Myths and Misconceptions*. New York: Consultant Press, 1991.

Applegate, Jane. *Jane Applegate's Strategies for Small Business Success*. New York: Plume Publishing, 1995.

Peterson, Mark. A. *The Complete Entrepreneur: The Only Book You'll Ever Need to Manage Risk and Build Your Business Wealth.* New York: Barron's Educational Series, 1996.

Cohen, William A. *The Entrepreneur and Small Business Problem Solver: An Encyclopedic Reference and Guide.* New York: John Wiley and Sons, 1990.

Merrill, Ronald E. and Henry Sedgwick. *The New Venture Handbook.* AMA-COM, 1993.

Problems and Solutions in Small Business Management. Denver: Upstart Publishing, 1995.

Frascogna, Xavier M. and H. Lee Hetherington. *Successful Artist Management.* Second edition. New York: Billboard Publications, 1998.

Finley, Michael. *TechnoCrazed: The Businessperson's Guide to Controlling Technology—Before It Controls You.* Princeton: Peterson's/Pacesetter Books, 1995.

COMPUTER MAIL ORDER CATALOGS

The Mac Zone: 1-800-248-0800
The PC Zone: 1-800-258-2088
MacWarehouse: 1-800-255-6227
Micro Warehouse: 1-800-367-7080
MacMall: 1-800-222-2808

5

Have You Thought of Starting
Your Own Record Label?

If the '80s was a decade characterized by big corporations, slick packaging, and Phil Collins' shining forehead, the '90s are experiencing a resurgence in the grassroots, do-it-yourself ethics that empower the little man and woman to get out and put their creative thumbprints on the world. The music industry is hardly immune to this climate, and small record labels have been springing up like lemonade stands in a suburban heat wave.

Some are launched by artist managers who want to organize the talent around them into a viable company. Others are launched by studio owners or producers wanting to expand their operations by developing their own indie label towards securing a production deal with a larger company. But the vast majority are started by artists themselves seeking to develop their musical product towards professionally presenting themselves to the music industry.

There are four factors contributing to the indie label resurgence today and each one is a door of opportunity for anyone who can offer good music, basic business smarts, and a load of perseverance.

Factor 1: Small is Beautiful (and profitable)

When rock 'n' roll exploded on the scene in the mid-50s, major labels scorned it. However, basement concerns like Chess and Sun made fortunes. Likewise, no one saw a buck in disco except Casablanca; again millions were made. More recently, rap, country, and to a lesser extent reggae, illustrate the same story. Why is this the case?

Major record labels are too large and ponderous to be in a position to discover and nurture great music and talent. Independents worldwide have been, and will continue to be, the lifeblood of the music industry. As a result, most significant musical trends have their origins in independent companies.

The *Billboard* charts of the last few years show an interesting, if not surprising, trend. Thanks to the installation of point-of-sale systems at most major music chain retailers, SoundScan's computers can poll music stores and get the exact number of each title sold (prior to SoundScan it was done by a highly corruptible method of polling music chains, wholesalers and independent record stores. Apparently lots of totals were "bought").

Here are the new results. In 1990 there were no independent labels ranked among the top 20 labels with titles on *The Billboard 200*. By '91 three indie labels had entered the top 20 list. Among them they placed 19 separate titles on *The Billboard 200* and represented 5.1% of the label chart share.

By 1992, the number of indie labels occupying places in the top 20 had increased from three to four, but more importantly, they represented 34 titles (an 80% increase) and 5.9% (a 16% increase) of the label chart share. The trend is even more dramatic if we look at Billboard's Top R&B Albums chart where chart share doubled between 1990 and 1992 to a total of 22.2%! During one week in 1996, indie labels occupied all top 5 spots on the chart!

Majors today seem to act more like film distributors than production houses. They have the organization and capital to take new music to the public, but little ability to create the music themselves.

"While the majors want to sell music like McDonald's sells hamburgers, we'd rather be a small chain of gourmet restaurants with a line going around the block," says Bruce Iglauer, founder of indie label Alligator Records. "It's the menu that counts—not how many are served." Independent labels are once again artistically and creatively on the cutting-edge of the new music. This new music is not a fad; it is the *fastest-growing segment of the music market*. It includes everything from rap, urban, and alternative to country, world, and folk.

I don't mean to set up a false dichotomy of goodies and baddies (independent companies and adventurous musicians vs. the multinationals and flavor-of-the-month clubs). There are still plenty of struggles and contradictions between these two groups. But increasingly, we are seeing a pattern of *symbiosis* emerge, where one can help the other, a fair deal can be struck, and *both* can profit. Indies are the highly valued testing grounds for the superstars of tomorrow.

Factor 2: Diversity is also Beautiful (and Profitable)

Growing market segmentation by music style is another significant factor for independent labels. Rock's share of music sales, so long the mainstay of pop music, has plunged 27% since 1987 to about 32% of the total. This new musical diversity is even reflected in the Grammy awards. Started in 1959 with a mere 28 categories, this year (1999) the number was up to 85.

A rapidly segmenting music market means more opportunity for independents whose releases detail the richness of particular or "niche" musical forms: the blues of Black Top and Alligator, the rap of Priority and Ruffhouse, the industrial dance meshes of Nettwerk and Wax Trax, the world folk of Green Linnet, the rock 'n' roll of Touch 'n' Go—the list goes on and on. Each began out of a love for a certain style of music—a style the majors didn't want anything to do with initially.

These companies didn't simply find a niche and fill it, as so many lesser new age and "fuzak" labels do. Nor did they just concoct one and market it, like so many major-label-forged "alternative" indies. They usually developed their label along with the music they presented, often as a hobby, bringing bands and artists to an ardent audience and then riding the crest of their influence. For a number of the smarter ones, yesterday's hobby has become today's gold mine.

Factor 3: Distribution is Consolidating

Recent years have witnessed a trend toward *consolidation in both music distribution and retail* that will likely continue. In distribution, the old system—where indie labels assigned their product lines to a different regional distributor in each market—is changing to one where a single distributor handles a label on a nationwide basis.

The consolidation of retail into megastores during the last five years is a reality in most consumer goods categories. Music has been no different. That development, coupled with significant merger and acquisition activity, has resulted in an overwhelming percentage of the music business being conducted by a small number of large chains. In other words, by linking up with key national distributors, independents can potentially reach about 90% of the U.S. record-buying public! The building blocks are all in place.

Record retail is only part of the story (albeit the largest part). Independents have long known that the best way to reach their niche audiences most effectively is to go directly to them through the mail. Direct marketing of music recordings accounts for about 10% of overall sales in the U.S. for major labels but up to 50% of sales for independents! Other record retail alternatives include bookstores, record clubs, specialty gift stores, TV home shopping, digital interactive TV, the Internet, and even vending machines.

Probably the greatest threat to traditional record retail will arrive through computers. Digital transmission of music via power line and satellite is poised to transform the recording industry as we know it. On-line opportunities for independent labels are multiplying rapidly and leveling a playing field that was decidedly tilted in favor of larger companies. "The accelerating trend," says Davitt Sigerson, former president of Island Records, "is putting much more control in the hands of the public, and much less control in the hands of the tastemakers and gatekeepers." The majors see it coming and many are worried.

Factor 4: Technology with a Human Face

Robin Hood would approve of what the purveyors of office equipment are doing these days—making powerful technologies affordable for rich and not so rich alike. They're giving small businesses the same tools and resources to which only large organizations once had access. And prices are plummeting! Today you can set up a modern office with computer, laser printer, copier, fax board, and all necessary software for under $3,000.

Prices are not all that are falling. What began as a trickle of high-end technology to the economy segment of the market has swelled to a flood of deluxe features now commonly available on low-cost machines. Upgradable computers, sophisticated voice-mail systems, and full-featured copiers and faxes are now available at prices that used to buy you only no-frills technology.

What all this hardware and software will give you is the look and efficiency of a professional business and, in the end, save you tons of time, money, and energy. The extraordinary strides made during the last five years in information gathering and communication enables even the smallest record company to obtain, analyze, and utilize sales and consumer data that are equal to that obtainable by large branch distributors and labels.

On a more basic level, these tools can help you manage projects, design your marketing communications, set agendas, track your schedule, build mailing lists, network coast to coast, keep records, print labels, and generally assist you in maximizing your resources as a small independent label.

Checklist for Starting Your Own Label

Okay, these are the factors making it an opportune time to start growing your own indie label. But opportunity alone does not equal success. As mentioned at the start of this chapter, great music, business smarts, and a load of perseverance are also required. Do *you* have what it takes? Check it out.

❏   **Great Music.** Don't even think of starting a label without great music. This may be your own music or that of bands and songwriters you know. Just be sure you've gotten enough feedback to know you're onto something special. How do you get this feedback? Ask! Get input from at least ten people you respect on what makes you or your artists different from others. Write a summary of the best original qualities, and try to think of ways you can enhance them. Originality is an all-important key to success. Look for it, and when you find it, nurture it.

❏   **Business Smarts.** Starting your own indie label is probably the ultimate entrepreneurial venture and, as such, demands a good amount of business know-how. Any skills you can acquire in project planning, bookkeeping, marketing, product development, writing, contract negotiation, and office management will go a long way toward insuring your label's success. Organizations like the Small Business Administration can be very helpful to young business start-ups in need of resources and information (see chapter 4).

Apart from the music, money will be the most important ingredient in launching your label. Some start their labels on a shoestring and end up very successful. But most ventures will require a minimum capital outlay of $3,000 to $10,000. Anything less and you're shooting yourself in the foot before the race begins. Banks and investors will be reluctant to capitalize such a risky venture but a well-thought-out business plan (and a good credit rating!) could make the difference in garnering the support you'll need. If you're a woman or a minority your chances of obtaining a loan are much greater. Look into grant opportunities too. A lot of grant money goes unclaimed each year and your chances are as good as anyone else's.

As a one-man or one-woman record company executive, you should be prepared at the beginning to wear a lot of different hats. Take stock of your strengths and weaknesses, and those of any partners you may have. Starting your company will be the easy part. Keeping it going will require long days and even longer nights. It will mean learning how to be a self-starter, taking risks, being creative, being calm amidst chaos, and taking responsibility for your actions and decisions.

It's the rare artist who can function alone effectively as businessperson without some conflict with their creative side. This is because the very qualities that make one the most sought after writer, producer, or musician may spell difficulties when applied to running a business. This is not to imply that business cannot be conducted creatively. It can and it should be. It simply means that the artist needs to strike a balance between the two, and should perhaps consider teaming up with a partner who can contribute those skills with which the artist needs help. If at all possible, the roles each individual will play should be clearly defined in advance with as little ambiguity or overlap as possible (see sidebar for some partnership guidelines).

❏ **Perseverance.** If you're planning on starting your own record label you will hopefully be thinking *long-term.* Overnight success is extremely rare in this business. Persistence and holding onto your unique vision are the golden keys that will often unlock future rewards.

It's important to remember that artists who are currently charting and labels that are "suddenly" news have usually been plying their respective trades a long time without fanfare. Joseph Brooks could have given up after the song he believed in was rejected three times, twenty times, fifty times, a hundred and thirteen times! It was only on the hundred and fourteenth attempt that a music publisher saw his song's hit potential and "You Light Up My Life" went to #1 on the pop charts in 1977, earned a Grammy award, and made Joe Brooks a multimillionaire.

Brian Epstein had a vision, but every record company in Britain, save one, passed on the Beatles. He stuck to it, picked himself up after each rejection, and finally landed a deal with an EMI subsidiary. The rest is history. Persistence and vision are the energizing factors common to both.

Trend-analyst John Naisbett's book, *Global Paradox,* has a provocative subtitle that has some relevance to this topic: "The Bigger the World Economy, *the More Powerful its Smallest Players.*" Our world has become friendlier to small business. The climate is right. With the right combination of talent, information, and energy, you too can become a powerful player in an industry dependent on small companies for tomorrow's sounds.

CREATE STRONG PARTNERSHIPS

- Find someone whose strengths complement your weaknesses and set up a trial period to see if you can work well together. The key is chemistry, and chemistry involves experimentation with different combinations of elements until the right formula is found.

- Define who will contribute the cash, property, or expertise. Each is needed and each has a value.

- Communicate regularly to avoid power grabs and misunderstandings. Talk openly, honestly, and relentlessly with your partners. Never let things build up to the point of explosion.

- Specify the percentage of ownership each person will have and define how, when, and in what order the profits will be distributed to partners.

- Prepare a business plan and financial forecast for the life of the partnership. This provides a map and an agreed-upon route to your goals.

- Provide a way to remove or buy out partners who fail to meet their obligations. Shit inevitably happens. People fall in love and leave town, another band snatches your drummer, a job with a steady paycheck becomes just too irresistible—in essence, people change. Prepare for this scenario beforehand and you'll save countless hours of heartache and stress later.

- Never forget you're dealing with people. Don't let the stupid biz stuff and tedium get to you. Stand back from the petty conflicts that inevitably crop up and try to see the big picture.

Further Resources

Naisbett, John. *Global Paradox: The Bigger the World Economy, the More Powerful its Smallest Players*. New York: William Morrow & Co., 1994.

Sweeney, Tim and Mark Geller. *Guide to Releasing Independent Records*. New York: Prentice Hall Trade, 1998.

Rappaport, Diane. *How to Make & Sell Your Own Recording*. Jerome Hedlands Press, 1999.

Schreiber, Norman. *The Ultimate Guide to Independent Record Labels & Artists*. Pharos Books, 1992.

PART TWO:
going forward

6

How's Your Net Working?
Increasing Your Contacts in the Music Industry

It has long been said that success lies not so much in *what* you know as in *who* you know. Implicit in this is the belief that this is somehow unfair. But it isn't. What we're talking about here is relationships. Relationships have been the catalysts of business practice forever. After all, it's not record companies that relate to each other, but *people* within these companies. Likewise, corporations don't hold conversations—people do.

This is good news for all ye who seek success in music. Your mouth is your most valuable marketing tool. No longer do we live in a society where one's set of acquaintances is fixed by one's family upbringing or education. In today's information-intensive world, you can contact virtually anyone you need to through networking. "Networking" is the process of building a connecting system of people working in the industry who know your talents, skills, and goals. These connections will alert and lead you to opportunities in your goal area.

The Challenges of Networking

Networking presents more of a challenge to some than to others. Those endowed with the gift of gab network with ease. Those of a more introspective nature, however, may need to work at developing those social and interactive skills so useful to networking. There are actually courses and workshops offered to help with this. Check out continuing and non-credit education programs at your local college. These courses are often great confidence boosters.

Time constraints are another barrier to networking. Networking is a high-time, low-money marketing strategy. That's why it's important to set realistic networking goals.

I suggest trying to meet and interact with just two new people a week. This can mean anything from talking to a booking agent on the phone, to visiting a recording studio for a tour, or writing a promotional letter to a music publisher. The music industry is huge. There is no lack of contact opportunities. Two contacts a week is manageable for most of us. Achieving two contacts a week will result in over one hundred solid contacts a year. If two, three or four band members each do this, your contacts will multiply dramatically.

How to Network

Here are some simple ways you can begin networking and increase your music industry contacts:

- **BECOME INVOLVED IN A SCENE.** Whether it's a musical genre (rap, metal, folk, etc.) or a political movement (Rock the Vote, National Association Against Censorship, etc.), immersing yourself in a particular musical community will enable you to meet and become known to others.

- **READ PUBLICATIONS RELATED TO YOUR SCENE.** Keep up with current events, people and issues. Read the music section of your local paper. You'll pick up what clubs, labels, and bands are hot in your area of interest. Your favorite record store should have a selection of magazines and papers.

- **GO TO CLUBS AND MUSICAL EVENTS.** A show is a magnet for different people working in a genre/community. Other people at the show will have similar interest and goals to your own. Get to know them.

- **ASK QUESTIONS.** People love to talk about themselves and their work. Expressing a common interest will create a bond.

- **DON'T ALWAYS TRY AND MEET THE HEAD OF THE COMPANY.** You're more likely to strike a friendship with a peer who works in the company who may call when they hear of an opportunity.

- **ATTEND CONVENTIONS** (CMJ Music Marathon, NEMO, South-by-Southwest, etc.). They offer a wealth of opportunities to meet and mingle with people working in all areas of the industry. Hit the booths and exhibit halls; you'll have a captive audience. Most conventions have volunteer programs that allow you to work in exchange for a free registration. Many people working in the industry will be volunteering alongside you, giving you an extra networking advantage.

- **GIVE AND GET BUSINESS CARDS.** Hand them out whenever you have the opportunity. Most people keep the business cards they collect and will know where to find you when the time comes. Keep a record of those you give cards to so you can send them updates when they occur.

- **FOLLOW UP.** When you are given a business card, or make an impression with someone in a position to help/hire you, follow-up the meeting with a letter and promotional materials.

- **JOIN CLUBS AND ASSOCIATIONS THAT ASSIST AND ADDRESS PEOPLE WITH YOUR INTERESTS.** There are songwriter organizations, producer associations, and others that provide opportunities for connecting. Many organizations have regular meetings that non-members can attend.

- **CONSIDER GETTING INVOLVED IN YOUR LOCAL MUSIC SCHOOL OR COLLEGE MUSIC DEPARTMENT.** You can take classes or work with student programs. School radio stations, bulletin boards, student organizations, and newspapers can be very tuned-in to local music scenes.

- **ELECTRONIC NETWORKING** is another avenue rich with potential for the working musician. With a computer, telephone and modem you can plug yourself into a vast sea of music-industry contacts and informational resources. See chapter 18 for more information on using the Internet and World Wide Web to boost your professional life.

These are just a few of the ways you can network and increase your music industry contacts. Networking takes commitment, but it is time and energy well spent. It's like planting a garden; there's no harvest until you've planted, watered and nurtured the seeds through the growing season. But when harvest time comes, it will be a bountiful one. This is when *contacts* hopefully become *contracts*. It's a big world out there, and there's a host of thousands waiting to meet you. Cast your net wide!

KEEP A PHONE CONTACT LOG

Name:

Company:

Title/Position:

Address:

Phone: (w)   (h)

E-mail:

Referred By:

Followed-up:

Notes:

Date:	Time:	Action/Outcome:

Fig. 6.1

Further Resources

Burg, Bob. *Endless Referrals: Network Your Everyday Contacts into Sales Money.* New York: McGraw Hill, 1993.

Kimpel, Dan. *Networking in the Music Business.* Cincinnati: Writer's Digest Books, 1993.

Olson, Eric. *The Business of Networking in the Music Industry.* Watson-Guptill Publications, 1999.

Boylan, Michael A. *The Power to Get In.* New York: St. Martins Press, 1997.

Lant, Jeffrey. *The Unabashed Self-Promoter's Guide.* Cambridge, MA: JLA Publications, 1991.

Wilson, Jerry. *Word-of-Mouth Marketing.* New York: John Wiley & Sons, 1991.

7

Impressive Promo Kits (with Valuable Tips on Dealing with Printers and Artists)

First impressions are crucial in the music industry. Bands and solo artists are made or broken on the basis of a first impression. Though this may seem unfair (often it is), the competitive nature of today's music business has resulted in an expectation of higher and higher standards from a band's presentation of itself. Today a band must grab attention and hold it. If you miss your first chance, you've blown it.

This is why putting together a winning press (or promo) kit is crucial. This kit can be viewed as your *graphic ambassador*, the one that goes before you, representing your music and act to the world. With such rich resources available today, in terms of printing and graphics, a contemporary promo kit should be nothing less than a visual feast leading the recipient step-by-step to the audio feast—your music.

The promo kit should be a tightly constructed sales pitch. There should be no confusion about what kind of band you are. Image must be crystal clear— it needs to shine through all the separate parts of the package, unifying printed, photographic, and audio materials. In fact, it is advisable that when constructing your kit you begin with the photo. Use it as the tone-setter for the entire project.

This will, of course, mean a significant financial outlay. High quality promo kits could end up costing anywhere between five and eight dollars per piece. Go for quality. Don't compromise! Be patient. Your high-quality act deserves high-quality representation. If you send out a half-baked kit expect a half-baked response, or even none at all.

A good thing to remember when assembling your presentations is that standout creativity is in short supply. The presentation of your image and essence is a tremendous opportunity to express your uniqueness and pique the imagination of your audience.

In this chapter we will look at each item that goes into a winning promo kit. Since printing and graphics are such a large part of the project, we'll conclude with some helpful tips on dealing with printers and artists. But first, who might want your promo kit?

Where Your Promo Kit Goes

You'll be sending your promo kit to three main groups of people that can help your career:

1. ENTERTAINMENT BUYERS. These can include club owners, booking agents, festival and fair coordinators, private party organizers, and student activities directors at schools and colleges.

2. MEDIA CONTACTS. These can include music magazine editors and writers, entertainment editors in the mainstream press, radio station music directors and key DJ's, and television and video music buyers.

3. INDUSTRY CONTACTS. These can include A&R (Artist and Repertoire) representatives from record companies, music publishers, multimedia producers, entertainment lawyers, and record pool directors.

Each group will require a certain slant that can be conveyed effectively in your cover letter. Kits going to clubs and colleges will want to stress the group's following and its powerful stage show. Those aimed at record labels will want to underline the band's staying power, original sound and success at selling records.

What Makes Up a Winning Promo Kit?

What does an attention-getting promo kit look like? Put yourself in the place of the one receiving your kit. They are likely to see its components in this order:

1. MAILING ENVELOPE. This is the first thing one sees. Avoid the typical brown manila envelope and go for some color. There are a lot more options available today than a short time ago. Check out a good office supply catalog for suggestions (a good one is available from Quill Office Supply; 1-800-789-1331). Also send for "Paper Direct's" catalog of very funky (and pricey) paper products. Call 1-800-A-PAPERS.

2. FOLDER WITH STICKER LOGO. This is the next thing to greet the eye. Again go for something unique. School report folders are also pretty typical. Try something marbleized or metallic, or perhaps a granite look to it. Go for glossy. Your logo will provide the first direct contact with your act's image and the graphic cue that unites your whole package. Office supply houses are again the place to look.

3. PHOTO. When the folder is opened there are a number of items a person can grab. Chances are the photo will be the first to catch their eye. Again, go for quality. Hire a pro and look for a "package deal" that includes a three-roll shoot and printed 8"x10" glossies of your photo with logo and contact information. If you can get three or four usable pictures per roll from your shoot, you're ahead of the game. It helps to get a lot of input from people you respect before choosing the photo for your kit.

4. DEMO TAPE. At this point the kit recipient will probably fish out the tape and pop it in the cassette player. Your demo should contain no more than three tunes with your best one up front. Have them duplicated professionally with creative graphics and all pertinent information printed on both the cassette label and (if included) the cassette case "j" card. Don't forget to put your contact address and phone number on the tape.

   Don't send shrink-wrapped tapes. It's better for the environment and easier for the listener to just open and play. Local duplication packages can be found in local music mags or you can call a complete CD, LP and tape production house like Discmakers in New Jersey (for a free catalog call 1-800-468-9353). Should you send a full-length CD? Not for demo purposes. Most people will not have a conveniently located CD player to play it on. Most expect tapes. It's a good idea to call and ask which format is preferred.

5. COVER LETTER. Here's the personal touch. A sincere individual letter works better than a form letter. Introduce yourself and your act. Be concise and make it professional (grammatically correct and typed on good bond paper with letterhead). Ideally, use a word processor so you can use mass mailing software and personalize each letter with just a few keystrokes. You don't even need to own your own computer to do this. There are plenty of word processor services listed in the Yellow Pages or your local classifieds. Call and compare prices. There's probably someone in your own neighborhood who can

79

help with this. Chains like Kinko's are another option. They have computers (both Macs and PCs) and software programs available to the public for an hourly charge.

6. ARTIST OR BAND BIO(GRAPHY). Give a brief history of the act and what the near future holds. The bio should be short (one page), neat and professionally written. It should reflect your musical identity, originality and style of music. Use a professional writer if you can possibly afford one (local music publications are, again, a good source). While its content should be true, you should present yourself as a likely candidate for success. Don't lie, but don't be afraid to exaggerate a bit either, because the people reading your promo kit will assume you did anyway! While preparing your bio, keep in mind the print media (magazine and newspaper writers) who will be receiving your kit. Well-written, creative sentences are often scooped up and reproduced whole from bios, saving time and getting your point across. Finally, since you want to be able to use the same bio over and over again, don't date it or link it to any particular record release. By all means, drop names. Pump it up!

7. BUSINESS CARD/ROLODEX CARD. This can be inserted in the pre-cut slot on the folder's inside pocket (make sure the folders you purchase have this feature). Most businesses use Rolodexes for fast retrieval and, again, you want to make it as easy as possible for those you contact to reach you. Some good deals on business cards can be found in "The Business Book," (for a catalog call 1-800-558-0220).

These are the seven *essential* items that should be in every promo kit. If your kit lacks anything from the above list, you're selling yourself short. They are the minimum daily requirement for your basic promo kit.

There are also a number of additional non-essential items that can make your kit stand out from the rest. These include:

8. GIG SCHEDULE. This lets people know you're getting around and where they can catch your act. Complimentary to this is a "Where We've Been" list, telling them where you've played—kind of a musical employment record.

9. RADIO AND PRESS QUOTES. Once you have a new release, you can send it around to music magazines for review. Hopefully you'll get good reviews! Then you can pull quotes from the review and use them for further promotion. Likewise with radio. You can include a "DJ Response Card" with your release, leaving a space on the card for comments. Any positive comments can also be pulled and used for promotion. This can lend your act additional credibility and assure the recipient that you're not just tooting your own horn, others are too!

10. SONG LIST. If you're sending your kit to an agent, school, or private party organizer, and you do some cover tunes as well as originals, it's a good idea to send a song list. These potential buyers look for both originality and familiarity when hiring talent. Well-selected covers go a long way towards getting you work, especially at schools and private parties.

11. VIDEO. A picture is worth a thousand words. But before you start enclosing expensive videos in your promo kit, make sure you have a standout product. If you want to use your video for simply making your act more attractive to entertainment buyers, then a low-budget shoot of your live performance or an in-studio, lip-synched shoot will be all you need. Expect to spend anywhere from $1,500 to $2,500 for a full ten-minute production. If your plan is to sell your video in stores, air it in clubs and/or get it on music television programs, then you should expect to spend upwards of $5,000 or more. Needless to say, those unfamiliar with video production should work with professionals from the planning stage onward. For some video producer contacts consult *The Yellow Pages of Rock*. Be sure to get references and talk to other bands about who they've used for their video shoots.

12. PROMOTIONAL NOVELTIES. Here is probably the ultimate way to make your promo kit memorable. Enclose an object with your name printed on it that's slightly off the beaten path. A creative button, or bumper sticker, or maybe a mock ticket to your band's performance at Madison Square Garden! I remember Pink Floyd enclosing an inflatable pink plastic cow udder in their promotion to radio in the early seventies. A little brainstorming can result in some great, untried ideas. There are a number of companies with catalogs available to stimulate your thinking on this. Check the Yellow Pages under "Advertising Specialties."

SPECIAL REPORT
Practical Tips On Dealing with Printers and Artists

WORKING WITH PRINTERS. Find a good print shop and stick with it. You'll be seeing a lot of your printer. Printing costs can vary greatly. I recently priced a print job with four different printing companies and these are the four prices I received for the exact same print job: $89, $175, $234, and $441! The lesson: ask around and compare prices. When I say "printing" I mean not only the traditional offset printing to which most of us are accustomed, but also desktop publishing (DTP) or computer-aided design and printing. A virtual revolution in the world of document creation, printing and distribution is occurring and the sooner you become acquainted with the potential of DTP for your project the better. For now, most of the following is written with more traditional print shops in mind. The economies and technicalities of the printing process must be factored in at the earliest stages. By first understanding the issues involved in getting ink on paper, you can determine whether or not a project is economically viable. It will also help you determine what designs can save you time, money and hassles. To discuss these issues realistically with a commercial printer, you'll have to provide certain information about your project and know the right questions to ask.

1. WHAT'S THE UNIT COST? The lion's share of cost goes to setting-up your project on the press. The higher the quantity printed, the cheaper the cost per unit.

2. WHICH PAPER IS BEST? A mind-boggling variety of papers are available. The best procedure is to determine the effect you are trying to achieve and ask the printer to show you samples (don't forget Paper Direct mentioned earlier). Also, ask the printer if the weight and finish of the paper are appropriate for the kind of text and illustrations you'll be printing. This is especially important if you are planning to use photographs or fine-line drawings in your printed materials.

3. HOW MUCH DOES COLOR COST? The colors you use for type and illustrations are a major expense in any printing job. A more economical way to add color is to add a single spot color with colored inks. You may be able to "piggyback" your additional color on another printing job that is using the same color, thus eliminating a separate set-up charge. Talk to your printer about these opportunities.

4. WHAT ABOUT PHOTO AND ILLUSTRATIONS? Images with areas of gray or color require several steps from the print shop. Compare prices.

5. ARE THERE OTHER DESIGN ELEMENTS TO CONSIDER? For example, you may want to run a photograph right out to the edge of a page. This is called a "bleed" and can be an effective graphic device. However, if you don't place your bleeds carefully they may interfere with printing. Similarly you may want a design element to "cross the gutter" and span two consecutive pages. Precisely aligning pages to make this work properly can be tricky. Definitely discuss it with your print shop.

7. WHAT ABOUT FOLDING, COLLATING, AND BINDING COSTS? These are additional costs. For your own peace of mind, get bids from several print shops on any given project.

Now that you know what questions to ask, you can do all this (or most of it) over the phone. Let your fingers do the walking and your mind do the talking.

WORKING WITH ARTISTS. Professionally designed printed materials create a successful image, but it doesn't come cheap. One way to make this more affordable is to seek out an art student whose style you like and see if you can work out a mutually profitable exchange. Some tips:

1. KNOW YOUR BUDGET. Request written estimates from designers you interview for a particular project (allowing a plus or minus 10% variation). Printing can be complicated and mistakes expensive. If you are unfamiliar with the process, have the artist check bluelines (the equivalent of photo proofs) and handle the press check (verification of colors and alignment as the piece comes off the press).

2. SCREEN ARTISTS CAREFULLY. Ask around for referrals and check the Yellow Pages under "Graphic Designers." Meet with three artists to review their portfolios, but discuss your budget with them beforehand. Though perhaps awkward, it will save both of you time and frustration if your financial expectations are worlds apart. Ask to see samples relevant to your planned project and make sure the artist was responsible for these samples from concept to execution.

3. GIVE THE ARTIST CREATIVE FREEDOM. Carefully describe the audience you want to reach and the message you want to impart. Show your artist design samples you like, then let him create. Establish checkpoints along the way so no one is running off in the wrong direction.

4. PERFECT MEANS PROFESSIONAL. Proofread! One proofreading tip that works: Hold a ruler under each line as you read. The ruler focuses your eyes on one line at a time and greatly improves your chances of catching errors.

5. APPROVE THE DESIGN IN THE EARLY STAGES. Be sure to ask your designer for "comps" before a job is done. Comps are true-to-life renderings of a finished piece. They're usually not cheap, but they are well worth the cost.

6. OBSERVE DEADLINES. Give you and your designer enough lead-time. Never assign a job without a deadline.

7. PAY AS YOU GO. Never pay an artist the entire amount up front. It's fair to pay one third at the start, one-third midway through a job, and one third upon completion and delivery. Your contract with an artist is a business agreement. Let mutual respect and fairness prevail.

Further Resources

BOOKS

Morgenstern, Steve. *Grow Your Business with Desktop Marketing.* New York: Random House, 1996.

Gibson, James. *Getting Noticed: A Musician's Guide to Publicity and Self-Promotion.* Writer's Digest Books, 1987.

Christensen, Glen, ed. *Compact Disc Packaging & Graphics.* Cincinnati: Rockport Publishers, 1994.

Baron, Cynthia. *Creating a Digital Portfolio: A Guide to Marketing and Self-Promotion.* Hayden Books, 1996.

PAPERS, FOLDERS AND NOVELTIES

Best Impressions: 800-635-2378

The Business Book: 800-558-0220

Paper Access: 800-PAPER-01

Paper Direct: 800-A-PAPERS

Quill Corporation: 800-789-1331

8

Creative Publicity and
Promotional Ideas for Musicians

Successful publicity and promotion involves a swirl of activities, but begins, first, with a positive mental attitude. This is because, unless you believe in your project and keep that belief in spite of what others say, unless you think about how to further and improve it all day long, and view it from the long perspective, it will lack the necessary energy to go the distance. A positive, dedicated attitude is the essential foundation of successful promotion (and a successful life).

What is your basic promotional goal? Answer: To let John and Jane Public know that you exist and that they should find out more about you. The way to achieve this is through strategic publicity and promotion. Sound strategy insures maximization of resources; non-strategic promotion, or "shotgunning," can waste gobs of time, money and effort.

There are thousands of bands out there promoting their projects, but only a handful are doing it effectively. It's the difference between hanging fifty posters that hundreds read and displaying one poster that thousands read. Strategy, or thoughtful planning, makes all the difference. So how does one go about it?

Publicity and promotion are really very simple jobs. All they require is a little intelligence, a little insight, a fair amount of tact, and a great deal of push.

The first step is to compile your key contact lists and continue to add and delete from these lists throughout your career. They are the "Grand Central Stations" of all your promotion and publicity and will allow you to feed the networking that is so crucial for success in today's music industry. There are three separate lists that you'll want to develop: a media list, a fan list, and a music industry list. Let's look at each.

Media List

Newspapers, magazines, radio programs, and television are all driven by common needs: To fill time and space with information of value to their readers, viewers, and listeners. They're eager for this information and quite willing, at their own expense, to publish or air it. They need your news.

You can begin this list with the local scene and then branch out regionally, nationally and even internationally, depending on your marketing goals. A good public library is your key resource here. Tell the reference librarian what you're looking for and you'll be guided to the media directories you need. Several good ones are listed at the end of this chapter. You can find most local media information in the Yellow Pages. Pay attention also to writers and radio DJs who have helped break ground for other independent musicians. When the time is right, you can contact them with a press kit.

Fan List

This is your grassroots support network. The best way to compile a fan list is at your gigs. Make it as easy as possible for people to join your fan list. Have pens and attractive cards on every table. Make them visible by announcing their existence throughout the night. Designate someone in the band or crew as the "Fan List Manager."

Once you have a substantial mailing list, you might offer to exchange it with other bands who also keep fan lists. Two or more good mailing lists will help draw greater followings—especially if their music appeals to similar audiences.

As with all lists, the best way to store them is on a computer disk with a "contact management" program. *Goldmine and Act!* (Symantec) are two excellent programs. Short of this, type the contact names and addresses onto masters that can be duplicated onto self-adhesive mailing labels. This will save you from having to write or type them every time you do a mailing. Speak to a printer about the best way to do this.

Industry List

Your Industry List will be made up of people and organizations that can promote your music, hire you, use your songs, or book performances for you. This includes club owners, promoters, booking agents, managers of groups who might invite you to be a warm-up act for their group, owners and managers of stores who might stock your record, record distributors, artist and repertoire (A&R) executives at record companies, and publishers and producers interested in buying new songs.

To obtain these contacts see *The Yellow Pages of Rock* or *The Recording Industry Sourcebook,* two excellent resources. More local industry contacts can often be obtained from published lists in local and regional music magazines. Lists and directories always cost something but they're well worth it. If time is a factor or you don't want to do the research yourself, let others do it for you. No sense reinventing the wheel. These contact lists are an informational gold mine for the independent musician. Whenever you have a gig, send a flyer or postcard announcing it to everyone on your mailing list. If you gig more than once a month you may want to do a monthly mailing. Don't forget to include any news about the band. Work to create a buzz.

Your Other Ambassadors

While your promo kit will be your chief graphic ambassador to the media, there are many other "ambassadors" you can employ to promote your music:

1. POSTERS AND TABLE TENTS. Develop a gig poster including blank space at the bottom where you can write in when and where you'll be performing. Post them wherever you can and don't forget the club where you are playing. Table tents are small index-stock papers folded in half and placed on the club's tables. They announce your upcoming shows. Strive to unite the designs of your posters and tents.

2. PROMOTIONAL NOVELTIES. These can be everything from bumper stickers to buttons, pens to mugs, scratch pads to calendars. They'll keep your name in front of people. Check the Yellow Pages under "Advertising Specialties" and compare prices. There are some good deals available out there but some atrocious rip-offs too.

3. PLAYING BENEFITS. Is pollution an issue you feel strongly about? How about violence against women? AIDS? Team up with organizations that need to raise money for these and other causes. They're always looking for entertainers for fundraisers. You may not get paid in money, but the publicity of the event with your name on the bill can be worth a lot in free advertising *and* you've contributed to a worthwhile cause. Always be thinking about these cooperative opportunities. To locate these contacts check the Yellow Pages under "Social Service Organizations."

4. PLAYING LIVE AT RADIO STATIONS. This is another non-paying gig with great publicity potential. Check out college radio stations especially for these opportunities. Try to combine your playing with a well-prepared interview. Always think in terms of *maximizing* each occasion.

5. PERFORMING IN RECORD STORES. This is a relatively new idea that was effective in boosting the careers of Suzanne Vega, Harry Connick Jr. and Lucious Jackson. The performer works for free, the only payoff being the extra sales his or her appearance generates. It works. Musicland, at the time the country's largest record chain, started the ball rolling and now Sam Goody, Borders Books & Music, and Tower Records have followed suit. When you have your CD or tape in-hand, look into this great promotional outlet.

There are many other promotional avenues for musicians. Your best resource, of course, is your own imagination. Bands (along with any support crew) should spend an hour a week together brainstorming on promotion ideas. You'll be surprised how many exciting thoughts spring from this kind of practice. Finally, remember this: There's no such thing as *too much* promotion and publicity. There's never enough!

Further Resources

BOOKS
Pettigrew, Jim. *The Billboard Guide to Music Publicity.* Second edition. New York: Billboard Books, 1996.

Levine, Michael. *Guerilla P.R.: How You Can Wage an Effective Publicity Campaign Without Going Broke.* Harper Business, 1994.

Soden, Garrett. *Hook, Spin, Buzz: How to Command Attention, Change Minds & Influence People.* Princeton: Peterson's/Pacesetter Books, 1996.

Yudkin, Marcia. *Six Steps to Free Publicity.* New York: Plume/Penguin, 1994.

Pinskey, Raleigh. *The Zen of Hype: An Insider's Guide to the Publicity Industry.* Citadel Press, 1991.

MEDIA DIRECTORIES

These are expensive so check your local library first!

Bacon's Publicity Checker. Bacon Publishing Co., annual.

Gale's Directory of Publications and Broadcast Media. Gale Research, Inc., annual.

Gebbie Press All-in-One Directory. Gebbie Press, annual.

The Musician's Guide to Touring & Promotion (a biannual "Special Edition" from MUSICIAN magazine). Available at most well-stocked magazine stores; excellent for setting up tours (also available on disk).

PRINTERS

Cameo Graphics, 917 Calhoun Street, Columbia, SC 29201. Good deals on posters.

9

Finding Gigs in All the Right Places:
Tapping the Sources of
Lesser-Known Music Work

The Changing Club Scene and New Opportunities

When most musicians think of "getting a gig," nightclubs are what usually come to mind. After all, clubs provide local forums for you to sharpen your stage act and spark that grassroots buzz so crucial for moving up to the next level of success. But clubs are not what they used to be and for some very good reasons.

First and foremost is population changes, or in marketing lingo, "demographics." Generally speaking, the largest portion of club-goers today are people in their twenties. There are approximately 46 million twenty-somethings in America at present—a large pool for sure. But just ten years ago, when the "baby-boomers" were clubbing, there were 76 million of *them*.

In other words there were 30 million *more* potential club-goers at that time. Correspondingly, the club scene was a lot healthier. Where are these 76 million now? Home raising families and grooving on their home-entertainment centers. This is slowly starting to change as baby boomer offspring begin entering college age.

While that's probably the most significant reason for a shrinking club scene, there are others as well. The lion's share of club profits is derived from bar receipts and people today are drinking less alcohol. Related to this are the numerous drunk-driving laws and drinking-age requirements, which have further eroded club profits and kept people home.

The heightened awareness of alcohol-related dangers has also affected liability insurance requirements for club owners. My father, for example, had a live entertainment club in Arizona that was put out of business because the state legislature (albeit controlled by a conservative, ultra-religious majority) upped the liability requirement for all Arizona bars (to the tune, for my Dad, of $24,000 per year!). While it hasn't gotten this bad in most other states, liability insurance does account for a big chunk of a club's expenses—one most musicians rarely consider when negotiating fees.

Before we start pitying the clubs for trends they can't control, it is also important to acknowledge how little clubs provide in terms of comfort, adequate ventilation, respect for musicians and general cleanliness. These too have kept potential patrons away. To battle shrinking profits, clubs have resorted to everything from mobile DJs to karaoke. These are some of the real factors affecting your attempts at securing club gigs. So what are musicians to do?

If you like to perform but feel a bit jaded against the club scene, you're in luck. There are hundreds, probably thousands, of hidden gig opportunities awaiting your act's performance. Besides a chance to play, these jobs will usually pay you more than a club date and also allow you to reach audiences who probably wouldn't set foot in most clubs. It's time to enlarge your borders.

Getting Ready

A key requirement for getting these new gigs is *professionalism*. You're aiming higher and dealing more with the "suit-and-tie crowd," so your presentation has to really shine. What does "professionalism" look like? Many things. First, the person that books your act should be a good communicator—someone who can succinctly and effectively deliver your sales pitch over the phone or on paper; has a high-functioning answering machine and upbeat message; possesses "people skills"; and is able to negotiate contracts and mediate between band members. With these skills, you'll make great headway. Without them, you're sunk.

Professionalism also means having all your "marketing communications" ready to go: promo kits, sales letters, business cards, contracts, confirmation letters, photos, testimonials from previous clients, demo tape, mailing labels, envelopes, etc. While we shouldn't judge a book (or, in this case, a band) by its cover, in reality we do. First impressions stick and they're very hard to unglue, especially in the world of business. Opt for the very best materials you can afford. Today you can save a lot of money in set-up by designing your promo materials on a computer with desktop publishing programs like *PageMaker* or *Publish It!* Be sure your materials have a clear theme and that all your contact information is clearly displayed on every component in the package. And keep good records!

Unlike club gigs, these will usually require written contracts between client and performer. In fact, you will find that some of these events will require two contracts—one from the client, and one from you (see Fig. 11.1 "Sample Performance Agreement," which you should feel free to adapt for your own needs).

The information you need in order to access these gigs won't be found in most gigging and club directories. Your public library will be the key resource in digging out these hidden opportunities. Libraries are repositories of useful information. Get to know the reference librarian. This person will be your guide through the many directories you're likely to consult.

As you find potential clients for your services, add them to your database. Software programs like Symantec's *ACT!* and Claris' *FileMaker Pro* help you manage your contacts. If you don't have a computer yet, make copies of the "Booking Research Worksheet" on the next page and use one for each | contact. Putting them in a 3-ring binder will keep them organized and handy.

Where to Look and What to Do

What follows is a list of gig possibilities with information on how to access them. It's not a complete list. Hopefully you'll be able to add your own ideas to it as you brainstorm with your bandmates. The gigs I'll be discussing cover a wide spectrum and won't apply to every musician. Some will match your act perfectly and others you'll want nothing to do with. A few may require more music than you have right now. But that doesn't mean you can't be preparing for them in the days ahead.

ASSOCIATIONS. Check out the multi-volume *Encyclopedia of Associations* and you'll find over 25,000 associations (read, similar interest groups) in the United States. Start with topical associations that strike your interest: environmental, arts, religious, media, educational, computer, social service, science fiction, etc. Virtually every association sponsors state, regional, and national meetings and conventions, and many of them hold dinners, programs, dances, or fundraisers that need music.

Call them and ask for two things: first, request they send you information about their association with a calendar of the coming years' events, and second, get the name of the association's Entertainment Coordinator or Chairperson of the Entertainment Committee. When you reach the enter-

BOOKING RESEARCH WORKSHEET

Package Out: _____   Follow-up Call: _____

                                              date

Name of Club/Facility: _____

Address: _____

_____

Phone Number(s): _____

Fax: _____

Contact Name: _____

Musical Style Preference: _____

Set Structure: _____

Budget Information: _____

Booking Procedure: _____

Past Acts: _____

Room Capacity: _____

Stage Size: _____

Sound System: _____

Monitor System: _____

Soundperson Name: _____

Lights: _____

Dressing Room: _____

Standard Amenities for Bands: _____

Additional Notes: _____

_____

_____

_____

_____

tainment person (after you've studied the information sent to you) be ready with a sales pitch tailored to their own special interests. The key is to create a "tie-in" with what they're all about. Begin with local associations and branch out.

BUSINESSES of all kinds are great possibilities for a wide variety of music work. Though business events are often booked by entertainment agencies or public relations firms, many are open to outside suggestions. Businesses need music for any number of functions including ground-breaking ceremonies, grand openings, seasonal sales, trade shows, promotions and retirements, company milestones, Christmas and New Year's Eve parties, and fashion shows. I once played a reggae gig for a Caribbean travel agency at a bridal fashion show in the Providence Civic Center in Rhode Island. Our job was to provide background music to entice brides to choose the Caribbean for their honeymoon spot. We were literally put behind a curtain, out of sight. So we just jammed some reggae grooves for two hours and walked away with $1500! This, and a few other gigs like it, helped us finance a recording we were making at the time. Can your act fit in with any of these events? Businesses are everywhere. The Yellow Pages is your best source for ideas. The possibilities are endless.

NON-PROFIT ORGANIZATIONS sponsor all kinds of events that need music. Again, begin locally with a directory from your public library and scope out those organizations with which you resonate. There are as many non-profits as there are associations, so it's a wide-open field. Don't forget civic orchestras, historical societies, health organizations, and foundations—all of which may sponsor dinners, dances or shows to benefit a cause. Some of these will be non-paying (basic freight and technical costs excluded), but what is lost in cash can be gained in publicity and important contacts. As with the business and association gigs, these jobs often lead to repeat business for your act.

CONVENTIONS make up one of the largest, fastest-growing markets in contemporary America. Just about every business, industry, government agency, social group, and professional association has, at the very least, an annual meeting or conference to discuss common interests, socialize with colleagues, make useful contacts, and plan for the coming year. And they all hire musicians for entertainment. Try to find out if there will be a particular theme for the convention and then tie-in your act with that theme.

The people you want to contact for these gigs are Events Planners. They specialize in organizing all the different components of a successful convention. Most work through entertainment companies but isn't that what you are? Again, the way you present yourself makes all the difference. There's a great annual resource called *Meeting Professionals International Directory* (214-712-7700, TX) that will give you the contact info on these people. You should be able to find it in a large public library. See also the Yellow Pages under "Convention Services and Facilities."

COUNTRY CLUBS need lots of music for an astounding variety of occasions. They have regularly scheduled dinners, dances, parties, and athletic events, as well as more specialized "theme" parties, seasonal activities, and shows. When you think of "clubs," however, don't limit yourself to just the big country clubs. Include every organized group you can think of, and you'll expand your market to include all kinds of non-public but well-paying gigs. Since country clubs are often linked to golf courses you can find a complete national list of them in a directory called *Golf Courses: The Complete Guide to over 14,000 Courses Nationwide.*

PARK PROGRAMS abound, and local government agencies are often in control. Begin with the "Recreation and Park Departments" in your region. If you want to check out parks programs outside your region consult *The Municipal Executive Directory* to put you in touch with key people in parks and recreation departments. Other government-sponsored work can include inner-city festivals, cultural-enrichment programs, officers and NCO clubs and even foreign tours. Some of this information can be found through the mayor's office in the city of your choice.

CRUISE LINES. Want to spend the winter jammin' on the warm waters of the Caribbean? Then perhaps cruise line work is for you. According to the Cruise Lines International Association (CLIA), the cruise industry is one of the fastest growing categories in the entire leisure market. The industry has tripled in size every ten years! New employees are needed to support the growing cruise vacation business, and this includes a wide assortment of musicians. Cruise lines rely on entertainment agents such as Marcelo Productions out of Miami (305-854-2228) and ProShip Entertainment out of Quebec (514-485-8823), who regularly hold auditions in various cities. Players should be able to

PERFORMANCE CRITIQUE WORKSHEET

COPY & DISTRIBUTE TO IMPARTIAL AUDIENCE MEMBERS BEFORE THE SHOW:

Band: _____ Date: _____

Type of Music: _____

Stage wear appropriate? _____

Was the band introduced? _____

Were the first couple of songs short, powerful, and to the point?

_____

Did the front person interact well with the crowd?

_____

Did he/she set the pace/tone of the performance?

_____

Did other members move well? _____

Were you entertained visually? _____

Was the key song announced? _____

Was there an obvious ending or did the performance simply die down?

_____

Was there a pitch for merchandise, mailing list, or future band info?

_____

Were you aware of the band's name from some aspect of the performance?

_____

PA/Sound quality? _____

Lighting quality? _____

Specifically, how could the performance be improved?

_____

_____

_____

Fig. 9.2   *adapted from "Doing Music & Nothing Else" by Peter Knickles*   **99**

read as well and have a wide repertoire to draw from. Salaries range from $350 to $500 per week and include food, lodging and transportation to and from the ship. For inside information on this job option, see *How to Get a Job with a Cruise Line* by Mary Fallon Miller.

HOTELS are a prime market for musicians and not just GB (general business) acts. Hotel-sponsored parties are frequent and a variety of music is sought for these. Much of this work comes through word of mouth. If you have a good relationship with the catering or sales staff, you'll get these jobs. A full list of a particular city's hotels can be obtained from that city's Convention & Visitor's Bureau or Department of Tourism.

PRIVATE PARTIES are another specialized but excellent market to pursue. Since many of these are held in well-to-do homes, it is important that you be able to relate socially as well as musically. How do you find out who's throwing a party? One way is to contact party organizers and caterers. Send them your business cards, letting them know what you can offer their clients by way of music. Stay in touch. You never know what will turn up.

PUBLIC RELATIONS FIRMS AND ADVERTISING AGENCIES can be good music clients because they are involved in creating and staging all kinds of events. A band I was playing with was approached by a PR rep for McDonald's to see if we'd be interested in performing at the grand opening of one of their restaurants. It's nice when they come to you, but you can also go to them. Whatever your musical specialty, you should let all the advertising and PR firms in your area know, so when they need your type of music they'll know where you are. Remember, public relations and advertising people thrive on innovation and are open to suggestions for new or unusual uses of music. Therefore, when talking with these firms, let creativity rule. Make suggestions that are too unusual to present to other clients, and you'll be treated as a kindred spirit.

SCHOOLS offer a broad market for all kinds of music, whether elementary, high school or college. Colleges, in particular, are rich with playing opportunities. They should be viewed as small cities with scores of events happening each week throughout the year. If you're serious about playing the college circuit you should definitely check out The National Association of Collegiate

Activities (NACA). NACA holds annual regional conferences (read: trade shows) where musical acts can exhibit their wares for the hundreds of college talent buyers passing through. Live showcase opportunities are also possible and, if you're liked, can result in "block bookings" along the college touring circuit. To book yourself at colleges, call the student activities office and find out who is responsible for hiring entertainment at that school. Call that person and inquire about specific events during the upcoming year that might be appropriate for your style of music.

For music opportunities on the elementary, middle, junior high and high school levels, check out *How to Make Money Performing in Public Schools* by David Heflick. Heflick discusses what schools are looking for, developing a program, how arts commissions work in relation to schools, promotion, scheduling, performance, payment and follow-up. An excellent handbook.

These are just a few of the thousands of "hidden" gig opportunities available to musicians. Musical jobs are everywhere and there's no reason you shouldn't enjoy the rewards of these less-common jobs. With the current slump in the club scene and surplus of willing bands, these lesser-known jobs should be all the more attractive.

Just remember, most of these jobs will bring you in close contact with the professional business world. The musician who can communicate on the same professional level will be the one who gets the gig.

Further Resources

BOOKS

Gibson, James. *Playing for Pay: How to Be a Working Musician.* Cincinnati: Writers Digest Books, 1990.

Buttwinick, Marty. *How to Make a Living as a Musician: So You Never Have to Have a Day Job Again!* Sonata Publishing, 1994.

McCord, Robert. *The Best Public Golf Courses in the United States, Canada, the Caribbean and Mexico.* Second edition. New York: Random House, 1996.

Snyder, Arthur Jack and J. C. Wright. *Golf Courses: The Complete Guide to over 14,000 Courses Nationwide* (Lanier Guide). Berkeley: Ten Speed Press, 1996.

Miller, Mary Fallon. *How to Get a Job with a Cruise Line*. Fourth edition. St. Petersburg, FL: Ticket to Adventure, Inc.

Smith, Darren L. *Parks Directory of the United States: A Guide to More Than 4,700 National and State Parks, Recreation Areas, Historic Sites, Battlefields, Monuments*. Detroit: Omnigraphics, 1994.

Heflick, David. *How to Make Money Performing in Public Schools*. Orient, WA: Silcox Productions.

DIRECTORIES
Encyclopedia of Associations (Gale Research)

Meeting Professionals International Directory, 214-712-7700, TX.

The Municipal Executive Directory (check your local library).

ORGANIZATIONS
The National Association of Collegiate Activities. 3700 Forest Drive, Suite 200, Columbia SC 29204; 800-845-2338.

Booking Club Gigs:
Getting Your Foot in the Door
without Getting It Slammed

You've been calling a club for months, and you finally get the booker on the phone. Don't celebrate yet—the real work is still ahead. That crucial conversation you're about to strike up is an art that requires skill. Luck and talent won't help you much on the phone.

What you say and how you say it is as important as what you shouldn't say. By understanding the needs of your market, you can anticipate a booking agent's response and turn a "no" into a future opportunity.

Getting Your Foot in the Door

As mentioned in chapter 7, the current club scene is experiencing a bit of a slump owing to a smaller club-going population and some anti-drinking legislation (see previous chapter). Despite these woes, however, the clubs still provide a crucial outlet for bands to hone their performance skills and catalyze local, regional and national followings. So how does one go about getting club gigs?

Selling your band on the phone is a tough proposition. Try to realize the volume of calls clubs receive, then imagine the booker's frame of mind. You want exactly what 100 bands a day want. What makes *you* worthy of the coveted slot?

Before you call, do some market research. Make sure your music is compatible with the club's entertainment focus. Check the local entertainment guides for info on who's booked where. If possible make a personal contact first. The music business, like most businesses, is *relationship*-driven. If you can meet someone eye-to-eye, you'll have a head start.

When you call, keep your tone friendly and relaxed. Get right to the point. Bookers are busy. They need to know exactly what you want right away. Get a feel for each person's style. Be very clear about the date you want, thank them for their time, and leave a number. It's important to specify a particular night. That way, if your date won't work, there's a chance to ask what date will.

Instead of too-frequent callbacks that can irritate the booker, tell him or her you'll call them back in a couple of weeks. Then use that promise to launch the next conversation. Don't vent your anger on the booking agent. Remember, they're in control and you're not. You're in a buyer's market. The only control you have is your following. If you're trying to develop a club following, incurring the wrath of a booker could be a terminal setback.

Even in music meccas like LA, the club circuit is small. Bookers and managers know when a band can draw a crowd. When you get to that point, a club that turned you down six months ago might call you.

But, nine times out of ten, clubs won't call you back. Accept this as the way it is. Be persistent, however. Give them a few weeks to hear your material, then call at least once a week, depending on the response. If they say they haven't received the tape by then, send another. Even when a booker is curt and abrupt, make a point of ending on a polite, friendly note. Cultivate a calm, hang-tough approach.

Talking Business

Your job is to convince the booker that it would be to the club's advantage to have you play there. How do you communicate this?

First, emphasize the crowd you will draw. Even if it's just fifteen people, let them know. Second, stress the uniqueness of your music—what makes it stand out from the rest? Third, let the booker know about your promotional plan for the show and all the *free* publicity the club will receive from your mailings, flyers, radio announcements and newspaper calendar listings. Show them you are organized, professional and thinking ahead. This alone will set you apart from the crowd.

Should you send a contract when you secure a date? Most clubs operate strictly on verbal agreement. Usually this is okay. As you get more popular it becomes easier to secure written agreements with clubs. Early on, however, there's little you can expect in the way of formal contracts.

Remember, a club is a *business*. It has to make financial sense for them to give you a gig. Bands that haven't developed a following yet should get some college airplay in the vicinity of the clubs they want to play first. You have to respect the club's position; if no one's ever heard of you, how can they make money from the show?

Here are a few ideas for how you can work together with clubs to bring in larger crowds.

1. Hook up with local promoters; there are dozens of promoters that would love to promote a club once a week.

2. Call local record labels, record stores, magazines, newspapers, radio and TV stations and see if they want to have a night at the club. Lots of radio stations promote clubs to their listeners and are always looking for new affiliations. Labels are always renting clubs to showcase their bands to the local media.

3. Call all the above people and talk to the promotion departments, especially at radio stations. See if you can send them tickets to your show. Make a habit of mailing them tickets.

4. Set up a contest with the club, like a legs contest, or during intermission announce, "The first person to the bar with a red T-shirt gets a free CD." Bands can donate CDs and tapes; clubs can donate free drinks. The point is to give everyone a good feeling about that club and that band.

5. Run co-op ads in local magazines and newspapers advertising the show and the contest. Give the ads pizazz. Put in coupons for free admission or a free drink with admission. This will make your ad a hundred times more effective and bring in a lot more people.

6. Encourage the club owner to have his employees to put names on the club's guest list. Their friends will add to the club's regular crowd. Request that the band have an unlimited guest list. This will make the job of getting all their fans to your club easier.

Don't start until you're ready. Make sure your vocals are strong, your arrangements tight, your equipment adequate and your promotion happening. Jumping the gun and taking gigs for which you're not ready can take months—even years—to repair. As the saying goes, "You never get a second chance to make a first impression." Prepare and come out strong.

Further Resources

BOOKS

Garbo, Liz. *Book Your Own Tour: The Independent Musician's Guide to Cost-Effective Touring and Promotion.* Second edition. San Diego: Rockpress, 1997.

Shagan, Rena. *Booking & Tour Management for the Performing Arts.* Second edition. New York: Allworth Press, 1996.

Scheff, Joanne and Philip Kotler. *Standing Room Only: Strategies for Marketing the Performing Arts.* Cambridge, MA: Harvard Business School Press, 1997. Good for organizing larger shows and concerts.

Barrell, M. Kay. *The Technical Production Handbook: A Guide for Performing Arts Presenting Organizations and Touring Companies.* New York: Samuel French, 1992.

PERIODICALS

Musician's Guide to Touring and Promotion. Musician magazine. This city-by-city booking guide is also available on disk.

ON-LINE RESOURCES

Deterrent DIY Tour Guide, http://www.deterrent.br.ca/tour.html. Maintained by bands for bands, a clearinghouse for bands who want to book their own tours.

Musi-Cal Performer Index, http://www.automatrix.com/cgi-bin/list-performers. Provides an international concert calendar for folk, bluegrass, blues, and world music performers, organized alphabetically by artist. Also, add your own concerts.

Performance Concert Tours Database, http://www.quest.net/performance/toursearch. Need to find out who is coming to your town, where your favorite band is playing or the schedule for your favorite venue?

Polaris, http://www.epn.com/polaris. Get the latest celebrity appearance and tour schedules.

Pollstar, http://www.pollstar.com/. Concert tour information database including all genres of music and other events.

World-Wide Internet Live Music Archive (WILMA), http://www.wilma.com/. Comprehensive, cross-referenced, and searchable database of concerts indexed by artist, venue, and city.

Live Deals:
The Ins and Outs of Performance Contracts

There is nothing worse than coming off the stage after a smokin' gig only to find that the club owner or event coordinator has decided to delay your payment. What's a band to do?

Well, hopefully, you will have *already* done something to avoid this situation: secured a signed performance contract.

Get it in Writing

The performance contract—an agreement between the band or its legal representatives and the venue operator or promoter—is the basic legal tool for staging a show. Not all acts sign such *written* agreements. This is especially true of young bands that haven't yet established a track record. But the critical points in both oral and written agreements are fundamentally the same, varying primarily in degree.

If at all possible the contract should be a written document. The problem with an oral agreement is that in the event of a dispute, it is difficult to prove the terms agreed to between the venue rep and the band. If the contract is written, then the agreed-to points are much easier to document. A sample written performance contract is shown in Fig. 11.1. Feel free to copy and adapt this contract to your needs. It should also be noted that a contractual relationship with clubs or promoters (presenters) is only as good as the relationship between the owner or promoter and the group itself. You should therefore make a threshold determination of whether the owners of the club are people with whom you really wish to deal.

Do not accept a contract written by the presenter. You want to insure that the interests of your group are primary. Consequently, you should send out your own contract. Some colleges require that their contract be used. If this is the case, insist that your own contract also be signed by the presenter

109

and made part of the presenter's contract. As long as your terms are reasonable there shouldn't be a problem with this arrangement.

Contract Essentials Checklist

Regardless of the type or size of performing group, there are a number of standard elements that all contracts should contain:

1. The date of the agreement.
2. The artist's name, address, phone and fax number, and primary contact person.
3. The presenter (hereafter referred to as "employer") name, address, phone and fax number, and primary contact person.
4. The date and time of the performance, including number and length of set(s) and duration of breaks between sets.
5. The location of the venue where your performance will take place.
6. The artist's fee, plus the time and manner of payment (check, cash, etc.); whether there is a deposit required; and a guarantee that there will be no taxes, union charges or other surprise deductions from the fee when it is paid.
7. Any technical requirements regarding stage size, lighting, sound, and dressing room amenities.
8. Arrival time, set-up time, and the time for sound-checking.
9. An "Act of God" clause which releases the artist from liability for failure to perform if such failure is caused by an event beyond their control. Such clauses are referred to as "boilerplate" (standard legal clauses common to most time-sensitive agreements).

Of course, what's standard for bands may not be for presenters. They may want the contract to include other "essentials" (from their perspective) such as a clause about decibel levels or a "radius clause" wherein your group can't play within three or five miles of his club within 30, 60, or 90 days. The latter, however, usually happens only when the group has a large following.

You might also want to find out if the club is liable for any damage to your stage-equipment by customers during your hours of employment (as stated in the contract) or any damage to the customers if, say, a speaker falls on one of them. If the club isn't liable, you'll want to check your own insurance coverage.

You are ultimately responsible for your own equipment.

Contract Riders

The above are the nine essentials of a performance contract, also known as the "contract face." This should suffice for most gigs. Any additional requirements fall under the heading of "Riders"—supplemental attachments to the standard contract face.

Contract riders can range from such simple requests as a meal and beverage for band members all the way to the picayune, like the removal of brown M&Ms from the mix (I kid you not)!

Riders are vital unless you wish to exist solely on the presumed generosity of club owners and concert promoters. On the other hand, you can't expect a club or a promoter to provide what you need unless they know what it is. It's best to make the rider part of the contract so you have only one document to sign.

When the Club Doesn't Pay You

If you are owed money by the club owner and the owner refuses to pay, you have recourse to the courts (and to your AFM local if it's a union club, but that's a whole other story). This obviously can be an expensive proposition and is not one to be pursued lightly.

For example, Massachusetts law in general provides opportunity if the claim is no more than $2,000 or if you are willing to limit your claim to that amount. You can bring your own action in the small claims court in the county where you reside or where the club is located.

The procedure requires you to go to the county clerk for your local court system and pay a small fee for filing, stamping, and serving the complaint (in MA, $14 for a claim under $500; $19 for claims over $500). The sheriff then serves the complaint on the defendant, setting forth a date, time, and place for a hearing. The defendant can file a counterclaim within forty-eight hours of the hearing, but it has to be verified, or sworn to (yours does not). If you lose, you cannot appeal, and that is the end of the case. Your cause will be greatly strengthened, however, if you can present a signed and dated contract to the judge. Similar small claims procedures are in effect in most states.

Getting Legal Help

The following Sample Performance Agreement (see Fig. 11.1.) can be used as-is or modified for your own use. If you are going to need some additional modifications for your own performance contract you will need expert legal advice.

In many cities you can find low-cost expertise through nearby Volunteer Lawyers for the Arts (VLA) groups. The VLA's stated purpose is to "provide legal assistance and educational programs to the artistic community, particularly those artists and arts organizations who are financially unable to obtain necessary legal services elsewhere." In order to access VLA services, it is necessary to fill out an application and pay a $50 application fee (this fee can be waived if your inability to pay can be demonstrated).

If you are eligible for pro bono services, the VLA will attempt to refer you to a volunteer attorney. If it's determined that you're not eligible, the VLA will assist you in locating an attorney who may be willing to provide legal services on a reduced fee basis.

The Massachusetts VLA can be reached at 617-523-1764. Outside of Massachusetts call the main office in New York at 212-977-9270 for the VLA office nearest you.

Making arrangements for performing deserves special consideration and planning. Keep in mind that your ability to get your music out there will be enhanced by getting your business act together.

Further Resources

ORGANIZATIONS

Volunteer Lawyers for the Arts (VLA), 1285 Avenue of the Americas, 3rd Floor, New York, NY 10019; 212-977-9270.

SAMPLE PERFORMANCE AGREEMENT

THIS CONTRACT for the personal services of musicians on the engagement described below, made this_____ day of _____, 20_____, between the undersigned purchaser of music and musicians.

ARTIST _____

LOCATION _____ DATE _____ TIME _____

ARTIST FEE $ _____ DEPOSIT _____

TICKET PRICE _____

PAYMENT Cash/School Check/Certified Check CAPACITY _____

PAY TO: _____ TYPE EVENT _____

SETS _____ ARRIVAL TIME _____

CONTACT PERSON _____ PHONE _____

FAX _____

REQUIREMENTS:

DRESSING ROOM One clean, well-lit room for ten persons STAGE SIZE _____

SOUND Employer/Band provides   LIGHTS Employer/Band provides

FOOD/BEVERAGES _____

This agreement shall be governed by and interpreted in accordance with the laws of the Commonwealth of _____. This agreement constitutes the entire agreement between the parties relating to the subject matter hereof, and all previous understandings, whether oral or written, have been merged here-in. No alteration, amendment or modification hereof shall be binding unless in writing signed by all of the parties. Upon its execution, this Agreement shall take effect as a sealed instrument in accordance with the terms and provisions set forth above.

The Agreement of the Artist to perform is subjected to proven detention by sickness, strikes, adverse weather conditions, acts of God, or any other legitimate condition beyond control for which the Artist will not be held responsible for any loss incurred by Purchaser as result thereof.

Kindly return contracts within ten (10) days in order to insure confirmation of date.

The Purchaser in signing this contract warrants that he/she is of legal age and has the right to enter into this contract.

If you have any questions regarding the Agreement, or if we can be of further assistance, please do not hesitate to call or write.

Thank you for allowing us to be or service, and best wishes for a successful show

AGREED AND ACCEPTED

ARTIST REPRESENTATIVE   PURCHASER

DATE _____   DATE _____

Fig. 11.1

WHEN YOU NEED A MUSIC LAWYER

Sooner or later, you'll have to bite the bullet and seek out legal counsel as a musician, so it's important to know how to select the best lawyer for your needs. Here are a few tips to help you with the screening process:

1.GET A SPECIALIST. The value of a music attorney is determined in large part by the quantity and quality of his or her contacts in the music/entertainment field. Artists should be cautioned against the natural inclination to use a friend, relative ("My Cousin Vinny"), or family lawyer to fill their entertainment law needs. This is fine if they're qualified. However, the trend today is toward greater legal specialization than ever before because of the increased complexity of our commercial society.

Unless a lawyer deals regularly with management, recording, and music publishing contracts; copyright protection and administration; and licensing of intellectual and artistic property, chances are that he or she won't understand or appreciate the entertainment industry and its peculiar problems sufficiently.

2. GET REFERRALS FROM OTHER MUSICIANS. A referral from a satisfied client is a good start, but also...

3. GET REFERENCES. Always ask the attorney for at least two client-references and their phone numbers. This is a perfectly reasonable request and any balking at this should be your cue to exit.

Be sure that the work the lawyer did for this client is similar to what you need, and also that the work was performed in the last six months to a year (this business changes too fast for sporadic legal excursions).

4. GET THE DIRT (IF THERE IS ANY). You can make two important phone calls to find out if there have been any complaints lodged in your city or state against this attorney. They're calls worth making:

A. Secretary of State's office (look for the phone number in the "Government" section of your phone book).

B. The Better Business Bureau (4200 Wilson Blvd., Suite 800, Arlington, VA 22203-1804. Phone: 703-276-0100; Fax: 703-525-8277; http://www.bbb.org/). The Better Business Bureau Online Directory lists the addresses and phone numbers of Better Business Bureaus in cities throughout the United States and Canada.

5. HAVE A MEETING. Most attorneys will waive their usual hourly fee for the first consultation. At this consultation meeting you'll want to:

A. Ask the attorney about his basic philosophy of life. Why? Because this will help you understand his worldview, a significant relationship component. If your worldview turns out to be diametrically opposed to the attorney's, it probably means you are not a good match for each other.

B. Inquire about the extent and quality of the attorney's pertinent industry contacts.

C. Find out how the fee structure would work to avoid any misunderstandings.

A note on legal fees: Sometimes you'll need legal counsel for short-term projects like putting together the appropriate performance and partnership agreements, trademarking your business/band name, incorporating your business, and copyright registration. These kinds of projects are usually paid for as a "flat fee" based on the attorney's hourly rate. Longer-term projects and legal representation to the music industry (to labels, publishers, merchandise companies, etc.) are often paid in "points" (percentage points) of contract advances and/or future royalties.

6. FEEL THE VIBE. Trust your instincts.

7. DO-(SOME OF)-IT-YOURSELF. A lot of groundwork can be done by yourself when it comes to short-term legal needs. For example, modern communication technologies like the Internet let you do a national trademark search from your desktop. For tips on this and other do-it-yourself legal resources contact Nolo Press (http://www.nolo.com/) or call 510-549-1976 for their free self-help law books and software catalog.

chapter

Twelve Things You Can Do to Get the Most Out of Every Gig

One of the keys to music business success is the ability to maximize limited resources. This simply means making the most of the time, money and effort available to promote your career. Though your resources may be meager, it's what you do with them that really counts.

This principle applies to every aspect of a musician's life, but I want to focus on just one of them: *How to get the most out of every gig you play.*

Gigs are one of the most potential-rich avenues for bands and musicians in terms of networking and exposure, yet few take full advantage of the opportunities they present. *Each gig should be seen as an occasion for expansion of your music and performing skills, your fan base, your media contacts and industry relationships, etc.* What follows are 12 ways to get the most out of every gig.

Things to Do Before the Show

You've just booked a gig at a new club and it's two months away. Let's look at some of the things you can do <u>now</u> to maximize this performance before, during and after the show.

1. *Find out all you can about* the room you're going to play. Know the stage size, what times bands are expected to sound check and to begin and end playing and whether or not there's a dressing room. Find out about the sound and lighting system, if it's provided, and talk to the engineers. If possible, ask other bands who have played the room for tips and pointers. Remember, you're there to perform a show, not worry about all these details. Get the right information before the gig and you'll have that much less anxiety during the gig.

2. *Rehearse your show straight through as if it were the real thing.* Pay attention to your stage presence as well as your stage sound. Practice any movements or dance steps you're planning to use at the gig. You may also want to hold a full dress rehearsal and have someone snap some Polaroids or shoot a low-budget video of the group to see what the audience will see. This is always educational (and often humbling!). Remember, you're trying to make the most of this gig.

3. *Publicize the show.* Print up a bunch of flyers with all pertinent information, including contact number. You're competing with a lot of other events so you want your flyer to stand out. Use colorful paper and eye-catching graphics. Seek the advice of a friend who's an artist or go the extra distance and have a professional create a killer gig poster for your act, leaving a blank space at the bottom for all relevant info. Once you have your flyer in-hand, it's time to send it out. First, send it to all your fans, your primary support base. Second, send it to all music writers in the local media. To obtain this information, visit the reference librarian at your public library. Tell them what you need and you'll be directed to a number of useful directories. Two particularly good ones are *Gale's Directory of Publications and Broadcast Media,* which lists over 36,000 print and broadcast media, and the *Broadcasting Yearbook,* covering radio, TV, and cable outlets in the United States and Canada.

Write down all dailies, weeklies, and monthlies within a 10-mile radius of where your show will happen. Your list should include music publications as well as mainstream press. Chances are you've already started such a list but you want it to be as comprehensive as possible. Jot down phone numbers as well as addresses. You'll want to call each publication to find out two things: first, the name of the arts and entertainment editor to whom you will send your notice, and second, how much "lead time" the publication needs for printing a concert listing (i.e., when you need to send in your listing for it to be printed before your show). For more insights into working the media, see chapter 13, "Media Power: Creating a Music Publicity Plan that Works."

You'll also want to send a good photo of your act, if available. Your gig listing will receive a hundred times more attention with a photo. It's worth the extra expense. Make it as easy as possible for the editor to use the photo by finding out the exact specifications required for photo submissions when you call about the other items.

The next list you want to assemble is that of local radio. Most stations have local concert listings as part of their news segment and you'll want to target a flyer to each. Be sure the station receives your notice at least a week before the show. If the gig is extra-special (i.e., a high-profile showcase room), you may also want to send out personal invitations and free tickets to local music industry representatives (record execs, booking agents, personal managers, entertainment attorneys, radio personnel, etc.). Remember, think *maximization*.

Besides your mailings, you'll also want to post your flyers in music stores, hangouts, inside the venue (don't forget the bathroom stalls!) and on all community bulletin boards in the area.

If you want to save money on the mailings, you can have your flyer reduced to one-quarter its size (from 8 1/2" x 11" to 4 1/4" x 5 1/2") and printed on postcard stock. This lowers your postal rate about 21 cents per piece. If you're doing huge mailings on a monthly basis, check with the post office about a "bulk-mailing permit" for additional savings.

Things to Do During the Gig

At last, the night has arrived. You walk into the club, greet the sound and lighting engineers (you already know each other), park your belongings in the appropriate space, and proceed to set up on the familiar stage. Smooth. Now here are a few more things you can do to make tonight's show a standout:

4. *Have a banner with the band's logo* hung up behind the act, high enough to be easily read by all (for banner sources, see Further Resources at the end of this chapter). You'd be surprised how many people will see and hear your act and never know who you are. A visible banner solves that problem.

5. Place *"table tents"* with band information (read, "hype") and gig schedules on each table around the club. Use sturdy, postcard stock for best results.

6. *Set up a visible area for merchandise* (T-shirts, tapes, CDs, etc.). The person (non-band member) running the merchandising can also oversee the new fan mailing list. Be sure there's plenty of writing instruments and paper on-hand.

7. Have plenty of *business cards* with a contact person's name and number in the pockets of all band members and support crew. Distribute them liberally.

8. When you're on stage, remember to *make your show visually as well as aurally stimulating.* You're on display and all your clothing, colors, movements and lines should blend with the music you're playing. Give the people what they want—a feast of sight and sound. This is an essential part of "working the crowd."

Things to Do After the Gig

You just had a great gig! Congratulations. A lot more people know about you now than before this evening. There's a small buzz brewing and now it's time to follow it up.

9. But first, before you leave the club, *try to secure another gig* with the owner while you're fresh in his mind. At the very least, seek a verbal commitment and call within a few days to confirm and formalize it.

10. Before leaving the club *make sure the dressing room is in the same condition as that in which you found it.* While this may sound trite, it's a basic human consideration and will speak well of your act.

11. *Strike while it's hot!* As soon as possible, follow-up on any industry contacts made at the gig. Call and thank them for coming to the show. Build rapport. Network.

12. Finally, *send a personal letter to all new fans,* thanking them for coming to the show and informing them further about the band and other ways they can support you (for example, calling club owners, calling radio stations to request your song, purchasing your music at local retail outlets, telling their friends about you, etc.).

Of course, you can forget about all the above suggestions and just play the gig. After all, you're musicians and that's what you do best. Granted.

But more and more, we are seeing the smarter bands being brought home because they know how to organize publicity, work the radio, boost promotion, and generally maximize and optimize their limited resources. After all, why should one gig equal *one* when it can equal *ten*? Maximization is the key. Go for it!

Further Resources

BANNERS

Bannerama, Waltham, MA, 617-899-4744.

The Banner Barn, 800-537-7469.

PART THREE:

rising up

13

Demo Diversity: Customizing Your Demos for Maximum Exposure

Here's a scenario that has happened to more than one band: You're a hard rock outfit with a killer demo tape of your most slammin' tunes. You've used this tape to secure a load of club dates in your region. You're also versatile musicians able to read and play almost any kind of music. One day you hear about this person looking for a band that can play '50s covers for a wedding reception. It's a fifteen-hundred-dollar gig. You think: "We can pull this off easy!" The person doing the hiring, however, wants to hear a tape *today*. All you have is your hard rock club demo. They need to make a quick decision. Somebody else beats you to it. You lose.

The Versatile Musician

"Versatility" is the key today for an active musician life. The music market is segmenting at a dizzying speed. People's musical tastes are diversifying. What was the traditional choice yesterday is just one of a kaleidoscope of choices today. Musicians who can diversify their repertoire today and adapt their offerings to this splintering market are the ones who will secure the most gigs tomorrow.

The best way to ride this market change is to make sure you have a variety of demo tapes prepared for the variety of gig opportunities that can arise. Perhaps you're a jazz band and able to play classical-sounding music as well.

Or maybe you're a reggae band that can also spice up your set with some salsa and calypso; or a country band able to lay down some bluegrass and zydeco too. Think about what styles you can offer and then put together a demo tape *designed for each*.

Targeting Your Demo Markets

Each music style demands its own representative tape. You'll be sending demo tapes to a wide variety of people and companies. In order to communicate most effectively, each opportunity will require a certain angle or slant. Let's look at the two most common targets for demos: Live performance venues and general career/industry gatekeepers.

1. PERFORMANCE. *Club* gigs are more easily secured if the demo tape has some covers mixed in with a band's original songs. By including covers you're telling the booker or club owner that your ultimate goal in playing that club is to communicate with the patrons and help them have a good time. Covers provide a familiar bridge between the band and audience. Once the connection is made the audience will more easily receive the original material. As with all demo tapes, this one should be front-loaded with your best tune first. It should include three or four songs at the most. A live-performance recording with cheering audience also helps.

The same goes for *private parties and events*. Demo tapes should be a mix of covers and originals with a slight emphasis on covers. It's also important to find out as much as possible about the audience at such events since this will determine what you should emphasize on your tape in terms of repertoire, decibel-level, etc. For example you'll probably choose a different set of tunes for a banker's retirement party than for a high-schooler's sweet-sixteen party. Let your tape reflect this.

Wedding gigs probably demand the most versatility. People often desire musicians for quiet background music before the procession, ceremonial music during the procession, and upbeat music for the party after the ceremony. I know a number of groups who can meet each of these needs and their demo tapes show it. The tape will usually have quiet music for background and ceremony on one side and more upbeat tunes for the reception on the other side. Of course, the person responsible for obtaining the music for the wedding event is thrilled to be able to secure all the talent they need in one place. The band is happy to have a full day's playing (and paying) schedule.

What if you're looking for *studio session work* as a player or vocalist? Again, versatility is the key. You want your tape to reflect your abilities in as many styles as possible with your own unique stamp on each. Excerpt 30 second fade ins/outs for each style and have two (a fast and a slow) excerpt for each in order to give the listener a well-rounded hearing of your abilities. Label the tape by song and style accordingly.

2. CAREER/INDUSTRY/DEMOS. While versatility is the key to landing a rich variety of paying gigs, *uniqueness* is what attracts industry attention.

Those who've secured thriving music careers have done so because they had something so special about their talent, music and/or songs that people could not *not* pay attention. A few copies and clones might make a splash occasionally but usually it is uniqueness that receives the highest awards.

Therefore if you're contacting *artist managers*, for example, put away your Bon Jovi covers and submit original material. Managers for the most part are seeking fresh talent. The same applies to *entertainment attorneys* who may be in a position to mediate between you and the rest of the industry.

While *record company* rosters may be littered with bands and singers that all sound alike, the ten percent that *do* go on to success are often unique in a sea of sameness. It is that uniqueness that often propels them to gold and platinum careers. Send A&R (artist and repertoire) contacts only that which reveals your distinctive sound.

A note here about sending unsolicited tapes to A&R: Don't do it; you'll just be wasting time and money. Unsolicited tapes are almost always pitched unopened. Heartless? No. There are simply not enough people hours to listen to every unsolicited tape coming through the mail.

Music publishers are looking for original songs. Keep the arrangements simple. The song is what must be highlighted. Publishers don't care about guitar solos, multiple synth tracks or how well you can play the zither. They just want to hear the song. Don't make it difficult for them by letting a lot of unnecessary stuff get in the way. One instrument and a voice can suffice if that's all the song requires.

How many songs should you send? John Redmond of Irving/Almo Music Publishers has this to say: "If it must be three songs...by all means. If it can be two songs...even better. *If it's one song...fantastic!*" More and more, I'm hearing music publishers say they want one great song submitted at a time. Be as objective as possible and only send your best. Send your song "triple-back"— that is, the same song three times in a row to facilitate efficient listening. Publishers also want to see a lyric sheet typed on 8 1/2" x 11" paper with title and author at the top, chorus indented and verses numbered. Include your name, address and telephone number at the bottom of the page under the copyright notice.

There are other industry targets to whom you may want to consider sending your demo tape that are beyond the scope of this chapter. They include *commercial music* and *jingle houses, AV* and *multimedia companies,* and *play producers* or *musical theater.* For some good information on pitching your music to these targets see *The Songwriter's Market Guide to Song & Demo Submission Formats* by the editors of Songwriter's Market (Writer's Digest Books). Each of the above markets has its own protocol and procedures for submitting demos. The more you're acquainted with these procedures, the greater your chances of successfully getting your music heard and hopefully placed.

More Tips for Effective Demos

- **USE FRESH, PROPERLY SIZED TAPES.** Cassettes are cheap enough that you don't need to be recording your demos over already-recorded tape. When you use the erase head on your own tape deck it will usually be in the same alignment with information recorded with the same machine. A separate deck can sometimes pick up a ghost of the previous signal. The tape may sound perfectly fine at home but sound unintelligible on another machine due to bleed-through. It's much safer to just use fresh tape.

  I've received many 90-minute tapes with only three songs on them. This is a waste of good tape. You can get high-quality blank cassettes at custom lengths (15 minutes on each side is usually adequate) from any number of tape wholesalers. Two good suppliers are Discmakers (1-800-468-9353) and Cassette House (1-800-321-KSET). Call for their free catalogs and tape samples.

- **CHECK EVERY CASSETTE** you make to be sure that the entire song or songs were recorded. Machines make errors. If you insist on reusing someone else's tape make sure that it's blank all the way through.

- **AVOID SLOPPY PACKAGING.** I have seen too many situations where someone has sent three songs on a cassette that looked like it had been in constant circulation since the early seventies. The titles were written in ballpoint pen on a misfitted cassette label. The outer case looked like it had been used as a hockey puck. Don't let your songs be eliminated on the basis of a sloppy demo package. Remember, a demo is your calling card. Computer desktop publishing has brought quality graphic design within reach of just about everybody. Present yourself professionally.

- **PROVIDE ALL NECESSARY CONTACT INFORMATION ON THE TAPE.** More often than not the tape will become separated from the other materials you send. Be sure the listener knows whom to contact.

- **NEVER "SHOTGUN"—TARGET!** Sending tapes to a random list taken from a directory is inevitably wasteful for you and annoying for the recipient. A record company that puts out country music does not want to hear avant jazz. A club booker for a top-forty venue probably doesn't want to hear world music. Send tapes only to those you have already screened through an introductory phone call.

- **FOCUS** your efforts so you can maximize your limited resources. Customize, follow-up and reap the rewards!

Further Resources

The Songwriter's Market Guide to Song & Demo Submission Formats. Editors of Songwriter's Market. Cincinnati: Writer's Digest Books, 1994.

14

Media Power:
Creating a Music Publicity Plan That Works,
Part 1

When psychobilly rockers The Cramps signed their first recording contract they didn't do it in the standard office setting like everyone else. Instead they marched over to the cemetery where Bela Lugosi is buried and ceremonially signed it on his grave. Needless to say a photographer and journalist were in tow and the event received major media attention. With such a creative idea how could the media resist?

Publicity is the art of using the media (radio, press, TV, advertising, blimps, etc.) to expose your cause or event. Publicity includes all of the ways you can get noticed without buying expensive ad space or time. Publicity makes people talk, think, read, and hear about you. And it costs little or nothing.

One thing all bands have in their favor as far as publicity is concerned is this: *The media has space to fill and depends on us to provide the filler.* Did you know that 75% of what you read in magazines and newspapers is "planted?" This means it came to the media vehicle from outside, *from people like you* and me. Publicity provides an open door for music promotion. The key to successful publicity is having a strategic plan that leaves no stone unturned. In this chapter we'll lay out the ingredients for a successful media plan. In the following chapter we'll look at developing this plan into a powerful ongoing publicity *schedule*, along with a treasure of useful resources.

Know Thy Audience

The first ingredient for a successful publicity plan is *a clear idea of your market audience: who* they are, *what* they read and listen to, *where* they go. Each style of music is a subcultural world with its own outlook, values, organizations, and media. Your job is to understand this world inside and out.

For example, a jazz musician should be aware of the publications *Downbeat, Jazziz* and *Coda*, organizations like the Jazz World Database, various cable TV and radio shows specializing in jazz performance, as well as the hundreds of generalist outlets for jazz music. Likewise a reggae band will be acquainted with *The Beat, Reggae Report* and *The Reggae Quarterly,* record labels like Mango, Heartbeat and Shanachie, and organizations like Reggae Ambassadors Worldwide. The same strategy applies to folk, metal, alternative, blues, classical, country, Latin, world, experimental, and all other music styles.

Through learning about the who, what, and where of your music's audience you also learn about the best ways to reach that audience. This is the foundation for an effective publicity plan.

How do you find out about your audience's preferences? Observe. Ask questions. Another good way is to go through one of the better industry directories (*The Recording Industry Sourcebook* and *The Yellow Pages of Rock* are excellent) and look for listings of organizations relevant to your style of music. These groups often serve as general information clearinghouses that can make your job easier. Also, don't overlook local sources relevant to your style-audience.

Know Thy Media

As you're doing this research, take notes. This leads to the second component of a successful publicity plan: *developing your media contact list.* By "media" I mean print, radio and television primarily. Figure 14.1 compares the advantages and disadvantages of these media choices and others.

Here is where a computer comes in real handy. Contact management programs like *Act!* or *Touchbase Pro* can help keep your publicity information organized. I highly recommend you become acquainted with one of these programs in your own publicity efforts. Short of this, get yourself a Rolodex for phone numbers and addresses; separate file folders for newspapers, magazines, radio, and television; and a big year-at-a-glance wall calendar. Staying organized is essential! Your media list should forever grow and change based on your coverage needs.

The best approach is to start locally and then branch out from there. You'll be surprised at the wealth of publicity opportunities lying right at your doorstep.

When checking out local *print media*, watch for names of music editors, writers, and record reviewers relevant to your particular area. Pay special

MEDIA CHOICES COMPARED

Media	Advantages	Disadvantages
Television	• Wide reach • Sight and sound • Attention getting • Prestigious • High info content • Select audience (cable)	• Short life • High cost • Clutter of ads • "Button pushers" • Ads annoy audiences
Magazines	• High quality ads • High info content • Long life • Choose audience	• Long lead time • Position uncertain in magazine
Newspapers	• Good local coverage • Good for price info • Can place quickly • Group ads by product • Good demographic • Cost-effective	• Poor quality presentation • Short life • Poor attention getting
Radio	• Music, reinforce airplay • Fair cost • Can place quickly • Can get high frequency • Select audience	• Audio only • Short attention span • "Button pushers" • Ads annoy audiences
Billboards	• High exposure frequency • Low cost	• Message may not be read • Shortness of message • Environmental blight
Direct Mail	• Best selectivity • Large info content • No interference from other ads • Gets noticed	• High cost per contact • Associated with junk mail • Environmental blight
Internet/ WWW	• High interactivity • Multimedia • High, targeted exposure • International • Low entry cost • 24 hour/7 day access • Large info content	• Demo-/Psychographic constraints • Technical constraints • Difficulty of being found

133

Fig. 14.1

attention to those writers who help break ground for new acts. Go to your local library to reference city newspapers, alternative weeklies, suburban publications and other regional papers with which you may not be familiar. While there, check out the various media directories in the reference section. Two good ones (already mentioned in chapter 8) are *Bacon's Publicity Checker* listing over 18,000 newspapers and magazines, and *Gale's Directory of Publications and Broadcast Media* which additionally covers radio, TV, and cable outlets in the United States and Canada.

Always call first before sending in your material to verify contact information. When you call, find out the names (with correct spellings!) and direct phone numbers of all editors and writers in the areas of music, entertainment, and the performing arts. Also request a copy of their editorial calendar for upcoming months. This will alert you to what themes and topics it is planning so you can scope out possible story tie-ins with your band or act well in advance.

Radio also requires some research. Learn about the different formats of the various stations in your area and the types of programs they air. Consider their target audiences. Listen to the stations. Consult program guides (a station will send you one upon request). Check media reference books like the ones above for station contact information. Talk with program and/or music directors, producers and DJs. Always ask if they feature local and new artists in any special programming section. Write it all down.

Information about commercial and college radio stations and the types of music they play can be found in *The M Street Radio Directory* and *The Yellow Pages of Rock*. There are also fairly complete lists of college stations on-line (see the end of this chapter for contact information). When you discover which radio stations play music from independents (usually called "open" or "varied" formats), phone to inquire about the configuration they use. Some will play only CDs. Others will also play cassettes. Some still play vinyl. Record all this information into your database.

When it comes to *television* forget about MTV (at least for now). It has the tightest playlist on the planet catering exclusively to major label and high-charting artists. Focus instead on your own best bets: public television, local cable stations, and community programs. If your research shows that there are specialized programs devoted to issues that appeal to your target audience (environmental, women's issues, etc.), add the names of the producers to your lists. If your project is "newsworthy" the person to contact is the Assignment

Editor. His job is to weed through the news and prioritize it for news programming. You can find out whom these people are by phoning the station and requesting their names.

If you're involved with a non-profit cause, organization, or event, you can get your event or program listed in broadcast public service announcements ("PSAs") for free. Check radio and TV (network affiliates and local cable) station deadlines and requirements. Submit all pertinent information to Public Affairs or the PSA Director. Work with the benefit coordinator to make sure he has your band's information.

Know Thy Publicity Tools

With a clear understanding of your audience and the media around it, you are now ready for the third component of your publicity plan: *assembling your publicity tools*. While some of this was covered in previous chapters, it bears repeating. These tools will include promotional materials, photos, tape/CD, press kit, and press releases. Each of these could fill a separate chapter. For now, I will simply list them with their most relevant features.

1. PROMOTIONAL MATERIALS. These include your band name, logo, letterhead, envelopes, business cards, labels, flyers, buttons, monthly calendars, posters, T-shirts, etc. Remember: You never get a second chance to make a first impression, so go for the highest quality affordable. These are "graphic ambassadors" sent before you to represent you to a select audience. If neither you nor your bandmates are artists, hire one. When designing your materials, think unity of color, tone, line, and texture. Use your logo prominently on all your pieces. This enhances your image and instills top-of-the-mind awareness.

2. PHOTOS. You can get a lot of publicity out of a good photograph. The 8" x 10" black and white glossy is the standard. Have some 5" x 7" color shots available too. This will maximize your exposure possibilities. The 8" x 10"s should have your band logo/name at the bottom along with current contact information. Soloists should have both headshots and full-body shots. When doing a photo shoot, count on going through at least three rolls of film. If you get three useable pictures from each roll, you're doing fine. It's also a good idea to have a number of 5" x 7" "action" shots of you performing at a high-profile event, receiving an award, or any other scene that's worthy of notice. Use a professional photographer if at all possible. If the budget won't allow for a pro, look elsewhere for less expensive talent. Check local art schools for students who want to earn a few extra dollars (and enhance their own portfolios).

3. TAPE/CD. Which is best? A CD undeniably lends your act more credibility. However less than seventy percent of American households and offices have CD players while over ninety-five percent have cassette players. For demo purposes a cassette with three or four good songs is all you need. For more general marketing of your act, or when you're intent is to impress, either a full-length cassette or CD is the best choice. In all cases, the music should be of the highest production quality affordable and the packaging (color, tone, line, etc.) consonant with all the other publicity materials. Be sure to include your name and contact number on all items! You'd be surprised how often promotional materials become separated.

4. PRESS KIT. A press kit contains most of the materials listed above. Journalists and DJ's use your press kit to obtain the background information they need to write an article or interview your band. A press kit is a just a promo kit until you have actual *press*. So this is your first task. Get reviewed. Court journalists for interviews. Find your publicity angle. What's special about your band or bandmates, your record, or your performance? To get mentions, you'll need to provide *newsworthy* information. What's the *hook* or human-interest pitch of your story? Give the media an angle that's fresh and informative and have your press kit reflect it.

5. PRESS RELEASES. How do you get the media interested in you and your projects? You send a *press release*, also called "news release." It's a standard tool that works better than letters and phone calls. It's universally used to publicize people and events. The release is essentially a pared-down news story that presents the outline of your event in a way that will grab an editor's attention.

Anything newsworthy should be publicized. You should define *newsworthy* as creatively as possible. Special upcoming shows; formation of a new band; record release parties; production of a video; signing a management, agent, distribution, publishing, or recording deal; recitals; formation of your new indie label; involvement in a benefit; winning a band contest. These are just a few of the events worthy of mention.

Always type and double-space the band's information preferably on the band's own letterhead. Include all the pertinent details (who, what, when, where, and why). Use a bold and creative headline. Be sure to include the date, your contact information, and the city where your act or news is based. At the top write "FOR IMMEDIATE RELEASE" and then send it off to everyone on your media list.

Today, a number of editors and journalists prefer either faxed or electronic press releases. When you call for current contact information, be sure to also inquire about preferred submission formats and obtain fax numbers and e-mail addresses as needed.

For most musicians, working on publicity is more work than they bargained for. Getting noticed is a survival skill. If your publicity works you'll flourish. If it doesn't your career may not survive. Read on for Part Two.

Further Resources

DIRECTORIES
The M Street Radio Directory, 304 Park Avenue S, 7th Floor, New York, NY 10010; 212-473-4626.

The Yellow Pages of Rock, Album Network, 818-955-4000.

SOFTWARE
Act! Symantec, 800-365-0606.

Touchbase Pro, Aldus Corporation, 619-695-6956.

On-Line Resources

COLLEGE RADIO DATABASES
http://www.jett.com/collegeradio/clgradio.html.

http://www.181-4.com/database/radio.

http://www.linkmag.com/pub/college_radio_stations.html#listings.
Contains special details as well as links to select college radio stations.

See Further Resources after Chapter 8, Publicity & Promotional Ideas for Musicians.

Media Power:
Creating a Music Publicity Plan that Works,
Part 2

In the previous chapter we looked at the basic ingredients of a successful music publicity plan. They are: *researching your niche audience* and the media preferences of this audience, *developing your media contact database* based on this research, and *assembling your publicity tools*, including photos, tapes, promo kits, and press releases.

This chapter lays out some guidelines for organizing your publicity efforts and then point you to some great publicity resources that will boost your efforts towards success.

Organizing Your Publicity Schedule

Before sending anything out, get yourself one of those "year-at-a-glance" wall calendars. They can be obtained at any well-stocked office supply house like Staples or Office Depot. This will serve as your publicity map for the whole year.

Let me ask you a question. Can you remember what the lead feature was on the evening news three nights ago? All self-promoting bands take heed! People have miniscule attention spans and memories that are even shorter.

This is why your publicity objectives can only be realized through successive "waves" of media exposure. Each wave "coats" your market, raising the consciousness of your audience. These waves must come at regular, considered intervals so that your offerings are perceived as inevitabilities.

How many waves should you launch and how often? Each wave needs a promotional spearhead. For musicians, this spearhead can take many forms: a high-profile performance, record release party, important contract signing, endorsement, contest award, etc. The more of these you have, the more waves you can organize. One every three months should be effective.

Of course, all of this assumes a good amount of *planning*. This is where your wall calendar comes in. Set some goals for yourself for the coming year and mark their realization dates on your calendar: I want to set up a small tour for my act; I will record a full-length CD; I will organize a show to benefit the environment. Whatever it is, you'll want to incorporate it into your publicity wave. Four or five strategic, well-organized waves per year will reap exposure aplenty for your act or business.

Timing a Music Publicity Campaign for an Upcoming Performance

Say you've booked a high-profile gig and it's a month away. Here's a sample publicity schedule you may follow to maximize the media exposure of this performance.

3–4 WEEKS PRIOR TO PERFORMANCE
- Mail out a press release and bio to everyone on your media and blue-ribbon "influencers and tastemakers" lists. Follow this mailing with a phone call, two to three days after you think your materials have been received.
- Put up posters and flyers.
- If you have a record, send it along with a press release and bio to radio stations that your research has indicated might play it. Include a personal invitation to the gig. When you make your follow-up phone call, ask if the station might be interested in interviewing a key person in your band.

2–3 WEEKS PRIOR TO PERFORMANCE
- Send out the same release (or a longer one with more information) and a photograph, captioned with time, place, date and price), and other graphic materials. Include a personal letter of invitation. The personal letter might also contain a sentence or two of blatant hype pleading for attention and saying why it is important for the person to show up. Keep it short. This is also the time to request an interview of longer feature story.
- Send postcards to your fans.
- To other than media people (i.e., club owners, record company executives), send a personal letter inviting them to the performance, together with the press release and other publicity materials.
- Follow up with phone calls.
- Check the places where you placed flyers and posters to make sure that

they are still there. Repeat if necessary.

DAY OF PERFORMANCE

*   Make sure that people who are invited are on the "guest list" (at the entrance to the bar or club or at the gate or ticket booth). I've seen quite a few embarrassing situations where key people showed up only to find that band had forgotten to place their names on the list.
*   When you get reviews, reprint them on your letterhead stationery. Include them in mailings. Hype breeds hype. When the media sees favorable reviews and articles on your band, it stimulates them to join the bandwagon.
*   Two other nice ways to use reviews: make up a page of favorable quotes; blow up a review so that words are more easily read. Use favorable quotes in posters, flyers and on the packaging of recording materials.

PERSEVERE

*   Do these steps for every gig until you get results. Perseverance and repetition works.
*   The eighth time a club owner or record company executive sees a press release about a band, they will realize that you are consistently performing. The fifth time a critic is invited to a gig, they may actually show up. The tenth time you send a press release and photograph announcing a gig, you may be surprised to open up the newspaper and see it printed word for word.

The Importance of Follow-up

Before turning to a trove of resources that will help you organize these waves, I want to address the importance of *following-up* on *all* your media publicity. Follow-up allows you to monitor your coverage, maximize the benefits of good reviews, and maintain good relations with the press even after less-than-favorable reviews. There will be a number of opportunities for follow-up when you:

*   **ACKNOWLEDGE GOOD REVIEWS** with a thank you note. Have a stack of these stamped and ready to go on your desk. Good manners go far in the world of business.

- **POLITELY CORRECT ERRORS IN REVIEWS.** All publications work under tight deadlines and many don't spend the time to check every fact in the article with the sources. That's a sad fact, but true.

- **RESPOND TO BAD REVIEWS.** Look as objectively as possible at what's being said in the review. Learn from it and thank the writer for the feedback.

- **BUILD ON POSITIVE REVIEWS.** The real value in a review, release announcement, or news story is not merely its immediate impact on the publication's readers. It's the impact you create by subsequently sending reprints of that article to anyone you choose: labels, distributors, retailers, new leads, outside contacts, etc. To stay on the right side of the law be sure to contact the publication to obtain the rights to reprint the article.

- **KEEP IN TOUCH.** Help media people remember you by calling them periodically. You won't develop rapport overnight—it takes time. Until you feel you've established rapport, call only when you have news. Always have a goal in mind and a legitimate purpose for your call.

Another good planning tip is to obtain the editorial calendar from the publication you're planning to contact. This document will tell you what articles the publication is planning to print, the deadlines, and in some cases, the editor in charge. By obtaining the editorial calendar you'll learn what the publication is planning to write, when, and who their audience is. Use this knowledge to submit appropriate information about your product or event well in advance of the publication's deadlines.

Maximizing Interview Opportunities

There will come a time in your dealings with the media when you will have an opportunity to be interviewed. Here are some pointers for making sure that interview sparkles:

- Prepare. Write out points or message you want to convey to the audience.

- Keep the audience in mind. Find out as much as you can about who will be reading, watching, or listening to your interview.

- Don't try to sell yourself or your business. Guest appearances and other interviews are not commercials, and the media is very sensitive to this distinction. Your job in an interview is to be informative and to do so in an entertaining way.

- Arrange in advance for the audience to be able to contact you. If appropriate, ask before the interview whether the interviewer would be willing to let people know how they can contact you for more information. Such a plug will be far more valuable to you than self-promotion.

- Restate the question in beginning your answer. For example:

  Q: "Which song is most requested when you play out?"
  A: "The most requested song when I play out is..."

  This helps the audience stay with you and gives you a chance to focus your thoughts.

- Keep your answers brief and to the point. Radio and television interviews are a conversation, not a monologue, so if your response to a question lasts longer than 30 to 60 seconds, you are probably over-answering. Print allows a bit more room for stretching out on answers.

- Talk personally, concretely, and colorfully. Avoid academic, theoretical, abstract, and clinical language.

- Be positive and speak with enthusiasm and conviction. Don't dwell on the negative aspects of your message. Provide info that inspires hope, encouragement, and confidence, and end each segment on an upbeat note.

Key Resources to Help Develop Your Publicity Program

Short of obtaining professional help, most musicians and songwriters are going to have to go it alone for a time. With patience, a few graphic skills, some basic tools, and the nuts-and-bolts information in the following resources, you'll have what you need to do it yourself.

BOOKS. One of the best overviews of publicity planning I've ever seen is Jeffrey Lant's *The Unabashed Self-Promoter's Guide: What every man, woman, child and organization in America needs to know about getting ahead by exploiting the media.* Besides tried-and-true strategies, the book's chief value lies in how the author helps the reader develop an ongoing consciousness of publicity possibilities for one's business or project. This is the book's most empowering feature. All who study this work will be encouraged and equipped for the task.

From a musician's point of view the best on the subject is still James *Gibson's Getting Noticed: A Musician's Guide to Publicity and Self-Promotion.* Gibson shows how musicians, with just a few simple secrets and very little cash, can create attention-getting publicity materials and then use them to make more money with their music. The book includes a wealth of business information on press releases, letter writing, and how to deal with people in the media.

SOFTWARE PROGRAMS. If you're the owner of a personal computer or have access to one, you're in luck. JIAN Tools for Sale, Inc. has come out with an expert information software package that helps users publicize their business, group, event or service.

"Publicity Builder" is a crash-course in entry-level PR that will help you obtain quick, effective, low-cost results. A wide variety of publicity topics are covered from developing new product statements and press releases to creating press kits and writing pitch letters. Even publicizing products and services at trade shows and conventions are covered.

The program includes more than 10 easy-to-use worksheets to help users refine their messages and focus their efforts. More than 15 sample press release templates cover topics like new product announcements, personnel changes, fundraising events, new business openings, service programs, award announcements, and more. *Publicity Builder* also discusses how to target and reach media contacts and get their attention by being professional and helpful, not annoying. The workbook is a great achievement. It guides the neophyte publicist through everything from goal-setting and pitch letters to effective follow-up. Highly recommended!

When to Seek Professional Help

There is only one correct time to seek a publicist: When you yourself have become thoroughly familiar with the self-promotional universe, but because of manifold commitments and the lack of time, you fail to access all the publicity opportunities available to you. It's crucial for the do-it-yourselfer to have at least introductory experience working with the media. That way you're in a better position to evaluate a publicist's record and, once having done so, realistically evaluate just what is being done on your behalf.

Where do you find a publicist? Start by asking for local recommendations. Also notice which bands and musicians are getting a lot of quality press coverage. Call the publication and ask who the artist's publicist is. Publicists specializing in music will often advertise in music magazines. Shop around. Never just take the first person who's available. You have nothing with which to compare his skills. Prices vary as does creativity.

Once you've found several possibilities, use the following guidelines to be sure you get exactly what you need. Consider:
• Is the publicist inventive? Can they create distinction and dimension?
• Is the publicist interested in what you're doing?
• Is the publicist so overwhelmed by current clients that their ability to take on new work is limited?
• Does the publicist now serve clients with whom you compete?
• What will it cost?

It's completely reasonable to request samples of their work and client references. After all, it's the musicians they've worked with who can give you the most relevant feedback about that publicist's work.

Understanding how the media works is not merely a matter of idle curiosity. Whether you're a band, a soloist, a personal manager, booking agent or other music professional, having access to the media on a continuing, positive basis is a decided advantage. A positive media relationship can be measured in enhanced prestige, greater recognition and larger profits.

Further Resources

BOOKS
Gibson, James. *Getting Noticed: A Musician's Guide to Publicity and Self-Promotion.* Cincinnati: Writer's Digest Books, 1987.

Devney, Darcy Campion. *Organizing Special Events and Conferences: A Practical Guide for Busy Volunteers and Staff.* Sarasota: Pineapple Press, 1993.

Yale, David. *Publicity & Media Relations Checklists: 59 Proven Checklists to Save Time, Win Attention, & Maximize Exposure with Every Public Relations & Publicity.* NTC Business Books, 1995.

Bly, Robert W. *Targeted Public Relations: How to Get Thousands of Dollars of Free Publicity for Your Product, Service, Organization, or Idea.* Owlet Press, 1994.

Fletcher, Tana and Julia Rockler. *Getting Publicity: A Do-It-Yourself Guide for Small Business and Non-Profit Groups.* Self Counsel Press, 1991.

Lant, Jeffrey. *The Unabashed Self-Promoter's Guide: What every man, woman, child and organization in America needs to know about getting ahead by exploiting the media.* Cambridge, MA: JLA Publications.

SOFTWARE
Publicity Builder, JIAN, 127 Second Street, Los Altos CA 94022-2745; 415-941-9191.

On-Line Publicity Resources

Public Relations On-line Resources and Organizations, **http://www.webcom.com/impulse/resource.html.** A great jump site to PR-related services, including the headings Organizations and Associations, On-Line Resources, Promoting Your Web Site, Finding People On The Internet, and On-line Publications.

Internet Publicity Resources, **http://www.olympus.net/okeefe/pubnet.** Similar to the above site. Created by Steve O'Keefe as a companion site to his book, *Publicity on the Internet* (New York, John Wiley & Sons, 1997). A terrific labor of love!

16

Getting Played on College Radio

Radio is still by far the most effective medium to break new musical acts. Approximately 70 to 80 percent of the public learns of a new record or artist through hearing it on the radio. More than 95% of Americans across all age groups tune into radio programs every week, with more than half of listeners checking in before 8:00 a.m. and after 7:00 p.m., reflecting the standard work day pattern, according to media and marketing research firm Arbitron. At the end of 1998, there were 10,802 commercial and non-commercial AM and FM stations broadcasting in the United States, compared to 10,313 at the beginning of the decade (see Fig. 16.1 "On the Radio Dial").

The radio industry is not in the music business, it's in the advertising business. Music is used merely to attract a particular population demographic that, in turn, is "delivered" to potential advertisers. Usually owned by large communication concerns, most commercial stations are strictly *bottom-line* minded.

Trends in Traditional Radio

With the passing of the 1996 Telecommunications Act, Congress eliminated most restrictions on broadcast mergers. Over the next twelve months, more than 4,000 of the country's 11,000 radio stations changed hands and more than 1,000 corporate mergers were proposed in broadcasting.

This arrangement reflects a fundamental shift of power in the music business. In the past, powerful record companies were accused of bribing DJs operating at small, independent radio stations to influence what songs were played. This practice was known as "payola" and it was finally outlawed in the 1960s.

Industry mergers have moved the balance of power to radio groups, which today have the collective clout to launch a song simultaneously in scores of markets across the country—or consign it to oblivion. In a quest to create new revenue streams, Chancellor Media will soon launch its own record label and sell music on the Internet. "We have this giant distribution system in place," says

ON THE RADIO DIAL

While the number of radio stations continues to grow, traditional formats like Top-40 and Adult Contemporary are being replaced by more rock, religion, and news.

NUMBER OF RADIO STATIONS BY FORMAT

Commercial Format	1989	1998
Country	2448	2491
Adult Contemporary	2058	1508
New, Talk, Business, Sports	308	1111
Religion (Teaching & Music)	696	404
Rock (album, Modern, Classic)	365	733
Oldies	545	755
Spanish & Ethnic	313	474
Adult Standards	332	551
Urban, Black	284	349
Top-40	951	358
Jazz & New Age	64	92
Easy Listening	328	49
Variety	134	50
Classical, Fine Arts	49	44
Pre-Teen	0	40
Comedy	1	0
total:	**8876**	**9009**

Noncommercial Format	1989	1998
Religion	302	335
Variety	387	376
Rock (Album, Modern, Classic)	226	284
News, Talk, Business, Sports	11	456
Classical, Fine Arts	306	117
Jazz & New Age	37	69
Top-40	71	43
Spanish & Ethnic	34	42
Urban, Black	32	27
Adult Contemporary	16	15
Easy Listening	7	3
Country	8	14
Adult Standards	0	7
Oldies	0	5
total:	**1437**	**1793**

Fig. 16.1

John Madison, senior VP of operations at Chancellor. "It only makes sense that we would consider expanding into the record business. Having our own record label would give us more control over the content we pump through the distribution channel."

Programming is also being affected by these new power blocks. It's common now for the parent company to produce one general show that is distributed to all its affiliate stations while allowing room for local customizations. The local DJ has little or no say in music selections and Music Director positions at local stations are gradually being phased out.

Technology is also driving new developments in conventional radio. According to an Arbitron listening survey published late last year (1998), "radio is on the verge of facing the kinds of challenges that print and television have been facing for years." Satellite radio in particular is opening new avenues to a now limited and local-driven single market. And the same report indicates that Internet radio is already impacting radio listening behavior as well (see the end of this chapter for more on Internet radio).

Payola, though in a different suit, has also made a comeback. Advertising rate cards are now available that sell airplay slots to record companies and others who can afford it. In one case, a document obtained by the *Los Angeles Times* showed that Chicago radio station Q101, owned by Emmis Communications, explicitly promises radio airplay as part of a promotional package. "For $3,500 you will receive 30 guaranteed spins the first week...20 guaranteed spins the second week…" and so on.

College radio, on the other hand, is music-minded to the extreme. Freed from commercial constraints and funded by school budgets, college radio has unbridled license to indulge every musical taste, and it does.

The State of College Radio

College radio represents an anomaly on the airwaves.

Back in the '70s—what many call the format's true "heyday"—most college stations were ignored by record labels, and much of the music that was wanted for a station was either purchased or serviced to the station after numerous attempts. But while servicing may have been a problem, many were content with the fact that the format was indeed a true alternative to the legions of AOR stations that dominated the commercial airwaves. Stations were relatively untouched by the giant corporate music monster, allowing them to blossom and develop their own styles and sounds.

There was still a sort of innocence to the format. That, however, is not the case today.

Since the late 1980s, more and more college stations have become marketing outlets for labels to promote their "product." College radio is now viewed as a "tool" that will gain their acts "credibility," perhaps making the transition to the next level—commercial radio—a little easier. Sadly, many college stations have accepted this role and lost sight of what the format represented in its glory days, when stations usually opted to play music that, compared to the standards set in the '70s, was rarely tame. Today, many share artists with the local commercial alternative station, and their play lists mirror those of MTV.

But college radio is still the most promising radio outlet for independent artists. Over the course of the last fifteen years, major labels have increasingly recognized college radio as a crucial talent source and as an important vehicle for breaking new bands into the mainstream. U2, REM, Midnight Oil and more recently, Jane's Addiction, Smashing Pumpkins, and Chumbawamba all got their first radio break at colleges. In fact, at a recent music conference in Texas, a major label rep told me that he now looks primarily to college radio DJs to provide the A&R service of scouting out new talent.

Since college stations receive dozens of CD and tape submissions weekly, you'll have to work smart to ensure that your music gets to the right person and that they will give it a chance for some airplay.

Where to Start

Getting the right information is your first task. There are literally hundreds of college radio stations in the United States alone. You'll want to *target* your efforts. To begin, pick a small number of stations (twelve or so) in a fifty-mile ratio of your base and concentrate on these.

You probably already have a pretty good idea which local stations would be receptive to your music. Contact these first. Identify yourself as a musician with a new release. Find out the names of the Program Director, the Music Director and djs who have shows that play your style(s) of music. Commercial radio formats are quite formal and inflexible (see Fig. 16.3 "Radio Formats"). College radio, on the other hand, is much less formal and its eclectic programming allows for a mix of formats or styles. But you should know generally where your music fits in with a particular station's programming.

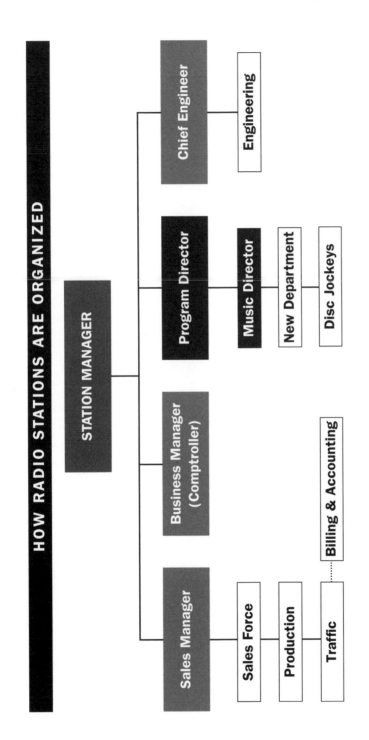

HOW RADIO STATIONS ARE ORGANIZED

STATION MANAGER

Sales Manager
- Sales Force
- Production
- Traffic

Business Manager (Comptroller)
- Billing & Accounting

Program Director
- Music Director
- New Department
- Disc Jockeys

Chief Engineer
- Engineering

Fig. 16.2

RADIO FORMATS		target age, ethnicity, & gender
Adult contemporary (AC)	**Subcategories:** Full-service stations: "soft hits," news, talk, sports; what used to be MOR (Middle-of-Road) "Gold": safe, inoffensive Rock 'n' Roll oldies (post 1955) "Lite": love songs, vocal-oriented Easy Listening Music-intensive: the mainstream AC subformat; emphasizes newer artists and crossovers; lack of non-musical services Adult Alternative: basic AC diet plus Jazz, Soft Rock, some Country, Quiet Storm, New Age	· 25-54 years old ("Boomers") · Mixed ethnicity and gender target · Primarily white women
Album-Oriented Rock (AOR)	**Subcategories:** Classic Rock, Soft Rock, Hard Rock, Heavy Metal, "Free Form" (e.g., noncommercial college radio stations)	· Primarily 18-25 · Whites · Men (Varies within subcategories)
Contemporary Christian Radio (CCR)	Musical, a format that is nearly indistinguishable from AC (except for the text content)	· Teens and young adults · Mixed ethnic target
Contemporary Hit Radio (CHR)	What "Top 40" became; a broad-based format that borrows from other contemporary formats; emphasizes the newest hits; ballads and conventional pop material are downplayed	· 35 and older; · Whites · Mixed gender
Easy-Listening Radio (based on non-rock music)	**Subcategories:** Beautiful Music (Muzak, "elevator music"),Big Band, Nostalgia (pre-Rock, excludes big band; e.g., 1950s popular song stylists) Music of Your Life (syndicated; mostly Big Band),	· 45 years and older · Ideally mixed, but mainly whites
Country	Relies heavily on oldies (but rarely pre-1970!); Subformats: Gradations range from traditional ("rootsier," old-time "rural" country) to upbeat (rock-influenced)	· 35 and older · Whites
Gospel		· Mixed ages · Black or white Christians
Hispanic		· Mixed ages · Hispanic
Urban Contemporary (UC)	A fullspectrum of "upbeat paced" Black music	· Young · Blacks
Quiet Storm	Less "upbeat paced" than UC (softer R&B, ballads, Mellow Jazz)	· Adults · Blacks
Classical	Generally older; mixed; mid-to-high economic standing ("upscale")	· 25 and older · Can attract an upscale audience base
Jazz	(Rarely found as a full-time format on commercial stations)	· Varied ages · Mixed ethnicity
New Age (Contemporary NAC)	Mostly instrumental, atmospheric; "beautiful music for yuppies." Often mixed with Jazz, AC, or Soft AOR	· 25 and older

Fig. 16.3

The key person on your list will probably be the Music Director (MD) since this is the person who often determines what gets played. But this isn't always the case. When you call the station ask for the name of the person who should receive your music. Be sure to get the correct spelling of that person's name.

Two good sources for radio personnel, addresses and phone numbers are *The Yellow Pages of Rock* and *The Recording Industry Sourcebook*. One or both of these can be found in a well-stocked city library in the Music Reference section. If you have Internet access, you can find a fairly comprehensive college radio list at **http://www.jett.com/collegeradio/clgradio.html**. Unfortunately, current radio personnel are not included. Always call the station to confirm and update directory information.

You also want to find out if the station is a "reporting station," that is, one that sends its play lists to the trade magazines that publish radio charts (see list of radio trades at end of chapter).

Keeping things organized is critical. Write down all information in a notebook. Provide a separate page for each station. Keep a phone-log for every station you contact and note all the names of those with whom you speak (see Fig. 16.4 "Radio Phone Log"). If you have access to a computer, store your data in a database file for easy retrieval. Once you've compiled a list of stations you're confident will give your music a hearing, you'll be ready to put a package together to mail out.

The Radio Mail-Out

Which format is most appropriate for radio airplay? By far the best is CD. Second best is vinyl (yes, vinyl) and, only as a last resort, cassette. The reason for CDs is the ease with which a song can be cued and the general durability of the product. Some stations may prefer DAT (digital audiotape) or reel-to-reel but these are the exceptions. If all you have is a demo cassette tape, state this to the MD when you call. However, you can include a cassette with your CD. Perhaps the DJ will listen to your music in their car.

Even though you'll be submitting a sound recording containing numerous songs you'll want to *select the one song you deem best for radio and push that one*. MDs and DJs are busy people. Make their jobs easier by telling them which cut to play.

The person receiving the package is going to want current information about the artist or band. You should include a brief cover letter referring to

RADIO PHONE LOG

Station call letters: _____ Station frequency: _____

Wattage: _____ Trade reporting: _____

Station owner: _____

Station address: _____

_____ Fax: _____

Station e-mail: _____

Station web address: _____

Program director: _____

Music director: _____

Key DJs:

name: _____ show: _____ date/time: _____

name: _____ show: _____ date/time: _____

Communication log:

Date:	Outcome:

Fig. 16.4

your initial phone conversation, a biography, photo (best to incorporate onto bio), and any favorable press about the act. Make each piece graphically interesting. Talk to printers for ideas. Also include mention of any other stations that have agreed to play your music as well as information on the record's availability in local stores. Make sure your name and address are on every item in your package.

Remember MDs receive tons of new music—twenty to fifty full-length CDs each week! One way to make your recording stand out is to enclose something unique in the package like a hip calendar with your logo printed on top or some other promotional novelty that will make your name memorable. Be creative. You're aiming for attention.

Another important item to include is a *DJ Response Card*. I use printed postcards, self-addressed and stamped. On the card you print three questions: Will the record receive airplay at your station? Which cuts? Would you be interested in an interview with the artist? At the bottom leave room for comments (to be used in subsequent promotion), their name, station address, phone number, and best time to call. The rate of return for these cards is about 30%. They can provide crucial feedback for your ongoing radio promotion (see Fig. 16.5 "DJ Response Card").

Follow-up all positive comments with a phone call. Use this to remind them of your recording. Tell them of other stations' response to it and any current information about your act. People talk. Work to create that buzz. Any invitations for interviews (in-studio or over the phone) should be followed up immediately and scheduled, preferably, in tandem with an upcoming gig in the area.

Maximizing Your Radio Airplay

Whenever you release a CD locally, your radio promotion should be tied into your other efforts encompassing retail presence, performances and publicity. This four-prong approach ensures the greatest amount of exposure for your music. Here are some additional ways to maximize your college radio airplay:

1. PUSH A SINGLE. Because of the sheer quantity of music at college radio stations and the natural time constraints of student DJs, it is wise to make their job easier by telling them the cut you want played. Some will ignore your choice and make their own selection, but most will take your lead and play that

DJ RESPONSE CARD
(also called "Radio Bounceback Card")

Side 1:

Thank you for taking the time to listen to **"Only When I Breathe"** from **Amanda Hunt-Taylor**. Please answer the following questions so we may service you better. A stamp is already attached to make it as easy as possible for you. Thanks again!

Will this CD receive air play at your station? _____

If so, which cuts? _____

Would you be interested in interviewing Amanda Hunt-Taylor either in-person or by phone?

    ❑ In person   ❑ By phone

Would you like to receive upcoming releases and news from Amanda? _____

What trades does your station report to? _____

Comments: _____

_____

Your name: _____   Phone: _____

Side 2:

return name
address
phone number

stamp

WMUS
100 Radio Street
New York, NY 11223

Fig. 16.5

cut. Having a single repeatedly play over several weeks is often more effective than airing multiple cuts. Your single should be the strongest song on the CD and should not exceed 3¹/2 minutes.

2. KNOW THE RULES. Most program directors and music directors accept calls only during specified hours. Ask their assistants for their "call hours," and call then and only then to pitch your material. These call hours apply to everyone—major labels, indie labels, independent promoters—so be prepared to be put on hold for an extended period of time. Call once just to make sure the PD or MD received your package. Don't bug them before they've had a chance to form an opinion!

3. LINE UP SONG REQUESTS. This should not be underestimated. Without getting obnoxious about it you, your brother, your mother, your boyfriend/girlfriend, your Aunt Sally and your band mates should all be on a "request schedule"—each person taking a different day to request your song. Even if the song isn't played when requested you've filled an ear with your act's name and song one more time each time.

4. GIVE THANKS. Send a letter to thank the radio station for playing your song. This proves you were actually listening, which will encourage them to play it again.

5. DISCUSS RELATED VENUES. Ask the MD what *other opportunities* exist for bands and artists at the station—live music weeks, benefits, annual fund-raisers, etc. Get involved!

6. PROVIDE PR FOR THE STATION. In exchange for airplay mention the station with thanks in all your promotional literature. Tell the Station Manager and MD you will do this. It can't hurt.

7. NETWORK. While working a college station, try to *network* yourself into the school's entertainment scene by contacting those who hire talent for various events and mention you're getting airplay at the college's radio station. You can locate these entertainment buyers through the student activities office.

8. DISTRIBUTE GIVEAWAYS. Provide the station with *giveaways*. Records, CDs, tapes, T-shirts, tickets to shows, whatever. Station personnel love this.

9. CONTINUE SCOUTING OUT KEY STATIONS. Subscribe to a national publication specializing in your music style to see what radio stations in your region are industry leaders. Make sure you send your record to them as well. For example, if your music is primarily acoustic, then check out *Dirty Linen* out of Baltimore. If it's thrash rock, look into *Maximum Rock N Roll* out of Berkeley, CA. If it's world music, check out *Rhythm Music* out of NYC. If it defies categories, see *Option* out of LA.

10. HIRE AN INDEPENDENT RADIO PROMOTER. If you really want to make a splash on radio you can hire an independent radio promoter. Independent promoters know the ins and outs of breaking a record on radio and can save you a lot of time. More importantly, independent promoters already have relationships with MDs and DJs. Getting a record played is a lot easier for them than it would be for you. Independent promoters aren't cheap (ranging from $300 to $500 per week for a 6- to 8-week period) and should only be considered once your distribution lines are established and you have money in the bank. You can find promoters in *The Yellow Pages of Rock* and *The Recording Industry Sourcebook*. Be sure to ask the promoter for references from recent clients so you can hear from artists themselves about their service and effectiveness.

11. LEVERAGE YOUR ASSETS. Be sure to include a list of all radio stations that play your music in future press kits.

Internet Radio

Recent years have seen the development of technology that allows Internet sites to transmit an uninterrupted wave of sound to listeners. Called "streaming audio," it resembles real radio in every way save one: the sound comes through computer speakers instead of over the airwaves. Users download a piece of software known as a "player," which acts like a tuner on a conventional stereo and allows them to access audio streams on the Internet. Accordingly, Web radio has grown from 178 stations in 32 countries in August 1996, to more than 1800 stations on the Net by mid-1999. Arbitron, radio's audience measuring service, has expanded its service to now include Internet radio. Information about the demographics of this audience is coveted by advertising firms, the financial engine behind conventional radio, and may lead to new interest in Net radio.

Part of the attraction of Net radio springs from real-world radio's current straits. As related earlier, consolidation has largely left over-the-air radio in the hands of multi-station networks, with computer-generated play lists, controlling consultants, and fierce competition for ratings. The results are cookie-cutter programming and stifled innovation, leaving a prime opportunity for competition on the Net.

Such Net radio companies as Broadcast.com (http://www.broadcast.com) and major players such as Spinner.com (http://www.spinner.com), Imagine Radio (http://www.imagineradio.com) and the *Rolling Stone* Radio Network (http://www.rollingstone.com) are building a strong presence. They offer artists and genres not heard on conventional radio, commercial-free programming, and the ability to break down the geographic boundaries of conventional radio. Particularly in music selection, such features are a big change and play very nicely into the segmentation tendencies of today's music market.

Further Resources

M Street Radio Directory. New York: M Street Corp., 1996.

Hustwit, Gary. *Getting Radio Airplay*. Rockpress, 1996.

RADIO TRADES

Album Network, 120 N Victory Blvd., 3rd Floor, Burbank, CA 91502; 818-955-4000; http://www.musicbiz.com/.

CMJ New Music Report, 11 Middleneck Road #400, Great Neck, NY 11021; 516-466-6000; http://www.cmjmusic.com/.

The Gavin Report, 140 Second Street, San Francisco, CA 94105; 415-495-2580; http://www.gavin.com/.

The Hard Report, 708 Stokes Road, Medford Lakes, NJ 08055; 609-654-7272.

Hits, 14958 Ventura Blvd., Sherman Oaks, CA 91403; 818-501-7900; http://www.buzznetonline.com/.

Radio & Records, 10100 Santa Monica Blvd. 5th Floor, Los Angeles, CA 90067; 310-553-4330; http://www.rronline.com/.

On-Line Resources

GLOBAL LISTS OF RADIO STATIONS:

The MIT List of Radio Stations on the Internet, http://wmbr.mit.edu/stations/list.html.

BRS Radio Directory, http://www.radio-directory.com/.

COLLEGE RADIO LIST:

http://www.jett.com/collegeradio/clgradio.html

17

Multimedia and Musicians:
What It's About and How to Get Involved

The hybrid or meeting of two media is a moment of truth and revelation of
which a new form is born… The crossings of media release great force.
—Marshall McLuhan, *Understanding Media*

Introduction

After two decades in the great technology incubator, the phenomenon we are
now calling multimedia has exploded onto the technological landscape with a
force that even its most vocal advocates had not imagined possible. But what
is it? Even the experts are often bewildered when pressed on this blunt question. It would appear that, in spite of abrupt and blaring pronouncements in
the media, the identity of this new medium is very poorly understood.

In essence, *multimedia is a catchall term for interactive software that combines at least two of these: text, still images, video, animation, and sound.* A multimedia program is *interactive* when it lets you explore its content in a variety of
ways, take action based on the program's information or contents (such as creating your own song from music fragments stored in a musical database), or
control the out-come of a scenario (as you do, for example, when playing an
interactive murder mystery game).

The development of multimedia is now happening so fast that it is difficult
to discuss our place in the procession of technological history. But there are a
number of reasonably cogent things that can be said about multimedia and
about where this emergent medium is heading. Based upon the reflections of
a handful of industry leaders and early conceptual pioneers, it is possible to
round up at least a thimbleful of useful ideas. I offer them here as a provisional
guideline of what's happening and then follow with some pointers on how
musicians can get involved.

Three Industry Segments

The early market for multimedia applications appears to have divided into three fairly distinct segments:

1. THE HOME MARKET, which owes its origins to the likes of Sega, Nintendo, and the other adolescent-oriented video games, is now on the verge of blossoming into a much more robust enterprise. The games themselves are becoming more sophisticated and intelligent and are now offering some of the first genres capable of attracting and holding an adult audience. Just around the corner looms the promise of interactive television, which threatens to turn the standard American couch potato into the newly rejuvenated couch commando (see Fig. 17.1 "Top Video-Game Producers").

2. THE SCHOOL MARKET, which owes its origins to the small-scale, curriculum-based programs that ran on Apple IIe's, has recently played host to the large-scale integrated learning systems that rank among the most sophisticated forms of instructional software yet created. These systems integrate the electronic delivery of course content across broad, multigrade spans of content, and deliver that content via network-based client server systems that monitor learner performance in specific, objectives-level detail. With all of the great debate over the declining quality of the American education system, the pressure to explore various forms of instructional technology will keep this market growing at a rapid pace into at least the near future.

3. THE BUSINESS MARKET, which is, ironically, the most backward segment of the interactive market, has great growth potential. The tremendous pressure to reengineer business practices and processes in almost every sector of our economy will likely elevate the attractiveness of interactive training solutions. Corporate America will be seeking ways to quickly and efficiently train large and geographically dispersed workforces as never before, and now that the corporate desktop is becoming occupied by MPCs (multimedia personal computers), rather than just plain old vanilla PCs, the inclination to use interactive multimedia should grow dramatically.

In sum, every segment of the multimedia market is growing. The business market will be driven by the need to constantly train and retrain a diverse

TOP VIDEO GAME PRODUCERS

Top 10 Publishers Ranked by Interactive Entertainment Software Units Sold, 1998

| | | Publisher's Sales Mix | |
| | | Percent of entertainment software units sold | |
Rank	Publisher	Video Game Console vs	Computer
1	Nintendo of America	100%	0%
2	Electronic Arts	62%	38%
3	Sega of America	98%	2%
4	Acclaim*	95%	5%
5	CUC International*	2%	98%
6	GT Interactive*	0%	100%
7	Sony	87%	13%
8	Midway Home Entertainment	100%	0%
9	Interplay	20%	80%
10	Virgin Interactive	29%	71%

*Corporate
Source: NPO Group Inc.

Fig. 17.1

workforce. The school market will be fueled by mounting pressures to modify—if not overhaul—an antiquated instructional delivery system. And the home market will likely be the liveliest of all, as the twitch-and-shoot design model of first-generation electronic games matures into several successor genres, including the first interactive forms of fiction and cinema, and various other forms of increasingly immersive media.

The hype is not foundless. The wave of mergers and acquisitions we are now witnessing between previously segregated portions of the information economy are nothing if not early harbingers of an explosively innovative future. Massive and cash-rich telecommunications firms are buying entertainment and computing companies. Print publishing firms are seeking alliances with software companies. In fact, virtually every permutation of linkage between these various stewards of information is being pursued with almost frantic vigor.

All of these enterprises must be positioning themselves for something. But for what?

Multimedia Is About Converging Industries and Technologies

In 1978, Nicholas Negroponte, one of the true savants of multimedia, used a Venn diagram and his intellectual track record as an MIT professor to raise $70 million to launch the Media Lab, an organization dedicated to contemplating the far-flung technological horizons of communications. In the Venn diagram, Negroponte showed that three industries were converging to form a single technological powerhouse, one that would dominate the future of human communications. Those three industries were the printing and publishing industry, the computer industry, and the broadcast and motion picture industry (he didn't mention the recording industry per se but he certainly implied it). (See Fig. 17.2 "Infomedia Convergence.")

He projected that the overlap between these three industries would approach a near union by the end of the century. And while many futurists would just as soon have us forget their projections once the time of their foretold future has arrived, Negroponte's premonitions seem increasingly worthy of acknowledgement. Clearly, these industries are converging.

If anything, that convergence is ahead of schedule. And the multifarious outcomes of that convergence are a large part of what we are calling multimedia. They involve new products, new services, and new genres of art and entertainment. In fact, the impact that can be attributed to the interindustrial

INFOMEDIA CONVERGENCE

T H E N

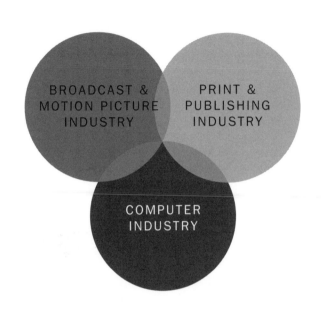

BROADCAST & MOTION PICTURE INDUSTRY

PRINT & PUBLISHING INDUSTRY

COMPUTER INDUSTRY

N O W

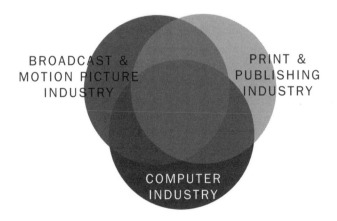

BROADCAST & MOTION PICTURE INDUSTRY

PRINT & PUBLISHING INDUSTRY

COMPUTER INDUSTRY

Fig. 17.2

convergence that is multimedia seems to broaden with each passing year and certainly with each new journalistic interpretation.

The span of topics covered by articles in the trade and academic presses that have the term "multimedia" in their titles is truly staggering. Much of what is written focuses on the enabling technologies, such as networking, transmission, and new forms of mass storage, playback environments, and the ever-expanding array of authoring tools. Many of these articles claim that in the final analysis content is king. They then suggest widely diverging interpretations of exactly what constitutes multimedia content.

Many writers think of multimedia as videoconferencing and its various derivatives, such as document conferencing, distance learning, and video mail. Others see multimedia technology as a new form of publishing, and thus see these media as those that are quickly replacing all major forms of paper documents with superior, interactive versions. Electronic catalogs and brochures replace their passive and inferior ancestors of the same name (sans the "interactive"). Likewise, electronic encyclopedias and computer-based training programs replace the static encyclopedia and textbook, respectively. And, not to forget the arts, interactive fiction and fantasy games replace the most venerated form of document in our cultural history, the novel.

Still others see multimedia technology as a natural step in the direction of increasingly sophisticated and immersive media. These writers and thinkers are concerned with such topics as 3-D audio and video, motion platforms and force feedback, even on to the exotica associated with cyberspace and virtual reality. Regardless of how one chooses to judge these various attempts to describe and classify the many forms of multimedia, one thing is absolutely clear: multimedia is a serious phenomenon.

It connects to our most salient historical arcs. The merging of computers and media now permits the author—or, as in film, the authoring team—to enlist and engage the audience as never before. Rather than watching the performance of a protagonist from a detached and safe-harbor seat in the theater, the listener-reader-viewer must now become something new and unprecedented in the history of the narrative arts. The audience member must now become an active participant, must now become the very protagonist whose performance is that which is judged.

The convergence of publishing with computers and media means that shoppers, learners and explorers will be able to take control of their media in

ways that enable them to find just the right advertisement relative to their immediate needs; to individualize their training experiences to match instructional content to personal skill and knowledge deficiencies; and to select entry points on the ladder of challenge that are most likely to lead to the optimal gaming experiences.

Multimedia Challenges

Increasingly, interactive forms of media appear destined to stand in the same relationship to the twenty-first century as film and TV have to our own. The current floodtide of journalistic interest is almost willing the transition from linear to interactive. But there are many factors that will make that transition difficult, expensive, and painful. In fact, at least two of the most significant problems have already made themselves apparent.

First, the most obvious, fundamental aspect of the interactive revolution is also currently its most problematic: the digitization of audiovisual forms of information. This relatively straightforward process holds the potential of unleashing some of the most powerful change agents in the history of the capitalist world. Unfortunately, there is no question about its having unleashed a tremendous set of technological problems.

If we consider the past three decades to be the formative years of computer technology—as most experts do—then it can be said that the formative period in the history of computing was all about the processing of symbolic forms of information, i.e., of text and numbers. As it turns out, digitally encoded forms of symbolic information are very compact, though this was certainly not the prevailing sentiment even just a decade ago, when personal computers were only capable of storing and manipulating a few million characters, or about the equivalent of a few healthy books. With the subsequent advent of hundred-plus megabyte hard drives, and then the 600+ megabyte CD-ROM, we now comfortably hold the view that computers have risen up to swallow our books and accounting records. The lone problem remaining seems to lie in getting this information better organized.

But when we move on to the task of digitally encoding audio, and especially video, sources of information, we re-enter the domain of the humble—the very humble. One second of uncompressed, television-quality video requires over 27 megabytes of storage. Pursuing this equation to some of its more painful conclusions, we find that the mighty CD-ROM player is capable of handling just about 30 seconds of uncompressed video, and that a full-length

167

motion picture would require close to 200 gigabytes, or approximately the amount of storage that one would expect to find handling the entire data processing needs of a medium-sized corporation. Cough.

The digitization of media—of audio, image, and video—has created a crisis in the computer and the communications industries. Though a multitude of compression/decompression schemes have entered the marketplace in the past half-decade, the problems associated with displaying and storing and transmitting the volumes of data needed to encode media are still immense. Computers are not fast enough. Storage devices do not have enough capacity. And the networks do not have nearly enough bandwidth. If you look at a multimedia title and wonder at the relatively poor quality of its media assets, consider it a manifestation of this larger problem. Barring some unforeseeable innovation, the challenge of mastering this undercapacitation will be at the center of the multimedia industry for at least the next decade.

But this technical problem is not the only one that threatens our transition into the age of multimedia. Nor is it perhaps even the most difficult. As one contemplates the convergence of media—of print and publishing with computers, and of both of these with film and television—the most tumultuous proposition would appear to be the imminent collision of the cultures that preside over these various media with decisively different styles, values, and vocabularies.

Take, for example, the separate cultures that preside over the computer industry, on the one hand, and the film and TV industry, on the other. Both are global leaders. Both require extremely large numbers of finely specialized and highly talented individuals. Both are proud to a fault, even ethnocentric. Neither tribe will take too kindly to the inevitable turf intrusions of the other. And lest we agree to fool ourselves, it is impossible to imagine that there will be many safe passages on the corporate battlefield that will serve to adjudicate the struggle for multimedia booty.

The coming decades will see the rise of multimedia, replete with opportunities and pitfalls. The convergence of multiple industries of the most powerful sort will further accelerate the forces of technology-associated change. New forms of media—electronic brochures, interactive fictions, system emulation programs, even virtual reality—will appear with clockwork regularity. Some of them quickly ascend to the role of major social change agent, much as telephony and television, for example, have done in our century.

There is no reason not to feel the same sort of excitement about the prospects of multimedia that one indulges in over such phenomena as major space exploration programs. This enthusiasm, however, should be balanced by some equally legitimate anxieties. As individuals with careers that will be impacted by these new media technologies, how should we govern our career path decisions?

Entry Points for Musicians

In a musical context, it's important to understand that record companies are re-positioning themselves as *entertainment* companies and are increasingly seeking artists who can express themselves in a *variety* of media. This allows the company to exploit the artist across the varied media holdings of the parent company. Even if you've taken the independent path as a musician, you will find increased opportunities if you can dance, act, paint, draw, design, as well as create and perform music.

Creative people are often creative in more than one medium. Think of Henry Rollins, former lead singer of punk outfit Black Flag. Henry continues to perform in The Rollins Band, but he also writes, publishes books, acts in films, and runs his own record label. Other musicians who've expanded their repertoire beyond music include Thomas Dolby, Laurie Anderson, Tod Rundgren, Peter Gabriel, and Madonna. Becoming a multimedia artist means expanding the definition of your identity as an artist.

In a certain sense, everyone who is in music is in multimedia whether they know it or not. A player who notates his music, a band that writes the liner notes for their new CD, and the musician who designs a poster for her upcoming gig, are all involved in multiple media. What's new today is the element of *interactivity* (which allows a user inside the work) and the *scope* (global) of multimedia.

Want to take a guess at which U.S. song logged the most listening hours last year? A Whitney Houston tune? No, the theme song to the Sega video game, Sonic the Hedgehog.

One major use of music in multimedia projects is to provide a soundtrack for a game or adventure program. This market now outgrosses the domestic motion picture industry. When a sequel to Sonic the Hedgehog was released three years ago, for example, it sold $300 million worth of copies during the first 90 days—more than any movie or album in history has done in a similar period.

The theme from the game Tetris actually reached number one on the English pop charts a few years back. Other game themes have also hit the

Top10. The boundaries between pop and computer culture are disappearing, offering great incentive to musicians with lofty ambitions. Before long, CD-ROM soundtracking may take on the luster of film and television soundtrack work.

Many people who are much more educated on this subject than I am see these changes as more significant than the Industrial Revolution. Here's an analogy: imagine the world without any roads and without any of the things that came with building roads—restaurants, shopping centers and the communities that sprang up around them. That's where we are currently with this technology!

The window of opportunity is NOW in multimedia. In fact, we are currently in the middle (not the beginning) of just such an "open window" time period in new media. Should you jump through the new media window? The short answer is: only if you really have a passion for it. You don't have to be a techie, but you do have to know in your guts what audiences want from new media and be ready to provide it.

Just as in the old media, there's a shortage of A-list talent and a glut of wannabes. One of the biggest problems in multimedia is getting people to go beyond traditional "linear" thinking. Multimedia requires people who can think outside of traditional media to come up with something that's fresh and different.

THERE ARE SEVERAL ROLES MUSICIANS CAN PLAY IN MULTI-MEDIA: Sound Producer, Composer/Sound Effects Specialist, and Voice Artist/ Vocalist. Let's look briefly at each.

SOUND PRODUCERS are a critical part of almost every multimedia team producing for CD-ROMs or to other delivery formats that feature sound in real time. Sound producers are part manager, part creative artist, and part programmer. Their responsibilities often include designing and producing all sounds within a product, including musical scores, vocals, voice-overs, sound effects, and ambient and/or navigational sounds.

A sound producer is often hired and managed by the art director, though they may work closely with the producer on budgeting and scheduling issues. Sound producers often find, hire, and direct composers, musicians, and voice talent. They may also use a sound engineer during recording sessions in order to let them concentrate on directing musicians and voice professionals. They also make use of a sound editor to edit, compress and integrate the various sound components. In other instances, sound producers may perform the roles of composer and sound editor themselves. Performing multiple roles may be a reflection of a sound producer having multiple talents or a reflection of a limited budget.

COMPOSERS, MUSICIANS, AND SOUND-EFFECTS SPECIALISTS

write, design, create (or sample) music scores, background sounds, and sound effects for interactive projects. These sounds are commonly edited and processed by sound producers or editors and then integrated into interactive products by programmers.

The opportunities for creating sounds and music for multimedia products are growing rapidly because many producers and designers are recognizing the value that great sound brings to a project.

Composers, musicians, and sound effects specialists are hired by sound producers. They enter a project, most commonly, after the storyboards have been created. Experienced composers and sound-effects specialists are often given lots of leeway to create appropriate sounds. The reason producers hire sound professionals in the first place is because their style matches what the sound producer needs. At the same time, though, this leeway does not mean complete carte blanche to create any sound whatsoever. It needs to fit what the art director or sound producer is seeking (not always easy to articulate). Two primary qualifications for a sound-effects professional are adaptability and inventiveness. They should be adept at identifying, creating and manipulating sounds in either the real world or in sound editing tools. The scope of the work usually means they have to be organized and able to handle multiple tasks at once. They also need to be fast.

Multimedia producers suggest that musicians interested in multimedia sound design should study scores by masters of film and TV such as Ennio Morricone, Elmer Bernstein, John Williams, and Danny Elfman to gain insight into the marriage of music, themes, dialog, and other sounds. Some multimedia producers expect the demand for ambient music to increase, while others in the industry see international music and the ability to use thematic composition as areas of growth. And don't worry if your work is too obscure or different sounding, because producers constantly seek new and exotic sounds.

VOCAL ARTISTS also have a number of opportunities. A *voice-over* is an off-screen oral delivery of scripted material. Voice-overs are used for many project types, especially those that address the audience or user personally. They are used for narration in special interest titles, dialogue in children's storybooks, games, and instructions for training pieces and help systems. Many CD-ROM titles—especially those influenced by the film and TV industry—make extensive use of voice-overs to help achieve the appropriate dramatic effect.

There is a wide variety in the type of work that voice artists do, mainly because interactive media projects are combining aspects from animated cartoons and films, documentaries, television commercials, instructional videos, theater, and many others. In addition, the increasing practice of including multiple languages in products and simultaneously releasing products around the world means there will be more need for voice artists capable of speaking foreign languages during the initial production of a product.

The need is not as great for singers as for general voice artists, but there is some work in multimedia. Only a fraction of voice artists can sing well, which can present a problem for sound producers who need vocalists. So if you can do both you will maximize your value to the producer and probably be called on more often.

Breaking into Multimedia

Here are some tips for preparing effectively for multimedia involvement.

*   **PUT TOGETHER A KILLER DEMO.** In the multimedia area, many rules that apply to demo production are no different than in the rest of the biz. You want it to be as professional as possible, packaged and presented nicely, and marketed with just the right balance of pure talent, business, and schmooze.

How should you assemble your demo? For the highest impact possible, I suggest listening to many of the demos available from music production companies offering buy-out libraries or licensed music (see the section "Music Libraries" in the reference book, *Recording Industry Sourcebook*). The presentation on these music library demos often follows a format using a wide variety of quick cuts with various cross-fades. This can be easily done using today's digital multitracks. Simply use assembly editing techniques to record the first cut on tracks one and two, back up and fly in your next section on tracks three and four, and so on. When you're done assembling, mix to another DAT, which becomes your new master, you can make duplicates from it.

• **NETWORK YOUR WAY INTO RELATIONSHIPS WITH PEOPLE WHO CAN SAY YES.** The word "networking" may be worn, but the process needs a name, and this one works. The likely candidate for your target audience is someone with the title "Sound Producer" or "Audio & Music Director," or "Audio Manager," or possibly "Music Director." In some cases there is no staff audio engineer or music director, in which case the recipient of your package may be the "Director of Product Development" or "Executive Producer."

When looking for new musicians, multimedia developers often call people they know for referrals, so get to know them. You should build relationships with sound producers and let them know you are not only musically gifted, but you deliver professional results when and where they need it. The Internet is an excellent starting point for networking. Referring to the directories following this chapter will also help though they won't always name the music or audio director.

Multimedia is a social art where you most commonly work in teams. The project leader may be primarily a programmer, graphic artist, or video editor, or sound designer. In multimedia you end up in collaborations you never dreamt of before.

And don't just look for collaborators in the most obvious places. Sometimes, the most interesting work comes from places you'd rarely consider likely for musical opportunity. I had the gratifying experience of seeing what this means while working on a couple of multimedia projects this past year. My partner and I (collectively known as Friend Planet) teamed up with some microbial scientists who were developing a middle-school educational project called "Microcosmos" at a local university. We provided the soundtrack to a film about the "dance" of microorganisms in pond water. Being a National Science Foundation grant-supported project, it paid well. The beauty of the project lay in our unusual collaboration. Audiovisual producers, scientists, musicians, film directors, and educators—people who did not normally traffic with each other—joined together to create the work. This project came about through informal networking.

173

Another great place to network is at industry trade shows, such as the Electronic Entertainment Expo (or E3, as it's called), Intermedia, and particularly the Computer Game Developer's Conference (see list of trade shows at the end of this chapter). There's a lot to learn at these events, and in the process you can create some of the one-on-one connections that could ultimately be just as important as the quality of your demo.

- **DON'T JUST READ ABOUT IT,** do it. By becoming a savvy "end user" yourself, you'll develop the all-important sense of what other users want from the product. In your search for work at a large production house, it never hurts to know about the whole production process. Become familiar with the key multimedia software programs beyond the audio realm: *Macromedia Director, Premier, Photoshop, Fractal Painter,* etc.

- **KNOWING WHICH PRODUCTION STUDIOS** do a lot of sound production is one of the first steps to take. Some companies have in-house facilities and staff for generating many of the sounds needed for their products. LucasArts and Sega, for example, have full-time staffs devoted to creating the sound for their products. Other companies "outsource" this work and contract with independent composers and sound creators.

- Here's **WHAT TO EXPECT** after you produce and send out your ultimate multimedia demo tape: a long wait. No response is typical in this business. Be politely persistent. Seek feedback and information. Is there a better time to call? Is there a more appropriate person in the company to whom you should send your tape? Would they mind if you periodically sent them revisions of your credits and keep your work on file? Are there any upcoming projects they can tell you about?

Even if you're flat-out rejected, don't lose heart. Because in the course of perfecting your demo, while you're busy getting rejected just as many times as the Beatles, you are becoming masterful at your craft. You are creating tracks in styles and genres you've never tried before. You are "pushing your own envelope," experimenting, reaching, discovering. In short, you are becoming a better, more professional musician.

TOP MULITMEDIA PRODUCERS (1996)

Company	Revenue in millions
Electronic Arts/Broderbund	$493.2
Acclaim Entertainment	$375.7
Microsoft Multimedia	$200.0
Software Toolworks	$129.7
Spectrum Holobyte	$ 66.1
Sierra Online	$ 61.3
Davidson Associates	$ 58.6
Learning Company	$ 32.9

Source: The New York Times; Company reports; Lehman Brothers' estimates

Fig. 17.3

TOP SOFTWARE GAME PUBLISHERS

Total software sales jumped more than 12% to $4.6 billion in 1996 from $4.1 billion in 1995, with 20 companies controlling about two-thirds of the market

Publisher, Ranked by Dollar Sales

Publisher	1996 $	1996 units	Mkt share $	Mkt share units
Microsoft	$929,749,431	10,375,133	20.37%	10.16%
CUC Software	310,183,384	9,545,182	6.80	9.35
Intuit	238,510,457	4,585,324	5.23	4.49
Symantec	190,830,779	2,304,093	4.18	2.26
Broderbund	174,346,681	4,304,885	3.82	4.22
Learning Co.	156,509,234	5,807,929	3.43	5.69
Corel	139,777,604	1,784,553	3.06	1.75
GT Interactive	133,000,491	5,417,542	2.91	5.31
Electronic Arts	121,239,843	3,349,740	2.66	3.28
Adobe	118,050,424	578,060	2.59	0.57
Disney	78,584,789	2,561,953	1.72	2.51
Virgin	62,894,373	1,745,149	1.38	1.71
Quarterdeck	60,996,422	1,260,187	1.34	1.23
LucasArts	57,234,467	1,629,398	1.25	1.60
MicroProse	49,494,055	1,334,355	1.08	1.31
Activision	49,168,924	1,306,505	1.08	1.28
Interplay	47,592,531	1,337,384	1.04	1.31
Maxis	43,124,844	1,243,480	0.94	1.22
Mindscape	42,101,420	1,487,189	0.92	1.46
Netscape	39,278,393	917,953	0.86	0.90
Total Software Sales	**$4,585,812,710**	**103,121,600**		

Source: PC Data

Fig. 17.4

Further Resources

DIRECTORIES

The *Hollywood Interactive Entertainment Directory* (annual), Hollywood Creative Directories, 310-315-4815.

The *Multimedia Directory: Software Producers, Publishers & Tele-Media Firms* (annual), The Corronade Group, 213-935-7600.

BOOKS

Rosen, David and Caryn Mladen. *Making Money with Multimedia*. Reading, MA: Addison-Wesley, 1995.

Goldberg, Ron. *Multimedia Producer's Bible*. Foster City, CA: IDG Books, 1996.

PERIODICALS

CD-ROM Professional, Pemberton Press Inc., Wilton, CT 800-248-8466.

Desktop Video World, IDG Communications Publishing, Peterborough, NH 603-924-0100.

Electronic Entertainment, Infotainment World, San Mateo, CA 415-349-4300.

Forbes ASAP, Forbes Inc., New York, NY 800-888-9896. A technology supplement to Forbes magazine covering how the digital revolution is affecting business.

Morph's Outpost, Morph's Outpost Inc., Orinda, CA 800-55 MORPH.

Multimedia Producer, Montage Publishing, White Plains, NY 914-328-9157.

Multimedia World, PC World Communications, Inc., San Francisco, CA 415-281-8650.

New Media, Hypermedia Communications, Inc., San Mateo, CA 415-573-5170.

ORGANIZATIONS AND ASSOCIATIONS
International Interactive Communications Society, 14657 SW Teal Blvd., Suite 119, Beaverton, OR 97007; 503-579-4427; http://www.iics.org/.

Interactive Multimedia Association. 410-626-1380. http://www.ima.org/. Holds multimedia forums; co-sponsors the National Association of Broadcasters' annual Multimedia World Conference; and publishes a membership directory, quarterly technical journal, and bimonthly newsletter.

The Multimedia Development Group, 2601 Mariposa St., San Francisco, CA 94110; 415-553-2300; http://www.mdg.org/.

Women's Interactive Entertainment Association, P.O. Box 1127, San Carlos, CA 94070; 415-568-1268; http://www.phillips.com/mmwire/associations/wiea.html.

CONVENTIONS AND TRADE EVENTS
There are hundreds of these around the world. Here are the biggies:

Intermedia, Reed Exhibitions, San Francisco, CA; 203-840-4800. *February.*

New Media Expo, The Interface Group, Los Angeles, CA; 617-449-6600. *March.*

Computer Game Developer's Conference, Computer Game Developer's Association, San Jose, CA; 415-948-CGDC. *April.*

COMDEX, The Interface Group, Los Angeles, CA; 617-449-6600. *Spring and Fall.*

Electronic Entertainment Expo (E3), Los Angeles, CA; 800-800-5474. *May.*

IICS Annual Conference, International Interactive Communications Society,

Anaheim, CA; 503-579-4427. *June.*

On-line Developer's Conference, Jupiter Communications, San Francisco, CA; 212-941-9252. *September.*

18

Using the Internet to Promote Your Music

> "For the music industry, the Internet is a blender that will shatter and enmesh the compartmentalized mini-industries that are dominated by traditional type cast players. Today, the business and logistical dynamics of concert tours, TV and radio stations and record sales are entirely separate. But over time, the Internet will render, as artificial, the distinctions we see today between performance, broadcast and distribution and this will have dramatic implications."
>
> —Gene deRose, Jupiter Communications, 1996

> "This is the culture industry's challenge of the 1990s: to build up an international network of information and sound that can act as an open and unpredictable alternative to that presently being put in place by the global leisure corporations."
>
> —Simon Frith, Industry Analyst, 1993

The impact of the Internet on everything musical is nothing less than extraordinary—from revitalizing dormant music careers to galvanizing global fan bases; from providing new DIY avenues for major-level artists to sparking, unlikely-yet-rich musical collaborations—the Net is taking the music biz in a whole new direction.

It is helpful to view the Internet within the larger framework of the "digital revolution," and also as a reflection of that world-changing cultural/economic trend introduced in the previous chapter, "convergence." These two developments are having vast effects, both positive and negative, on both music creation and the music business, and are worth exploring.

By "digital revolution," I refer to the vast changes to society that have been brought about by the spread of computer (particularly *desktop* computer) technologies around the world. One of the most promising features of the

179

desktop revolution is the empowerment it brings to microbusinesses. It allows the smallest office to have the professional look, market reach, and management efficiency of larger companies.

This digital revolution enables convergences to happen on all levels. In essence, convergence is the coming together of different technologies and industries. The new technologies and products that result from convergence are greater than the sum of the original parts—and the two most powerful and pervasive technologies—*information* and *media*—are converging today. Books and audiocassettes, songs and greeting cards, news networks and the Internet are blending on the digital common, while traditional media boundaries are disappearing.

Information technology consists of computers and information-storage devices. *Media* technology is audio and visual appliances like television, radio and the telephone. In the past, each technology had been separated from the other with a clean line between them. Computers were used to manage and process information—numbers and text—while television, radio and the phone were used to convey pictures and sounds. Now the line between the two is rapidly blurring, and soon it will disappear altogether. As computers, TVs and telephones fuse, new products are emerging (teleputers?)—different, more powerful and with much more potential than any before.

Cross-industry alliances are also forming. Communications and media companies are pairing up. Communications companies historically focused on carrying voice or video traffic. Media companies produced print, films, shows and music. One industry produced media (content); the other delivered it to consumers (carriage). The barriers between content and carriage are now breaking down. Giant cross-corporate power blocks, spanning the *production and distribution* of media, are being formed.

Several factors are contributing to this cross-industry realignment. First, networks have become *multi*media carriers. Everything from movies to music to books and magazines can be translated and communicated in the binary language of computers—zeros and ones. In turn, communications carriers and others are getting together with media companies (including record labels) that can provide media content. Two examples of this corporate convergence is the 1996 merger of Disney with ABC, and the 1998 takeover of WebTV by Microsoft.

Media in all its diverse forms is the oil of the next century. The Internet (or whatever else it's going to be called) is the pump that will deliver it to our

OUR TECHNOLOGY CULTURE

A Gadget Generation
Share of U.S. Households with the following:

Television	98%	Pager	28%
Radio	98%	Electric car alarm	27%
Cordless Phone	66%	Camcorder	26%
Telephone answering device	65%	Computer with CD-ROM	21%
Stereo component system	54%	Modem or fax/modem	19%
Home CD player	49%	Caller-ID equipment	18%
Personal computer	40%	Direct-view satellite dish	10%
Computer printer	38%	Fax machine	9%
Cellular phone	34%		

Note: Figures are for January 1997
Source: Consumer Electronics Manufactures Assn.

The Speed of Change
How many years it took each of these technologies to spread to 25% of the U.S. population.*

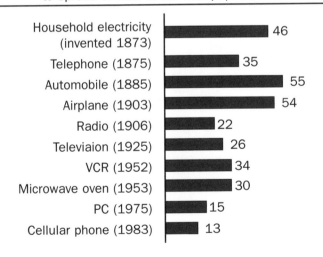

Household electricity (invented 1873) — 46
Telephone (1875) — 35
Automobile (1885) — 55
Airplane (1903) — 54
Radio (1906) — 22
Televiaion (1925) — 26
VCR (1952) — 34
Microwave oven (1953) — 30
PC (1975) — 15
Cellular phone (1983) — 13

* Defined as 25% of households, except for airplane, automobile and cell phone. Airplane:25% of the 1996 level of air miles traveled per capita. Automobile: The number of motor vehicles reached 25% of the number of people age 16 and older. Cellular phone: The number of cellular phones reached 25% of the number of registered passenger automobiles.
Source: Dallas Federal Reserve Bank

Fig. 18.1

homes. And the players are lining up to have as much influence on this evolution as possible.

Digital Democracy

The Internet ("Net," for short) is the fastest-growing communications network on the planet and the most effective at delivering multimedia content globally.

In essence, a network collapses distance. From my desktop in Boston, I can connect simultaneously with a guitarist in Zaire, a promoter in Australia, and a fan in Poland. For musicians, these developments bring tools to their cause that allow an extended reach on a playing field growing increasingly more level and accessible. On the Internet, you can appear side-by-side with multimillion dollar companies twenty-four hours a day, seven days a week.

What makes it especially suited to the music community is the navigational and viewing tool called the World Wide Web. Some have described the Web as "the Internet on steroids." Why? While the traditional Net (say from 1969–1992) was primarily a monochromatic *text*-based system, the Web opened the door to full-color graphics, CD-quality sound, and real-time video. The Web turns every owner of a computer, a modem, and a telephone line into a publisher, a radio station, and soon enough, a TV studio. Hey folks, we're talking 'bout a revolution! Personal and commercial empowerment at its finest.

SOME FACTS (CURRENT AS OF MARCH 1999):

- The Internet has about 90 million users in over 200 countries, and is growing at a rate of about 8–10% per month, almost doubling in size each year.

- According to a study by Nielsen Media Research and CommerceNet, music was the third most-purchased item on the Web in 1998 after computers and books.

- On-line users tend to be better educated and wealthier than other consumers, and can be efficiently reached via the Internet itself. As a result, an estimated $1.5 billion worth of Web advertising was placed in 1998 according to the Internet Advertising Bureau (http://www.iab.net), a 97% increase over the previous year. This is expected to soar to $2.5 bil-

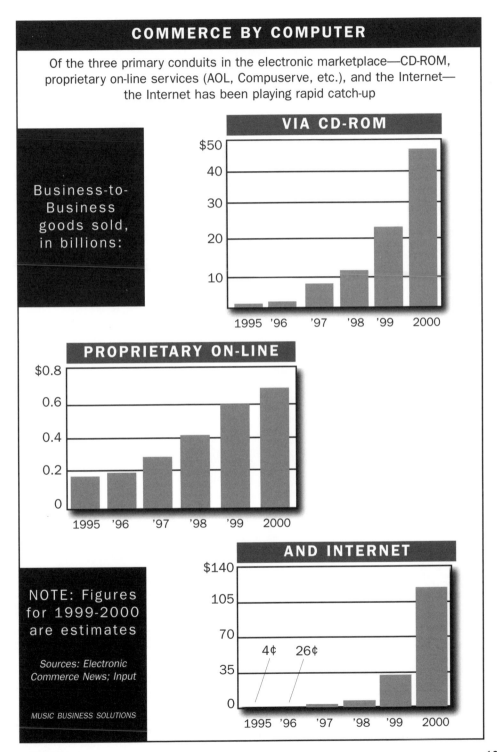

COMMERCE BY COMPUTER

Of the three primary conduits in the electronic marketplace—CD-ROM, proprietary on-line services (AOL, Compuserve, etc.), and the Internet—the Internet has been playing rapid catch-up

Business-to-Business goods sold, in billions:

VIA CD-ROM

PROPRIETARY ON-LINE

NOTE: Figures for 1999-2000 are estimates

Sources: Electronic Commerce News; Input

MUSIC BUSINESS SOLUTIONS

AND INTERNET

4¢ 26¢

Fig. 18.2

lion by 2000 says Simba. By then, advertisers will be able to reach as many as 340 million eyeballs (170 million Internet users) glued to the Web. [International Data Corp.]

- Global personal computer ownership grew from less than 20 million in 1993, to 120 million by 1998.

- In 1998, the wires of the world hit a crossover benchmark as they began transmitting more *data information* than voice. Andy Grove, chairman of Intel, calls this a "strategic inflection point"—the moment when the paradigm shifts and conventional wisdom no longer makes sense.

For the music industry, this moment has arrived.

But before fleshing out the finer features of the Internet for promoting music and music careers, let's first debunk some myths about the Net.

Unmasking Cyberlore

With the persistence of a spider, misinformation and myths about the Internet seem to crawl out of nowhere. These myths obscure the basic functions of the Net and actually sell short its true potential. Let's get a few of these out of the way first.

MYTH #1: *The Internet is just like commercial services like AOL, CompuServe and Prodigy.* Not quite. Commercial on-line services are proprietary computer networks of select informational databases. They're centralized and monitored. The Net, on the other hand, is a patchwork of commercial, educational, government, and public and private networks, all cooperating to achieve an open, interconnected communications system based on trust and goodwill. It's decentralized and relatively unregulated. But that doesn't mean...

MYTH #2: *The Internet is free.* Don't believe it for a moment. For people who receive Internet access as part of their employment or student status, the Internet may seem free. However, organizations pay for the infrastructure, equipment, and connections to gateways (exchange points for trading Internet traffic), and hire commercial providers to supply their connections to the

WEB'S WORLD WIDENS

Though the United States may dominate the World Wide Web, accounting for 60% of the 18.9 million host computers on the Internet, other countries are coming on strong, according to a survey of machines hooked up to the network. Here's a look at the fastest-growing nations in cyberspace.

COUNTRY	NUMBER OF INTERNET HOSTS AT 7/96	NUMBER OF INTERNET HOSTS AT 3/98
China	11,282	16,322
Russian Federation	32,022	94,137
Singapore	38,376	57,605
Brazil	46,854	117,200
Japan	496,427	1,168,956
Finland	277,207	450,044
Italy	113,776	243,250
Poland	38,432	77,594
Mexico	20,253	41,659
Greece	12,689	26,917

Sources: Network Wizards; I/PRO

Fig. 18.3

Internet itself. Interestingly, being the child of the Department of Defense, *your* tax dollars paid for it in the first place and, until recently, maintained it.

MYTH #3: *Internet users are cyberpunks and the content they create is cyberporn.* Thanks to some ill-gotten "research," the mainstream press (as usual) has made a mountain out of a molehill on this issue. While some consider portions of the material on the Internet to be immoral, obscene, or useless, much of it is no more controversial than what's found at a public library or in a bookstore.

MYTH #4: *The Internet is chaotic.* There's simply no way to find anything. While no Internet resource-searching tool is flawless, there *are* landmark directories and search tools on the Internet (e.g., Yahoo or Hot Bot, respectively) that you can use to find what you want with little, if any, hassle.

MYTH #5: *The Internet is hostile to newcomers.* Not many beginner tennis players would even consider running onto the court at Wimbledon and joining a match in progress. Instead, a new player typically seeks out information and support—by taking a class, learning from a teacher, watching tennis videos, or reading books about playing. Newcomers to the Net should spend some time learning its behavioral standards (see sidebar "Netiquette"), not just its technical necessities.

The Internet has any number of different "cultures." The liveliness of the Net derives from the people who take part in it, and different communities of people have different social norms. While not really applicable to the world of the World Wide Web, such subcultural sensitivity is crucial for participation in Internet newsgroups, mailing lists, and chat sessions.

The Essential Components of Internet Promotion

The Internet offers an ever-expanding banquet of opportunities, resources, and services for both the musician and the music fan. As of mid-1999, there are over 85,000 music-related newsgroups, mailing lists and Web sites on the Net.

On the Internet you'll find a lot more conversation *about* music than actual music, but this is changing fast. Compression technologies like MP3 and streaming audio are easing the once time-intensive process of listening to sound files on the Web. Right now, though, most of what you do on the Web is read, click, and type. Communication is its main use. There are two basic styles of computer communication: real-time chatting (like being on a party line) and bulletin-board posting (where a conversation on a topic, or "thread," can span months). Who are you talking to? You can never be sure.

NEWSGROUPS. The Internet's massive bulletin-board system is referred to as Usenet. Usenet is composed of "newsgroups," but it shouldn't be confused with a wire-service feed, such as the Associated Press or UPI. A newsgroup can best be pictured as a discussion group where participants post "articles" to the shared newsgroup "space" for all to see and to which others may either read or respond. Given the scope and speed of the Net, it is possible to carry on discussions on any subject with participants around the world in (almost) real time.

Topical areas vary widely. Looking for a review of Burning Spear's latest release? Try the rec.music.reggae newsgroup. Have questions about Coltrane's improvisational technique? Chances are somebody reading or posting to alt.music.bluenote can help you. Hoping to locate the lyrics of an obscure Californian folk song? Then check out the rec.music.folk newsgroup. Curious about what music's hot in Hawaii, Australia, or Vancouver? rec.music.info will definitely have the charts you are seeking. There are specialty newsgroups for Afro-Latin, a cappella, Celtic, funk, bagpipe, industrial, hardcore, ska, trance, karaoke, even "filk" (fantasy-related folk music)! Each one is a "cybercultural space" in which you can share ideas and make your opinion known. Chances are you'll find your own particular musical or extra musical interest represented in some newsgroup.

There are three important points to make about Usenet: make sure (1) your Internet access provider receives a full news feed, (2) that it provides a decent means of viewing the news, and (3) that it allows you to "post" to the server. If you can't post your own contributions to Usenet, you'll be limited to being an observer, not an active participant.

MAILING LISTS. In addition to newsgroups, you can locate over 700 music-related and subject-specific "mailing lists" on the Net. Mailing lists are different than newsgroups in that you can participate in electronic discussions only if you actually "subscribe" (for free, of course) to a given list. The range and scope varies from list to list, and there are many artist—or genre—specific lists on the Net. For example, lists for fans of bands and artists like Yes, Miles Davis, Celine Dion, Elton John, Busta Rhymes, Jewel and many others are available for subscription.

Mailing lists, like newsgroups, allow participants, no matter how distant geographically, to exchange concert and record reviews, tour schedules, discographies, and gossip, among other things. To get the most current list of all e-mail music lists, go to the "Musical List of Lists" at http://www.shadow.net/%7emwaas/lomml/. It's a huge file so you may want to cut and paste the lists you prefer onto another document instead of printing the entire directory.

WORLD WIDE WEB. Then, of course, there's the World Wide Web. The Web opened the door to full-color graphics, CD-quality sound, and real-time video—an ideal communications channel for musical artists.

When the World Wide Web hit the scene, early musical adopters became drunk with its possibilities. The promises were indeed intoxicating: Post your own multimedia press kit for all the world to see! Give your fans twenty-four-hour-a-day, seven-day-a-week global access to your musical goods! Allow Hottentots and Polynesians to hear sound clips of your Brooklyn-produced tunes!

Added to these prospects are technical features like animated GIFs, Java applets, ever-improving audio streaming technology, *and* the opportunities for full artistic control, and you have the makings of self-contained mini-music empires. In this new marketplace, smaller players are able to compete.

How Musicians and Music Businesses are Using the Net

In the area of music, e-mail, mailing lists, and newsgroups are among the most popular tools for individual users on the Net. Consider these examples:

- Artists and managers regularly use the Internet to announce new releases and tour itineraries. And when a gig is added or cancelled at the last minute, the Net makes it possible to get the word out quickly.

- DJs are posting play lists to share with each other and record companies, getting ideas for shows from each other and discovering artists and recordings they wouldn't otherwise know about.

- Songwriters are collaborating by e-mail by exchanging MIDI song and sound files.

- Musicians regularly put out "barter calls" for gear (e.g., amp for a sequencer).

CYBERMARKETING

Not all of these will apply to you and your music, but they will show some of the vast possibilities for business uses of the Internet.

MINING NEW PROSPECTS
- Post your own Web page on the Internet.
- Bait the Web site: put something exciting, amusing, or valuable at the Web site to attract potential customers to it.
- Use a service firm with good skills in designing World Wide Web facilities with color pictures and sound.
- Display the Web page address on all print advertisements.

NARROWLY FOCUSED MARKETING
- Do "micromarketing" linked to individual requirements, tastes, and profiles.
- Do highly focused marketing targeted at narrow communities with specific interests.
- Use on-demand infomercials, tailored to customer needs, that potential customers can explore when they want, rather than traditional advertising, which transmits the same message to everybody.

SELLING
- Offer goods for sale on World Wide Web shops and malls. There are numerous online record stores that sell independent music. For a directory of these on-line stores see CD Stores On-Line (http://www.geocities.com/RodeoDrive/5860/index.html) and The Ultimate Band List: Stores Online (http://www.ubl.com/store/)
- Facilitate impulse buying: allow customers to order goods as soon as they find them on the Web.
- Convert advertising and infomercials directly into orders and transactions wherever possible, using credit cards, smart cards, or e-cash.

HELP WITH ORDERING
- Encourage customers to do electronic order entry rather than having order-entry clerks decipher customer requests or using expensive fulfillment services.

Fig. 18.4 —continued— **189**

NEW INFORMATION TO FANS
- Announce new products or features by sending e-mail to existing customers. Enable these customers to explore details about the products on bulletin boards.
- Send customers information about discounts and lower prices.
- Provide free upgrades (e. g., software companies can distribute version changes over the Net).
- Create a news bulletin board containing stories about the product.
- In paper catalogs and literature, describe how new information can be found on the Net.

BULLETIN BOARDS FOR FANS
- Enable customers to access bulletin boards of product details.
- Where products have many pricing options, make these accessible on a bulletin board.
- Enable customers to access bulletin boards of service information, diagnostic information, and technical manuals.

PRESS RELATIONS
- Distribute news releases to the press by e-mail rather than regular mail. Most journalists would prefer news releases to go directly into their computers.
- Set up a bulletin board for the press.

SPREADING NEWS
- Complement information in the company magazine with more detailed or variable information on the Net.
- Provide information on product-related seminars or conferences, possibly making the proceedings or papers available on-line.
- Offer contests or sweepstakes on-line. As well as creating news, this can be a way to troll for new e-mail addresses.

PRODUCT SUPPORT
- Use person-to-person video communications via ISDN to provide better support to customers.
- Offer technical support via e-mail.
- Offer advice by e-mail (e.g., a blues band can offer a Chicago Blues discography).
- Offer e-mail services for customers to find out about add-on products or other models.
- List answers to FAQs about the products or services.

- Send customers stories about the company, its service philosophy, its new directions.
- Try to make customers feel like part of the family.
- Send reminders to regular customers (e. g., send suggestions before a spouse's birthday).

FEEDBACK FROM WEB SITE VISITORS
- Collect information for qualified leads.
- Reward Web site visitors for providing information that can be used in marketing (with discounts, free offers, promises of information, etc.).

FEEDBACK FROM FANS AND CUSTOMERS
- Obtain user feedback: product comments, information about problems, suggestions, concerns—worldwide.
- Obtain data for market research; learn about related products.
- Solicit knowledge of customer wishes (e.g., color or features).
- Create an electronic suggestion box. Invite all customers to send comments and suggestions.
- Provide survey forms to customers for electronic response. For mass-market products a large amount of feedback can be obtained cheaply.
- Prompt customers for comments on specific items ("We've just added a new option on...Is it useful to you?").
- Print your e-mail address prominently with every product shipped, and ask for comments.

USER GROUPS
- Start newsgroups where customers can exchange information and help one another.

FAN CLUBS
- Create an electronic fan club where fans can trade information and tell other fans what they like.
- Provide fans with interesting trivia, and ask for comments about future directions
- Ask fans for testimonials.
- In a company that sells information, books, music, or anything that can be transmitted, allow fans to download snippets.
- Offer product users a chance to have their names on the bulletin board by inviting them to say what they like about the product.

Breaking the band Korn was something the band attributes to their grass-roots efforts on the Internet. Korn's manager, Jeff Kwatinetz has said, "Many label people do not understand how we did so well...and still don't understand...The thing that makes the Internet so powerful is the control of information. Record companies love to control information...but by using the Net, managers and bands can find out their own information." For instance, he said bands can now go back to the record companies and say, "Here's the single we want, and here's our own research to back that up." Information empowers and artists are using this power to leverage better deals and strategies for themselves and their teams.

In 1994, when the Web was young, Virginia-based band Everything teamed up with their Internet Provider (I-Tribe) and broadcast a two week tour over the Net, one each night. For software, they used the relatively new (at the time) videoconferencing product called "CUSeeMe" out of Cornell University. The band promoted this "Internet Tour" via e-mail to cybercafés all over the world (which were new at the time and looking for promotional ideas) and sent them posters and CDs ahead of time, for advertising the shows. They also made a CD-ROM that told all about the band, along with Everything's music playing in the background. The CD-ROM was authored by some fans who were trying to launch their own multimedia company (Mouse Up Productions). On one of those nights, The Internet Café in London had over 200 people watching their concert, each paying $10 to view the performance. Since then, their Web site (http://www.ecolon.com) has drawn an international audience and the CD-ROMS are still generating calls and letters from around the world.

Of course, the big news on how the Net can affect a band's live performance opportunities happened early in 1998. Fans of British band Marillion began communicating with the group's bass player Mark Kelly via e-mail and found out the band was willing to tour the States but unable to capitalize the venture. A man on the list, Jeff Pelletier said, "Why don't we raise the money?" Though skeptical, Kelly gave Pelletier the go ahead.

This meant dealing with incoming mail, donations, accounting, and a myriad of other details. Another fan, who proposed to his wife at a Marillion show in London the previous year, opened the bank account. The Marillion fund took off. In the first week, worldwide donations totalled about $9,000. "We were using the fan base like a Marillion army," Kelly said. "People wanted to see the band succeed in America. It was like a crusade."

The crusade had no trouble raising $50,000, allowing Marillion to tour 22 North and South American cities. This story is a testimony to how the Internet enables those outside the orbit of big business to create their own support network based on belief and enthusiasm, rather than just achieving a sizable return-on-investment.

The Internet is also beginning to affect record sales. According to a 1998 study by Jupiter Communications, music and books gross more money than any other industries on the Web (excepting computers), and Macey Lipman Marketing found that 41% of major music retailers had been noticeably affected by the on-line world. Cowles/Simba Information estimates that revenue for the top five on-line music retailers jumped over 269% in 1998 to $135 million from $36.6 million the year before, and is expected to break the $300 million mark in 1999. Although on-line sales currently account for an estimated one-tenth of one percent of total prerecorded music sales, there is a very strong relationship between audiophiles and Web surfers.

If data from Fairfield Research and Soundata are correct, 75 million "active music buyers" buy 90% of all music sold in the United States, a little less than half have PCs in their homes, and about a quarter of these PC audiophiles have access to the Internet. With Web penetration increasing at a rate of anywhere from 80–100% per year and total Web commerce growing from $200 million in 1994 to $4 billion by 1998, trends suggest that on-line distribution will play a major role in the music world in the years to come.

Many artists have decided to use the Net to market their music and forego record company involvement altogether. For example, Canadian alternative rockers the Tragically Hip have repeatedly failed to break into the U.S. market, so the band left its U.S. label, produced its own CD, and sold it through Music Boulevard. Only 15,000 Tragically Hip CDs were sold, but half of the proceeds went to the band, about four times the standard artist's royalty.

If it wasn't for the Internet, the Artist Formerly Known as Prince may not have had the resolve to leave his record company of seventeen years and launch his own label (New Power Generation Records), sign his own artists, make his own manufacturing and distribution deals, and sell his label's music over the Net. Though the Artist's sales have come nowhere near those of when he was at Warner Bros., he nets more per record than before and is very happy to have full control over his own recording career. His example is also a straw blowing in the wind. As the record industry continues to grapple with issues such as digital distribution, consolidation, and stagnant sales, artists are increasingly hoisting the DIY flag and declaring their secession from the mainstream.

Radio shows and networks are joining the action fast and furious, especially with the debut of "RealAudio" which allowed FM quality sound transmission in real time over the Internet. RealAudio allows radio stations to broadcast worldwide, via the Internet, without the limitations of broadcast transmitters or short-wave radio's thin, patchy sound. See chapter 16 for more developments about Internet Radio.

The next generation of audio transmission can be seen in companies like Liquid Audio, a2b (AT&T), and the Madison Project (IBM) which aim to provide all-in-one delivery systems for music producers. As of January 1999, Liquid Audio promised delivery of forty-five minutes of CD-quality music in twenty minutes using a 28.8 bps modem. And it's only going to get quicker.

Ultimately, on-line music delivery offers advantages consumers will like: low prices, convenience, free promotional music, and the comfort of their own homes. Taking into account the not-so-distant future of high-speed cable modems and telecom Internet hook-ups with lightning speed, it's easy to see why so many companies and individuals are pondering how this development will affect the world of music. Red-button issues such as rights and royalties are finally being addressed and sorted out as well, creating a new confidence throughout the industry.

What is also fairly certain is that the Internet will, in the end, be most beneficial to smaller companies that specialize in a particular market segment or niche, rather than to larger companies trying to cater to the broadest possible audience. This may mean greater power and influence for the indies and less power and influence for the majors and their corporate owners. Time will tell.

A Home of Your Own: Do-It-Yourself Web Page Design

But say you wanted to go it alone and design your own Web pages. What would you need?

Your Web page construction costs and hosting can range from free to more than $1000 per year, depending on the information included, the complexity of the design and how long it takes you to become acquainted with an HTML software editor. Here is a list of things you'll need to create your own Web page:

- **A COMPUTER AND A MODEM.** For best results, use a Pentium II or PowerMac with at least a 28.8 Kbps (kilobytes per second) modem. Anything less powerful can make cruising the Web and downloading data feel more like creeping in rush-hour traffic.

- **AN HTML EDITOR.** A top-notch HTML (hypertext markup language) editor will give personality to the text of your Web page. HTML is essentially plain ASCII text with embedded codes that enable you to create links, fill-in forms and clickable images—all elements of a great Web page.

- **A WEB BROWSER.** Almost any browser will do—Netscape, Internet Explorer—even the ones built into one of the commercial on-line services, such as AOL or CompuServe. The only requirement is that the browser include an option that allows you to view files stored on your computer's hard drive before you add them to your Web pages.

- **GRAPHICS SOFTWARE.** If you want your Web page to get noticed, it has to have cool graphics. You'll either have to create them yourself or find a good clip art program. You'll also need a graphic converter program, such as HiJaak Pro, to convert images you've created into GIF and JPEG formats that Web browsers use.

- **A PPP OR SLIP CONNECTION AND SERVER SPACE.** A PPP or SLIP is your connection to the Internet's World Wide Web. You can obtain a SLIP or PPP connection through an Internet service provider, such as Earthlink, Netcom, or UUNet (see Special Internet Resources at the end of this chapter). This is the most expensive part of setting up your Web page, so shop around. These also provide server space for your home page. They thus become the "host" to you, the "client." Search out and critique potential hosts using http://www.budgetweb.com/.

- **MASTER OF YOUR OWN DOMAIN.** Your first decision is whether it's worth $70 up front for two years, and $35 per year after that, to have your own domain name, such as http://www.MyCoolBand.com. This works out to $3 per month, which is chump change, so I highly recommend it. Pick a domain name that you can yell into the mike at the end of a set, or tell all your drunken fans, and have a good chance that they will be able to remember it the next day. Also use the nifty lookup feature at http://www.internic.net/ to verify that nobody else has taken your domain name. Do not attempt to apply for the domain name at this time. Do not mistakenly go to http://www.internic.com/, who will cheerfully charge you $200 so you can fill out the same form on their site, which they automatically forward to http://www.internic.net with $75. Their profit: $125. They are raking in the dough from the uninformed.

- **FINDING A HOST FOR YOUR SITE.** You can have your site hosted for free on a service like Geocities (http://www.geocities.com/) or BandHost (http://www.bandhost.com/), but you won't get your own domain name, such as http://www.MyCoolBand.com/, or you can pick a hosting company and pay them to host your domain. Fees range from $10/month to $500/month, and it is NOT the case that higher-priced hosts are always better. Honest. You just have to do a lot of homework to figure out who's good.

One good way to find inexpensive providers is to use http://www.budgetweb.com/. It also provides all sorts of other criteria to narrow your search. One you definitely want is RealAudio and/or MP3 streaming. Visit each of the suggested hosts and verify their price. Pay careful attention to the different "packages" they offer, since some of the low-end packages won't actually have all of the features you need. Also see if they have any music clients that you can check out their Web site and verify that their music servers are not dog-slow. Contact their clients, and see how satisfied they are.

There is a lot of help out there for amateur Web page designers. A number of excellent shareware (and *freeware*) programs can be downloaded from http://www.oamag.com/on-line/access.html. Keeping updated on the cool tips and tricks requires a little more effort, but you can learn a lot by seeing what other Webmasters are doing on their pages. Getting involved in newsgroups and mailing lists or utilizing the resources mentioned in the Yahoo directory (http//www.yahoo.com/Computers/World_Wide_Web/Authoring/) will also go a long way toward helping you keep abreast of the developments in HTML authoring. Books like Laura Lemay's *Teach Yourself Web Publishing with HTML in a Week* and Ian Graham's *HTML Sourcebook* will answer most of the do-it-yourselfer's questions about building a Web page.

If you've been hesitating setting up a Web site because learning HTML is about as attractive as sticking your head in a beehive, take heart! This past year has seen a flood of "HTML Editors" come to market and their target market is you (and me!). No need to learn HTML coding or any of the other cryptic formatting commands early Web authoring demanded! If you can handle word processing, you can now author your own Web pages including graphics, audio and even video. Drag-and-drop commands and WYSIWYG (what you see is what you get) interfaces go a long way toward making Web design a snap. Some are freeware (like "Page Spinner"); others are packaged by software companies (Claris "HomePage," Adobe "PageMill"). Any of these programs will do the job, and for under $100. What are you waiting for?

You may also wish to include "sound bytes" of your songs on your Web page. There are two ways to deliver music on the Web. The first is to make your song into a downloadable file. There are four mail file types: wav, aiff, au, and MPEG3 (a.k.a. "MP3"). The sound quality for all file types is decent, with MP3 being practically CD quality. To convert your music to one of these types of files, use CoolEdit (**http://www.syntrillium.com/**) or Sound Forge XP (**http://www.sonicfoundry.com/**). The downside is the user has to wait to download the file, which can sometimes take a while.

To avoid making the user wait, your can "stream" your audio by using software like RealAudio, QuickTime3, LiquidAudio, or Netshow. The sound quality will suffer slightly but the music starts to play at the click of a button, so it's a sacrifice a lot of Web-site owners are willing to make.

Once you've finished your masterpiece, you'll need to transfer the files you created to your Internet access provider's Web server. This usually means that your access provider opens an account on its file server for you. Then you use the Internet "FTP" (file transfer protocol) function to upload your home-page files to the Internet provider's computer. Voila. Your home page lives.

You can also put your home page on other servers as well. The benefits of going with a commercial music site provider (like IUMA, for instance) are many: you get a built-in music-loving audience, Web-design expertise, in-house familiarity with the on-line music market, and relatively inexpensive hosting for your data.

A Dozen Design Tips for Creating a Great Web Page

1. GET ORGANIZED. Start visualizing your Web page before you ever turn on the computer. Think about what you want to put on your home page, what you want the reader to get out of it, how the information will relate, and how you want everything to look. Some Web experts recommend creating a storyboard—small sketches of each page in outline form—before you start writing.

2. TAKE A LOOK AT OTHER WEB SITES. Check out which ones you like the best. What features make the site easy for you to use? What content appeals to you? What designs do you like best. Select the best elements of your favorite sites and incorporate those features into your site.

3. GIVE PEOPLE A REASON TO VISIT. Don't waste people's time with a page that provides only a list of links to other Web sites. For example, if you're an avid blues lover and want to create a Web page on the subject, tell visitors where the best blues clubs are in your area and provide directions. Pull people in with useful information.

4. KEEP IT SIMPLE. The home page is to the rest of your Web site as a book's cover is to its contents. The design should be bold and understandable at a glance. Don't clutter it up with unnecessary details or over-complicated layouts.

5. GET VISUAL. Use imaginative layouts and good-looking typography to give your Web pages a unique and identifiable look. Graphical content should be of some practical value. Avoid empty window dressing. To save time, many users set their browsers to ignore graphics; all they see is text. It's essential that any important messages or links contained in graphics be duplicated in textual form. Test-drive your page in text-only mode to make sure it works.

6. OBSERVE LIMITATIONS. Many people have "technologically challenged" hardware. The WWW becomes the World Wide Wait when huge graphics files are downloaded for viewing. Keep graphics to no more than 50k and your site will be a delight to visit.

7. MAKE IT EASY TO NAVIGATE. One of the home page's primary roles is as a navigational tool, pointing people to information stored on your Web site or elsewhere. Make this function as effortless as possible. Also, don't bury information too deep in the page hierarchy. Stepping through five or more links can get pretty tedious.

8. INCLUDE THE ESSENTIALS. Here are a few things most every home page should have: a header that identifies your Web site clearly and unmistakably, an e-mail address for reporting problems, copyright information as it applies to on-line content, and contact information, such as mailing address and phone number.

9. MAKE IT FUN. What causes people to come back for return visits? According to IntelliQuest, 56% return to entertaining sites, 54% like attention grabbing sites, 53% extremely useful content, 45% information tailored to their needs, 39% imaginative sites, and 36% highly interactive sites.

10. BE SURE TO TITLE YOUR HOME PAGE with a headline that will attract the most viewers to your Web site. Many search engines use the title as one of their main ways of selecting sites to show to requesters. The first paragraph of text after your title is also often used by search engines to rank listings, so be sure your first paragraph contains key words about the contents of your site. As a matter of practice, you should add proper titles to the rest of your pages as well. Follow the same basic principles for all your pages.

11. ALSO GO TO DR. HTML (http://www2.imagiware.com/ RxHTML) for a free testing service that will test a single URL and report back to you on spelling, form structure, link verification, and other aspects of your Web page. Your entire site can be checked for a fee.

12. KEEP IT FRESH. Users could get jaded if your Web site never changes. Encourage return visits by giving them something new to look forward to. Include your Web site in your established publicity program, so that new information (such as press releases) appears concurrently on your Web pages.

Marketing Your Music on the Net

When it comes to "marketing," the Net is a "soft sell" medium. Unlike traditional media (TV, radio, magazines, etc.) which "push" information at us, the Internet "pulls" us in through the added dimension of interactivity. While traditional media is unidirectional (one-way), the Net is bi-directional (two-way) and, as such, is nothing short of revolutionary.

You "sell" on the Net by providing useful information to people. For example, say you're a rock band from Boston. Instead of just promoting yourself and your CD, you can also have some cool, hard-to-find info about Boston at your site (e.g., a list of your favorite live music clubs with reasons why). Don't forget, people will be checking you out from all over the world and some "inside" information about Boston's music scene will be much appreciated by the out-of-towner, as well as locals.

Record labels, retailers, manufacturers, and talent agencies can also use the Net to increase their customer base and market their brands. The Web, in particular, offers a powerful forum to dispense product and service information, raise awareness, and generate brand loyalty in a global environment. On-line marketing offers some significant advantages over traditional ads and catalogs:

- You are not limited by the price of printing and postage, which makes on-line selling extremely economical.
- You can change your content quickly, easily, and at virtually no cost.
- An on-line catalog is easily searchable. All shoppers have to do is type in a key word or two to get the info they want.
- Technology allows you to offer audio and video clips with product demonstrations for "deeper" marketing.
- You can provide your customers with an essentially infinite amount of product information.
- The cost per exposure/per month is extremely reasonable compared to full-page print ads.

The Net is also a great medium for offering customer service, dispensing company information, and even soliciting employees and interns. Any business with a mail-order component is especially well-positioned for on-line success. If it will sell in a mail-order catalog, it will work on the Internet, if you *target* your market/audience (see Fig. 18.4 "Cybermarketing").

NETIQUETTE

Both newsgroups and mailing lists are very sensitive about blatant self-promotion. The quickest way to make a bad name for yourself on the Net is to send obnoxious e-mail or news. This is called "spamming" the Net and usually results in being "flamed" (being sent nasty or insulting messages for your violation of cyber-manners). So mind your netiquette. Here are some good ways to do this:

- Before posting a message, make sure your post has a point to make. If you do not have a point, there is no need to post because it will waste other people's time, bandwidth, and disk space. Also, when responding to a message, if you include a copy of the original message, trim it down to the minimum needed. Again, there is no sense wasting bandwidth.

- Know the difference between the address you use to get on or off a mailing list and the address you use to send messages to the list itself.

- Read a mailing list or newsgroup for at least a week before you try to send anything to it so that you understand what topics it covers and grasp the level of discussion.

- Most lists and groups have an introductory message, and most newsgroups periodically post FAQ (frequently asked questions) messages that introduce the topic and answer the most common questions. Before sending in your question, make sure it's not already answered for you.

- If you are arguing with someone on Usenet, keep to the facts and avoid personal insults. If you are angry, wait until you cool down to post (it may even be a few days). If you cannot cool down and must send something, do it in e-mail and keep it private instead of using Usenet.

- Include a short signature file that contains at least your name and your e-mail address.

By following these guidelines, you will have a better reputation on Usenet than you would otherwise. Also, it will save other people's time.

A banquet of Web site promotion resources can be found at Virtual Promote, http://www.virtualpromote.com/.

For Those New to the Net

So how does a band or music entrepreneur get started with this new medium? First, total up everything you've spent this past year on promotion and marketing—paper, copying, postage, gas, phone, etc. What did you come up with? $500? $1000? $2000? Now realize that a small piece of this can get you a presence on a medium that's always turned on reaching millions around the globe. Here are some simple steps to help you get acquainted with the Net as a new promotional tool:

1. SEE THE NET FIRSTHAND. The first and best thing to do is play on the Internet yourself. This will give you a sense of the possibilities. For beginners, the Web is probably the easiest entry point. There're a lot of other areas to explore on the Net but they can wait. Either set up your own hardware for an Internet connection (see sidebar 18.2 "Getting Wired") or go check it out at a friend's house or office that's connected. You can also visit one of the many "cybercafés" springing up where, for a few bucks, you can explore the Web while sipping your mocha latte. Remember, this is an *emerging* technology. There are few rules and those that do exist grow more flexible every day. You yourself can contribute to the Net's overall makeup and development as you apply your imagination to the medium's vast possibilities.

2. DECIDE WHAT YOU WANT TO DO ON THE NET. Are you interested in posting notice of some high-profile gig you're involved in or just generally promoting your band? Do you want to communicate via e-mail with your customers or is a "snail-mail" address sufficient? How about actually selling your tape or CD over the Net? Most artists choose to post their "electronic press kit": bio, gig schedule, photo, album art, press reviews, sound byte and video clip (if available). Including all contact information lets people contact you if they like what they see and hear (and sometimes if they don't!). Remember, the Net is worldwide.

Also, think about how Internet marketing fits in with your traditional marketing mix of advertising, mailers, performances, press, and airplay.

The Net shouldn't *replace* these ongoing efforts but instead, *supplement* and *enhance* them.

3. CHOOSE AN IPP (Internet Presence Provider) and a site location for your Home Page *carefully.* A presence provider (different from an *access* provider which helps you get connected) acts like a design house for your site. It can digitize your music and video, scan your graphics and translate your bio and everything else into "hypertext markup language" (HTML) so it's readable on the Web. HTML is relatively easy to learn which has resulted in a sudden explosion of people willing to "do your Home Page." But watch out. There's a lot more to effective Web design than mere HTMLing. Layout, color, tone, backgrounds, ease of navigation, clarity, and uniqueness are other components that make a Web site shine, rather than merely exist. And with thousands of new Web sites coming on-line every month, it's more and more important to truly shine.

Once your Page is designed you'll next need a "server" to store it on so it can be seen. Most IPPs also have a server and a Web site where you can "post" your Home Page. For example, IUMA (http://www.iuma.com) *and* Kaleidospace (http://www.kspace.com) provide both Web design and site hosting. Some model themselves after stores or malls: you bring the ready-made site, they supply the "space." Others choose a magazine format. Still others seek to create the atmosphere of a club or venue.

The key thing to look for in a hosting site is traffic. After all, why be siting on a site no one visits? Fortunately, with the Internet you can know exactly how many times your page is seen. These viewings are called "hits" in Net parlance and a Web site's traffic is measured by how many "hits" it gets in a given day or week. But this can be deceiving. Some equate hits with people, whereas in actuality a hit is a "click," the action of clicking on an image or "link" on a Web page. Since most people average seven clicks per visit, the overall hits should be divided by at least this number to obtain a realistic measure of unique site traffic.

When choosing a host site look also for extra values—contests, promotional opportunities, cyberpublicity, order fulfillment, statistical reporting, helpful information, special programs, etc. For example, Kaleidospace sponsors an Artist-in-Residence program where, once a month, a high-profile artist's work is featured prominently on their site. The key is to get the most mileage possible from your site. **203**

4. FINALLY, MAXIMIZE YOUR ON-LINE PRESENCE. Once you're residing on a chosen site (or a number of sites—this is possible too), use your new Internet address on all your mailers, flyers, album and tape covers, photos, and business cards. Send out a special press release to everyone on your media, fan, and industry mailing list letting them know you've gone on-line. Remember, one of the Net's key features is interactivity. Contests, polls, trivia questions, and other devices get browsers involved and interested. Use you imagination and work with your IPP to design these elements for your Page.

---

sidebar: 18.2

GETTING WIRED

A list of national Internet access providers and how to choose one.

EARTHLINK, 800-395-8425
NETCOM , 800/501-8649
UUNET, 800-4UU-NET4

HOW TO CHOOSE AN INTERNET ACCESS PROVIDER:

Send for information from each of the above and then ask the following questions:

Q. What's the total cost?

The true cost of Internet service is made up of several elements: a monthly charge, which may include a fixed or unlimited number of hours online; an hourly fixed charge for additional time; and a charge for the connection itself, which may require long-distance telephone calls or access through a data network such as Sprintnet.

Q. Can you connect easily?

The lowest cost is not always the best choice. If you spend more time listening to busy signals than you do online, it's time to cancel your account. System downtime also holds up connections. It's true that modems, servers, and routers sometimes fail, but if you suffer frequent and prolonged stretches of time when the system does not answer, you need a different service provider.

Q. Is support available? Is it useful?

Sooner or later, you'll need some kind of hand-holding. You might want to configure a new modem, or a program that has worked flawlessly for months might mysteriously die. What happens when you call for help? Calls to tech support tend to come in bunches, especially when some part of the service provider's setup crashes. If you can't get an immediate answer, does someone return your call within a couple of hours?

Q. What kind of extra services do you get?

Many service providers offer a plain vanilla connection and nothing more, but if you look around, you might find some added hot fudge and whipped cream. For example, some accounts include space on a Web server or an FTP server. Other providers might offer their own conferences or newsgroups, or a toll-free telephone number for access from out of town. Especially in competitive markets like Seattle and Boston, it's worth asking about extras. And don't ignore the commercial online services. Some hard-core Internet heads may sneer at @aol.com or @mci-mail.com e-mail addresses, but these services are relatively easy to use, and their prices can be competitive with those of other Internet access providers.

Further Reading

BOOKS

Chase, Larry. *Essential Business Tactics for the Net.* New York: John Wiley & Sons, 1998.

Allen, Cliff, Deborah Kania and Beth Yaeckel. *Internet World Guide to One-To-One Web Marketing* (Internet World Series). New York: John Wiley & Sons, 1998.

Janal, Daniel S. *On-line Marketing Handbook 1998 Edition: How to Promote, Advertise and Sell Your Products and Services on the Internet.* New York: John Wiley & Sons, 1998.

Yudkin, Marcia. *Marketing On-line: Low-Cost, High-Yield Strategies for Small Businesses & Professionals.* NY: Penguin, 1995. An older work but full of relevant ideas and tactics.

Lemay, Laura. *Teach Yourself Web Publishing with HTML in a Week.* SAMS Publishing.

Graham, Ian. *HTML Sourcebook.* New York: John Wiley & Sons, Inc.

PERIODICALS

The Net, Imagine Publishing, Inc., 150 North Hill Drive, Brisbane, CA 94005; http://www.thenet-usa.com/.

Internet World, Mecklermedia Corp., 20 Ketchum Street, Westport, CT 06880; http://www.iw.com/.

Internet Resources

Each listing below is followed by its "URL" (Uniform Resource Locator). This is the company's World Wide Web address. "http" stands for Hypertext Transfer Protocol and it allows World Wide Web (www) pages to be transferred over the Net. With most browsers today you don't have to type the "http://" prefix anymore; they automatically resolve it. Cool.

MUSIC WEB SITES SAMPLER

See plenty more recommended Web sites in the "Musicians' Resource Directory" at the end of this book

GENERAL INTERNET INFORMATION

General Net info and terms explained: http://www.zrhome.com/iwc.

How big is the Internet and who uses it? http://arganet.tenagra.com/howbig.html.

FIRST-STOP MUSIC JUMP SITES

Yahoo, Music & Entertainment Directory, http://www.yahoo.com/Entertainment/Music.

Indiana University, http://www.music.indiana.edu/music_resources.

POPULAR SITES ON WHICH TO POST YOUR WEB PAGE:
Billboard's TalentNet, http://www.billboard.com/.

IUMA (Internet Underground Music Archive), http://www.iuma.com/.

Kaleidospace, http://www.kspace.com/.

RockWeb Interactive, http://www.rockweb.com/.

Ultimate Band List, http://www.ubl.com/.

MAJOR RECORD COMPANY SITES:
BMG, http://www.bmg.com/.

EMI-Capitol, http://www.emirec.com/.

Polygram, http://www.polygram.com/.

SONY Music Entertainment, http://www.sony.com/music/musicindex.htm.

Universal, http://www.mca.com/mca_records.

Warner Bros. Records, http://www.wbr.com/.

SOME INDIE RECORD LABEL SITES:
Delicious Vinyl, http://www.dvinyl.com/.

Knitting Factory, http://www.knittingfactory.com/.

Mammoth Records, http://www.mammoth.com/.

Higher Octave, http://www.higheroctave.com/.

Rykodisc, http://www.rykodisc.com/.

Rounder, http://www.harp.rounder.com/.

Ruffhouse, http://www.ruffhouse.com/.

INTERNET RADIO:
Broadcast.com, http://www.broadcast.com/.

Imagine Radio, http://www.imagineradio.com/.

Net Radio, http://www.netradio.com/.

RealNetworks, http://www.real.com/.

Rolling Stone Radio Network, http://www.rollingstone.com/.

Spinner.com, http://www.spinner.com/.

Virtual Radio, http://www.vradio.com/.

OnRadio, http://www.onradio.com/. A search engine hub that lets users find any station on the Net by call letters, format or location.

OTHER COOL MUSIC SITES
Daily Music & Entertainment Industry News
    http://www.newspage.yahoo.com/newspage/yahoo2/003idx.html.

    http://www.la.yahoo.com/external/hollywood/today_news.html.

    http://www.addict.com/html/lofi/MNOTW.

Music Resources on the Net
    http://sun.goddard.edu:80/students/wgdr/kalvos /musres.html#top.

Harmony Central, http://harmony-central.mit.edu/.

Liquid Audio, http://www.liquidaudio.com/.

Web Wide World of Music, http://american.recordings.com/wwwofmusic.

Music Business Solutions, http://www.mbsolutions.com/.

Indie Music Resources, http://www.kathoderay.org/music.

Digital Music Network, http://www.dmn.com/dmn.

Music News Agent, http://imusic.interserv.com/newsagent.

BUSINESS & MARKETING ON THE NET

Information and resources to help bring you up to speed on commercial use
of the Net.

The Internet Business Center, http://www.tig.com/IBC/index.html.

Cyberpreneurs Guide to the Internet, http://asa.ugl.lib.umich.edu/chdocs/
cyberpreneur/Cyber.html.

Techniques for Internet Acceptable Marketing & Advertising, http://arganet.
tenagra.com/net-acceptable.html.

PART FOUR:
staying fed

Books, Magazines & Journals, Organizations & Associations, and On-line Resources for:

- **All Musicians**
- **Music Performing & Recording Artists**
- **Music Composers & Songwriters**
- **Music Industry Careerists**
- **Music Technology Careerists**
- **Music Educators & Music Therapists**

There are THOUSANDS of music-related resources available, but alas, not all are created equal. The emphasis here is on those resources I believe are most helpful in the above-listed areas. General music and entertainment books, Web sites, magazines, etc. are not included except where relevant to the above purpose.

See www.mbsolutions.com for a continually updated version of this directory.

Resources for All Musicians

A. BOOKS

Baker, Bob. *One-Hundred One Ways to Make Money Right Now in the Music Business.* San Diego: Rockpress, 1993.

Levine, Mike. *How to Be a Working Musician: A Practical Guide to Earning Money in the Music Business.* New York: Billboard Books, 1997.

Rapaport, Diane Sward. *How to Make & Sell Your Own Recording: A Guide for the Nineties.* Englewood Cliffs, NJ: Prentice-Hall, 1998.

213

Baskerville, David. *The Music Business Handbook and Career Guide*. Second edition. Denver, CO: Sherwood Publishing, 1995.

Kimpel, Dan. *Networking in the Music Business*. Cincinnati: Writers Digest Books, 1993.

Clevo, Jim. *Networking in the Music Industry: Making the Contacts You Need to Succeed in the Music Business*. San Diego: Rockpress, 1993.

Coxson, Mona. *Some Straight Talk About the Music Business*. Toronto: CM Books, 1989.

Passman, Donald. *All You Need to Know About the Music Business*. Third edition. New York: Simon & Schuster Trade, 1997.

B. MAGAZINES AND JOURNALS

Billboard, 1515 Broadway, New York, NY 10036; 212-764-7300; http://www.billboard-online.com/. Weekly. Get it and study it!

Music Connection, 6640 Sunset Blvd., Suite 210, Hollywood, CA 90028; 213-462-5772. Focused on Los Angeles, but includes general articles as well.

Option: Music Alternatives, 1522-B Cloverfield Blvd., Santa Monica, CA 90404; 310-449-0120.

Rolling Stone, 1290 Avenue of the Americas, New York, NY 10104; 212-484-1616.

C. ORGANIZATIONS & ASSOCIATIONS

AFM (American Federation of Musicians), 1501 Broadway, Suite 600, New York, NY 10036; 212-869-1330. The number 1 musician's union in the United States.

American Music Conference, 5140 Avenida Encinas, Carlsbad, CA 92008; 619-431-9124. The American Music Conference (AMC) is the only national organization dedicated to the promotion of music, music making and music education to the general public. Major AMC initiatives include the National Coalition for Music Education and major public relations initiatives that reach hundreds of millions of individuals each year, furthering AMC's goal to build credibility for music and music education and to expand that portion of the population that enjoys and makes its own music.

The Good Road Network, 1201 First Avenue, Suite 304, Seattle WA 98134; 206-583-0838; http://www.GRN.net/. The main purpose of this organization is to provide affordable resources to the music community for purposes of promotion, performance and distribution of innovative music.

International Alliance for Women in Music, George Washington University, Academic Center B144, Washington, DC 20052. A coalition of professional composers, conductors, performers, musicologists, educators, librarians, and lovers of music.

D. ON-LINE RESOURCES (CAUTION: subject to change at the blink of an eye!)

Creative Musicians Coalition, http://www.aimcmc.com/. CMC is an international organization dedicated to the advancement of new music and the success of the independent musician.

Indie Centre, http://www.indiecentre.com. A well-organized site designed for musicians who want to retain control of their own careers.

Musician's Assistance Site (MAS), http://www.musicianassist.com/. A smorgasbord of links to on-line resources for developing artists.

Music Equipment Mail/Phone List, http://www.cis.ohio-state.edu/hypertext/faq/usenet/music/addresses/faq.html. This not only has addresses for major manufacturers, but also for mail-order companies.

Music Planet's Musicians Connection, http://www.music-planet.com/muscon/muscon.shtml. Free Web site of music-related classifieds. Lots of categories including Musicians Available, Musicians Wanted, and Instruments and Gear for Sale.

MusicPro, http://www.musicpro.com/. A good jump site to other music sites on the Web.

Musical Web Connections, http://www.columbia.edu/~hauben/music/web-music.html. Another great jump site for a tremendous variety of music-related sites.

Outer Sound, http://www.outersound.com/. An on-line community established to promote music created by and for independent-minded individuals. Provides information, research tools, news, educational resources, and communication capabilities to help you meet your music and business needs.

Ultimate Band List, http://www.ubl.com/. Offers links to information about any genre or style of music, and much more.

Resources for Music Performing & Recording Artists

A. BOOKS

Shagan, Rena. *Booking & Tour Management for the Performing Arts*. Second edition. Allworth Press, 1996.

Liz Garo. *Book Your Own Tour*. Second edition. San Diego: Rockpress, 1997.

MacLeod, Bruce. *Club Date Musicians: Playing the New York Party Circuit*. Champaign: University of Illinois Press, 1993.

Buttwinick, Marty. *How to Make a Living as a Musician So You Never Have to Have a Day Job Again!* Glendale, CA: Sonata Publishing, 1994. Great for general business music gig development.

Heflick, David. *How to Make Money Performing in the Public Schools*. Orient, WA: Silcox Productions, 1993.

Weissman, Dick. *Making a Living in Your Local Music Market: How to Survive & Prosper*. Milwaukee: Hal Leonard, 1989.

Clynes, Tom. *Music Festivals From Bach to Blues*. Farmington Hills, MI: Visible Ink, 1996.

The Musician's Atlas. Montclair, NJ: The Music Resource Group, annual.

Stanfield, Jana. *The Musician's Guide to Making and Selling Your Own CDs and Cassettes.* Writer's Digest Books, 1997.

The Musician's Guide to Touring & Promotion. Nashville, TN: Musician magazine, semi-annual. Also available on disk.

Shoemaker, Joanie, ed. *Note by Note: A Guide to Concert Production.* Oakland, CA: Redwood Cultural Work, 1989.

Gibson, James. *Playing for Pay: How to Be a Working Musician.* Writer's Digest Books, 1990.

Cunningham, Glen. *Stage Lighting Revealed: A Design & Execution Handbook.* Cincinnati: Betterway Books, 1993.

Kotler, Philip and Joanne Scheff. *Standing Room Only: Strategies for Marketing the Performing Arts.* Cambridge, MA: Harvard Business School Press, 1997. Resourceful but a bit on the academic side.

B. MAGAZINES
Alternative Press, 6516 Detroit Avenue #5, Cleveland, OH 44102; 216-631-1212.

Canadian Musician, Norris Publications, 23 Hannover Drive, St. Catherines, ON L2W 1A3 Canada; 905-641-3471; http://vaxxine.com/cm/.

CMJ New Music Monthly, 11 Middle Neck Road, Great Neck, NY 11021; 516-466-6000; http://www.cmjmusic.com/.

Gig Magazine, Miller Freeman PSN, Inc., 460 Park Avenue South, 9th Floor, New York, NY 10016; 212-378-0400.

Maximum Rock'N'Roll, P.O. Box 460760, San Francisco, CA 94146; 415-648-3561.

Music Connection, 6640 Sunset Blvd., Suite 201, Hollywood, CA 90028. Focused on Los Angeles but with general articles as well.

Performance, 1101 University, Suite 108, Fort Worth, TX 76107; 817-338-9444. Covers the touring industry.

Performing Songwriter, P.O. Box 158159, Nashville, TN 37215; 615-297-6972.

C. ORGANIZATIONS & ASSOCIATIONS

AFTRA (American Federation of Radio & Television Artists). Recognized as the union representing professional singers. It defines its jurisdictions as including "live and taped television, radio transcriptions, phonograph records and non-broadcast material." In addition to singers and actors, AFTRA's membership includes dancers, announcers, news reporters, sportscasters, sound effects people, and "specialty acts."

AFTRA-New York, 260 Madison Avenue, New York, NY 10016; 212-532-0800.

AFTRA-Hollywood, 6922 Hollywood Blvd., 8th Floor, Hollywood, CA 90028; 213-461-8111.

Chamber Music America, 545 Eighth Avenue, 9th Floor, New York, NY 10018; 212-244-2772. The organization of professional chamber music groups in the United States and Canada. It promotes the welfare of chamber music by advocating and coordinating funding for the field. It also serves in an advisory, informational, consulting, and referral capacity to professionals in the field and the interested public. Its publication is *Chamber Music Magazine*.

Creative Music Foundation, P.O. Box 671, Woodstock, NY; 914-338-7640. Sponsors and develops musical expression in all forms. Includes colloquia, workshops, seminars, residency programs, performances and artists management services. Publication: *Outlook, The Creative Music Quarterly* (free).

HEAR (Hearing Education & Awareness for Rockers), P.O. Box 460847, San Francisco, CA 94146; 415-441-9081; http://www.hearnet.com.

International Entertainment Buyers Association, P.O. Box 100513, Nashville, TN 37224; 615-259-2400.

International Fan Club Organization, P.O. Box 40328, Nashville, TN, 37204-0328; 615-371-9596. Clearinghouse for fan clubs that assists in the planning, setup, and operation of a fan club. Sponsors fan-artists tours and stages showcases for up and coming artists. Publication: *International Fan Club Organization.*

Musicians Contact Service, P.O. Box 788, Woodland Hills, CA 91365; 818-347-8888. A referral service for bands and musicians seeking each other.

Musicians National Hot Line Association, 277 East 6100 South, Salt Lake City, UT, 84107; 801-268-2000. Helping to increase the employment of musicians. Operates a telephone hotline, computer search file and newsletter to help musicians find bands and help bands find musicians. Publication: *Hot Line News*.

NACA (National Association of Campus Activities), 13 Harbison Way, Columbia, SC 29212-3401; 803-732-6222. A good organization to join if you're interested in performing on college campuses.

Society for Electro-Acoustic Music in the United States, 2550 Beverly Blvd., Los Angeles, CA, 90057; 213-388-0476. A non-profit organization interested in the composition and performance of fine arts electro-acoustic music.

D. ON-LINE RESOURCES (CAUTION: subject to change at the blink of an eye!)
The Deterrent DIY Tour Manual,http://www.islandnet.com/~moron /deterrent/tour_gd.html. Has listings of where to play and who to contact about playing all over the United States and Canada. Has most of the notable clubs listed with various musicians' comments about the clubs.

Listing of Open Musical Jam Sessions, http://www.cis.ohio-state.edu/hypertext/faq/usenet/music/jam-sessions/faq.html. This edition (4/97) of the list has been (1) sorted by State/Province/Country, (2) mostly tagged with musical genres to make searching a bit easier, (3) partially tagged with dates to help keep track of how current the various bits of information are.

A Nationwide List of Independent Record Stores, http://www.novia.net/~landphil/indies.html. Indie record stores, listed by state, where you can sell your records and tapes.

Pollstar, http://www.pollstar.com/. Pollstar is an industry trade publication that follows the national concert scene. Club owners subscribe to Pollstar to see what bands are planning to come to their city.

Resources for Music Composers & Songwriters

A. BOOKS

Kohn, Al and Bob Kohn. *The Art of Music Licensing.* Englewood Cliffs, NJ: Prentice Law & Business, 1994.

The Complete Handbook of Songwriting: An Insider's Guide to Making it in the Music Industry, Second edition. New York: NAL/Dutton, 1993.

Iossa, Lauren and Ruth Dreier. *Composers in the Marketplace: How to Earn a Living Writing Music.* New York: Meet the Composer, 1989.

Braheny, John. *The Craft & Business of Songwriting.* Cincinnati: Writers Digest Books, 1995.

Northman, Mark and Lisa Anne Miller. *Film & Television Composer's Resource Guide.* Milwaukee: Hal Leonard Publishing Corporation, 1998.

Lax, Roger and Frederick Smith. *The Great Song Thesaurus: Songs and Where They Come From.* New York: Oxford University Press, 1984. Lax and Smith organized their reference to cover 10,000 works spanning more than 400 years. Details are provided on the year the song was written, the writers, the various media sources (such as musical theater, radio, television, etc.), as well as brief narrative information introducing more recent years' works, with notes on how the music and the news interacted.

Fisher, Jeffrey P. *How to Make Money Scoring Soundtracks and Jingles.* Emeryville, CA: MIX Books, 1997.

Stone, Al. *Jingles: How to Write, Produce & Sell Commercial Music.* Cincinnati: Writers Digest Books, 1990.

Lissauer, Robert. *Lissauer's Encyclopedia of Popular Music in America 1888 to the Present.* New York: Paragon House, 1991. This reference contains information on 19,000 songs that have had major popular appeal. Specifically included is information on the composers and authors, the year the song was first written and became a hit, the performers, and incidental information such as any motion picture use or chart positions which may be significant, or multiple recordings by different performers. The information is sorted in three different ways, which facilitates the use of the book:

* alphabetic by song title;
* chronological by year; and
* alphabetic list by writers' names.

Faulkner, Robert R. *Music on Demand: Composers and Careers in the Hollywood Film Industry.* New Brunswick, NJ: Transactions Publications, 1982.

Whitsett, Tim. *Music Publishing: The Real Road to Music Business Success.* Emeryville, CA: MIX Books, 1997.

Karlin, Fred and Rayburn Wright. *On the Track: A Guide to Contemporary Film Scoring.* New York: Macmillan, Inc., 1990.

Roach, Martin. *The Right to Imagination & Madness: An Essential Collection of Candid Interviews with Top UK Alternative Songwriters.* London: Independent Music Press, 1994.

Jordan, Barbara L. *Songwriters Playground: Innovative Exercises in Creative Songwriting.* Boston: Creative Music Marketing, 1994.

Film, TV & Advertising Industry Guides:

Directors Guild of America Directory, Directors Guild of America, 7920 Sunset Blvd., Los Angeles, CA 90046; 310-289-2000. A directory of members, including contact info. If you are looking for a particular director, this is a great place to start.

Film/TV Music Guide, SRS Publishing, 800-377-7411. Excellent guide to film/TV departments at record labels, music publishers, music supervisors, and composer representatives.

Hollywood Blu-Book, 5055 Wilshire Blvd., Suite 600, Los Angeles, CA 90036; 213-525-2000. Published by the Hollywood Reporter, this is a virtual "Yellow Pages" for the entertainment industry. Includes an A-to-Z listing of individuals and organizations in film, television, music, and related services.

Hollywood Creative Directory, 3000 Olympic Blvd. Suite 2413, Santa Monica, CA 90404; 310-315-4815. Provides contact information and brief credit histories for major studios and film and television production companies.

Pilzer, Herbert R. *Motion Picture, TV and Theatre Directory.* New York: Motion Picture Enterprises Publications, Inc., semi-annual. This directory guide has a comprehensive index of production services and offers information about a wide variety of resources.

The SHOOT Directory for Commercial Production & Postproduction. BPI Communications, 1515 Broadway, New York, NY 10036, annual. Covers ad agencies, film commissions, interactive media, music production houses, and much more. To purchase copies of the SHOOT directory call 212-764-7300.

Horton, Tara A., ed. *Songwriter's Market.* Cincinnati: Writer's Digest Books, annual. Directory that goes beyond mere listings by providing annotations regarding kinds of music companies are looking for and tips for breaking in.

B. MAGAZINES
Advertising Age, 740 N. Rush Street, Chicago, IL 60611; 312-649-5200.

Film Music Magazine, Film Music Publications, 1146 N. Central Avenue #103, Glendale, CA 91202; 818-507-5377.

Millimeter—The Magazine of the Motion Picture and Television Industries, 826 Broadway, New York, NY 10003; 212-477-4700.

The Music Report. Attn: Adam Wolff, 1120 S. Robertson Blvd., Third Floor, Los Angeles, CA 90035; 310-276-9166. This biweekly publication is available to established music publishing companies and lists film, television, and multimedia projects currently seeking songs and original music.

New On the Charts, Music Business Reference, Inc., 70 Laurel Place, New Rochelle, NY 10801; 914-632-3349. Provides writer, publisher, performer, booking agent, producer and manager associated with all currently charting songs in *Billboard.*

Performing Songwriter, 6620 McCall Drive, Longmont CO 80503; 800-883-7664; http://www.performingsongwriter.com/. Internationally-distributed bimonthly periodical dedicated to the art of songwriting and the business of making music.

SHOOT: The Leading Newsweekly for Commercial Production & Postproduction. BPI Communications, 1515 Broadway, New York, NY 10036.

The Score, Society of Composers and Lyricists. 400 South Beverly Drive, Suite 214, Beverly Hills, CA 90212; 310-281-2812. Quarterly newsletter of the Society of Composers and Lyricists includes articles by and interviews with music industry professionals, as well as a calendar of upcoming industry events.

Songwriter's Monthly, 332 Eastwood Avenue, Feasterville, PA 19053; 800-574-2986.

Songtalk, National Academy of Songwriters, 6381 Hollywood Blvd., Suite 780, Hollywood, CA 90028; 214-463-7178.

Variety (Daily), 5700 Wilshire Blvd., Suite 120, Los Angeles, CA 90030; 213-857-6600. Variety is a prominent national trade publication that emphasizes films and television productions. Its Friday edition features film and television projects currently in production.

C. ORGANIZATIONS

NOTE: There are numerous regional songwriter & composer organizations, associations and workshops scattered throughout the United States and the world. See the annual *Songwriter's Market* (Writer's Digest Books) for one of the most complete listings anywhere.

American Association of Advertising Agencies, 666 Third Avenue, 13th Floor, New York, NY 10017; 212-MU2-2500. Trade association of approximately 650 member advertising agencies. Offers information and advice on all aspects of commercial production. Facilities include an extensive research library.

American Composers Alliance, 170 West 74th Street, New York, NY, 10023, 212-362-8900. Membership organization founded in 1937, representing over 300 American composers of concert music. Offers personal assistance for publishing, promotion, networking, licenses, contracts, royalties, copyrights, and more. Grants the annual Laurel Leaf award for "distinguished achievement in fostering and encouraging American music."

American Society of Music Arrangers and Composers, P.O. Box 11, Hollywood, CA, 90078; 213-658-5997.

American Society of Music Composers, P.O. Box 11, Hollywood, CA, 90028. Represents arrangers and composers with the AFM (American Federation of Musicians). Educates the public to the function of arrangers and composers. Promotes interaction between members through social functions. Presents the Golden Score Award for outstanding achievement.

American Society of Music Copyists, Box 2557, Times Square Station, New York, NY, 10108. A professional society of music copyists.

Association for the Advancement of Creative Musicians, Inc., P.O. Box 5757, Chicago, IL, 60680; 312-752-2212. Encourages the cultivation of musicians in order to create music of a higher level.

Composer's Recordings Inc., 73 Spring Street, Suite 506, New York, NY 10012-5800; 212-941-9673. A recording company whose mission is to produce high-quality sound recordings of performances of contemporary American works and to distribute mechanical royalties.

Film Music Network, 1146 N. Central Avenue #103, Glendale, CA 91202; 818-771-7778; http://www.filmmusic.net/.

International League of Women Composers, P.O. Box 670, 3 Mile Bay, NY 13693; 315-649-5086. Non-profit organization devoted to expanding opportunities for women composers of serious music. Promotes members' music through a tri-annual newsletter, concerts, a radio series and advocacy activities. Sponsors an annual Search for New Music by women student composers. Publication: *ILWC Journal.*

Meet the Composer (MTC), 2112 Broadway, Suite 505, New York, NY 10023; 212-787-3601. This organization fosters the creation, performance and recording of music by American composers and develops new audiences for contemporary music. Through its network of affiliates, MTC distributes composer grant funds and resource information nationwide.

MPA (Music Publishers Association), 130 W. 57th Street, New York, NY 10019; 212-582-1122; http://host.mpa.org/. Trade association for the music publishing industry.

Nashville Songwriters Association, Intl. (NSAI), 803 Eighteenth Avenue S, Nashville, TN 37203; 615-321-5004.

National Academy of Songwriters (NAS), 6255 Sunset Blvd. #1023, Hollywood, CA 90028; 213-463-7178 (call for chapter locations); http://www.nas-song.org/. A non-profit organization acting as a resource base for songwriters, putting them in contact with publishing companies and the industry. Offers educational workshops and printed materials. Offers legal help and collaborator matching services to help songwriters enter the industry.

PERFORMING RIGHTS SOCIETIES
ASCAP (American Society of Composers, Authors and Publishers), http://www.ascap.com/.

ASCAP—New York. One Lincoln Plaza, New York, NY 10023; 212-621-6000.

ASCAP—Los Angeles. 7920 Sunset Blvd., Suite 300, Los Angeles, CA 90046; 213-883-1000.

ASCAP—Nashville. Two Music Square West, Nashville TN 37203; 615-742-5000.   **225**

BMI (Broadcast Music International), http://bmi.com/. Performing Rights.

BMI—New York. 320 W. 57th Street, New York, NY 10019; 212-586-2000.

BMI—Los Angeles. 8730 Sunset Blvd., 3rd Floor, Los Angeles, CA 90069; 310-659-9109.

BMI—Nashville. 10 Music Square East, Nashville, TN 37203; 615-291-6700.

SESAC, http://www.sesac.com/.

SESAC—Nashville (headquarters). 55 Music Square, East Nashville, TN 37203; 615-320-0055.

SESAC—New York. 421 W. 54th Street, New York, NY 10019; 212-586-3450.

The Songwriters Guild of America, http://www.songwriters.org/new/home.htm. Association of 4,500 songwriters. Helps educate members and represents them in dealings with publishers and record companies. TSG provides copyright services and sample contracts. Publication: *AGAC News* (semi-annually, free)

West Coast office: 6430 Sunset Blvd., Suite 705, Hollywood, CA 90028; 213-462-1108.

East Coast office: 1500 Harbor Blvd., Weehawken, NJ 07087; 201-867-7603.

Nashville office: 1222 16th Avenue S, Nashville, TN 37203; 615-329-1782.

D. ON-LINE RESOURCES (CAUTION: subject to change at the blink of an eye!)
American Music Center, http://www.amc.net/. Classical/jazz archives, includes a list of composer organizations and contacts.

Cassette House, http://www.tape.com/. Blank cassettes, DAT tape, CDR's, books, videos and full songwriter services. On the net since '89!

Glade's Lyric Workshop Message Board, http://www.zapcom.net/~glade. A songwriter resource site with lots of on-line tools for the amateur and professional songwriter.

Harvestworks Composer Contact Service, http://www.avsi.com:80/harvestworks/ccs/ccs.html. Designed to connect composers with prospective collaborators in dance, as well as the film, video, radio and performance mediums. The program is currently housed in a stand-alone computer-based system, with digital sound files, biographical, and other descriptive text information in a cross-relational database.

Jeff Mallet's Songwriter Site, http://www.lyricist.com/. A huge directory of songwriter resources on the Web. Another great labor of love.

K & D's Music Resources for Composers, http://www.goddard.edu/wgdr/kalvos/musres.html. Helping to bring composers to the wider world through their music. Great links database for composers, radio show and much more.

Lyrical Line Songwriting Resources, http://www.lyricalline.com/. Offers places to market your songs, critique service, industry news and more.

The Muse's Muse: A Songwriter's Resource, http://www.musesmuse.com/. Articles, hints and advice for songwriters plus a wealth of links to other sites, including songwriter and industry associations.

NMPA's Music Links, http://www.nmpa.org/links.html. An assortment of Publishers, Organizations, Copyright, General Music Resources, Performers & Composers, On-line Publications, Labels, and Fun Stuff!

Songwriters Collaboration Network, http://websites.earthlink.net/~songmd. Consultant Molly-Ann Leikin's songwriter site offers lots of advice and information.

Songwriters Resource Network, http://www.songpro.com/. On-line information and services designed especially for songwriters.

TAXI, http://www.taxi.com. The independent A&R vehicle which helps unsigned bands, artists and songwriters get tapes directly to major record labels, music publishers and film/TV music supervisors.

United States Copyright Office, http://lcweb.loc.gov/copyright. Everything you wanted to know about copyrighting your tunes, plus downloadable copyright forms. You'll need the Adobe Acrobat Reader software to view and print the forms (available free at http://www.adobe.com/).

Resources for Music Industry Careerists

A. BOOKS

Avalon, Moses. *Confessions of a Record Producer: How to Survive the Scams and Shams of the Music Business.* San Francisco: Miller Freeman Books, 1998.

Brabec, Jeffrey and Brabec, Todd. *Music, Money & Success: The Insider's Guide to the Music Industry.* New York: Schirmer Books, 1994. Especially good on the music publishing industry.

Burnett, Robert. *The Global Jukebox: The International Music Industry.* New York: Routledge, 1996.

Dannen, Fredric. *Hit Men: Power Brokers and Fast Money Inside the Music Business.* New York: Vintage, 1991.

Goodman, Fred. *The Mansion on the Hill: Dylan, Young, Geffen, Springsteen, and the Head-On Collision of Rock & Commerce.* New York: Times Books, 1997.

Knoedelseder, William. *Stiffed: A True Story of MCA, the Music Business and the Mafia.* New York: Harper/Collins, 1993.

Haring, Bruce. *Off the Charts: Ruthless Days & Restless Nights Inside the Music Industry.* New York: Birch Lane Press, 1996.

Negus, Keith. *Producing Pop: Culture and Conflict in the Popular Music Industry.* New York: Routledge, 1993.

228

Chapple, Steve and Rebee Garafolo. *Rock'n'Roll is Here To Pay: The History &*

Politics of the Music Industry. Chicago: Nelson-Hall, 1978. An older work, but important in tracing the roots of current industry practices.

Eliot, Marc. *Rockonomics: The Money Behind the Music.* Revised edition. New York: Carol Publishing Group, 1993.

Wacholtz, Larry. *Star Tracks: Principles for Success in the Music & Entertainment Business.* Nashville: Thumbs Up Publishing, 1996.

Franscogna Jr., Xavier and H. Lee Hetherington. *Successful Artist Management.* Revised edition. New York: Billboard Books, 1998.

B. INDUSTRY DIRECTORIES

Billboard Directories (annuals), P.O. Box 2015, Lakewood, NJ 08701; 800-223-7524.
- International Talent & Touring
- International Buyer's Guide
- Record Retailing Directory
- Nashville 615/Country Music Sourcebook
- International Recording Equipment & Studio Directory
- International Latin Music Buyer's Guide

Performance Guide Series (annuals), 1101 University, Suite 108, Fort Worth, TX 76107; 817-338-9444.
- Facilities
- Talent/Personal Managers
- Manufacturers/Production Personnel
- Promoters/Clubs
- Booking Agencies
- International Markets
- Country Talent/Variety
- Concert Production
- Transportation/Accommodations

The Recording Industry Sourcebook, 6400 Hollis Street, Suite 12, Emeryville, CA 94608-9889; 800-472-7472.

Taylor, Barbara. *National Directory of Record Labels & Music Publishers.* Atlanta, GA: Rising Star Music Publishers, 1996.

Phonolog, 10996 Torreyana Road, San Diego, CA 92121; 619-457-5920.

Europop Book: International Rock & Pop Music Directory (available in the United States through the MIX Bookshelf catalog, 800-233-9604).

Australasian Music Directory, in the United States: 310-659-0596; http://www.immedia.com.au/amid/index.html. Covers Australia and Pacific Rim countries.

C. MAGAZINES

Billboard, 1515 Broadway, New York, NY 10036; 212-764-7300; http://www.billboard-online.com/. Weekly. Get it and study it!

Cashbox, 6464 Sunset Blvd., Suite 605, Hollywood, CA 90028; 213-464-8241; Weekly.

CMJ New Music Report, 11 Middle Neck Road, Great Neck, NY 11021; 516-466-6000. Weekly college radio and alternative music tip sheet.

Entertainment Law & Finance, 345 Park Avenue S, 8th Floor New York, NY 10010; 800-888-8300.

The Gavin Report, 140 Second Street, San Francisco, CA 94105; 415-495-1990; http://www.gavin.com/. Weekly listing of radio charts.

Hollywood Reporter, 5055 Wilshire Blvd., 6th Floor, Los Angeles, CA 90036; 213-525-2000. Covers news regarding U.S. and international developments in the entertainment industry. Often prints special supplements on events or topics of special interest including periodic features on film and television music. The Tuesday edition features a list of film and television projects currently in production.

Internet World, Mecklermedia Corp., 20 Ketchum Street, Westport, CT 06880; 203-226-6967.

Music Business International (MBI), U.S. office: 460 Park Avenue South, 9th Floor
  New York, NY 10016; 212-378-0406. Monthly.
Music Merchandise Review, 100 Wells Avenue, Box 9103, Newton, MA 02159.

Pollstar, 4333 North West Avenue, Fresno, CA 93705; 800-344-7383.

Radio & Records, 10100 Santa Monica Blvd., 5th Floor, Los Angeles, CA 90067;
  310-553-4330.

Variety, 5700 Wilshire Blvd., Suite 120, Los Angeles, CA 90036; 213-857-6600.

D. ORGANIZATIONS & ASSOCIATIONS

NOTE: Web site addresses are included where available. There are also numerous genre-specific and regional organizations. Please consult *The Recording Industry Sourcebook* or *Yellow Pages of Rock* for a fairly comprehensive listing.

AFIM (Association for Independent Music), 601-482-8999; http://www.afim.org/. Formerly NAIRD. An international organization of independent record companies, wholesalers, and retailers which provides legal assistance and acts as a go-between with major retail record chains and the music unions. Sponsors the Indie Awards.

AMC (American Music Conference), 303 E. Wacker Drive, Suite 1214, Chicago, IL 60601; 312-856-8820; http://www.amc-music.com/. This service organization distributes music-industry information to amateur musicians and encourages their participation in various musical activities. Its supporters include record companies, ASCAP and BMI, and radio and television networks.

American Mechanical Rights Agency, Inc., 333 South Tamiami Trail Suite 295, Venice, FL 34285, 813-488-9695. Issues mechanical licenses to record companies on behalf of its composers and publisher members. Collects and distributes royalties from record sales.

CPM (Conference of Personal Managers), 964 Second Avenue, New York, NY 10022; 212-421-2670.

Harry Fox Agency, c/o National Music Publishers' Association, 711 Third Avenue, 8th Floor, New York, NY 10017; 212-370-5330. Issues mechanical licenses on behalf of members. Collects from record companies and distributes to members. Issues synchronization licenses for many members.

MPA (Music Publishers Association), 130 W. 57th Street, New York, NY 10019; 212-582-1122; http://host.mpa.org/. Trade association for the music publishing industry.

NAMM (National Association of Music Merchants), 5140 Avenida Encinas, Carlsbad, CA 92008-4391; 619-438-8001; http://www.namm.com/. Members are musical instrument stores and their suppliers.

NAPAMA (National Association of Performing Arts Managers & Agents), 137 East 30th Street, Suite 3B, New York, New York 10016-7333; 212-683- 0801; http://www.napama.org/.

NARM (National Association of Recording Merchandisers), Three Eves Drive, Suite 307, Marlton, NJ 08053; 609-596-2221; http://www.narm.com/. NARM members are retailers, rack jobbers, one stops, independent distributors, independent record labels, and major labels and distributors of recorded entertainment products, including music and video. NARM sponsors annual promotions in support of various televised awards shows such as the American Music Awards, the Grammy's, the Soul Train Music Awards, the Academy of Country Music Awards, the Gospel Music Association Dove Awards, the MTV Video Music Awards, and the Country Music Association Awards. NARM hosts a large annual convention, various conferences and conducts research projects.

NARAS (National Association of Recording Arts & Sciences), offices in New York, Chicago, Atlanta, San Francisco, Nashville, Burbank and Memphis. New York: 212-245-5440; http://grammy.com/.

NMPA (National Music Publishers Association), 205 E. 42nd Street, New York, NY 10017; 212-370-5330; http://www.nmpa.org/.

RIAA (Recording Industry Association of America), 1330 Connecticut Avenue NW, Suite 3000, Washington, DC 20036; 202-775-0101; http://www.riaa.com/.

The Recording Industry Association of America is a trade group whose member companies create, manufacture and/or distribute more than 90 percent of all legitimate sound recordings sold and produced in the United States. The mission of the RIAA is to protect and defend artistic freedom; promote strong intellectual property protection; combat record piracy; expand market access opportunities worldwide; meet the challenges of technology; facilitate the development of voluntary industry standards; and foster awareness of industry issues and products. The RIAA also administers the Gold, Platinum, and Multi-Platinum Awards Program. Publishes the "Statistical Overview and Annual Report" each Spring. Available for FREE with a phone call.

TEIA (Touring Entertainment Industry Association), 1203 Lake Street, Fort Worth, TX 76102; 817-338-9444.

United States Copyright Office, Library of Congress, Washington, DC, 20559, 202-707-3000; Forms Hotline: 202-707-9100. Provides blank copyright forms of all types. Provides booklets explaining copyright topics. Current fee for each copyright submission is $20 but a planned increase for 1999 is in the works.

VLA (Volunteer Lawyers for the Arts), Main office: 1285 Avenue of the Americas, New York, NY 10019; 212-977-9270. Has branch offices in most major cities.

E. ON-LINE RESOURCES (CAUTION: subject to change at the blink of an eye!)
1212, http://www.1212.com/. European music industry directory

All Music Guide (AMG), http://www.allmusic.com/index.html. An encyclopedic database of music. Includes artist biographies, album reviews, and fully cross-referenced discographies that allow the user to browse from artist to artist.

Ari's Simple List of Record Labels, http://www.geocities.com/Hollywood/Academy/2899/index.html. Don't let the name fool you; this is a fairly comprehensive list of labels with Web sites.

Indie Label List, http://www.cs.ucl.ac.uk/external/T.Wicks/ill. The list contains label names, addresses, and other details. Perhaps more importantly, it also contains comments about the labels to give the reader some idea of the range of material a label has released, it's genre and ethos.

Music Business Search Engine, http://www.mbig.com/.

Music Yellow Pages, http://www.musicyellowpages.com/. Manufacturers, wholesalers, distributors and nationwide services.

Webnoize, http://www.webnoize.com/. On-line publication that monitors the effect of Internet technologies on the music industry.

World Access to Music Merchandising, http://www.exposhow.com/wamm/wammhp1.htm. Listings of manufacturers, merchandisers, and distributors of instruments, clothing, and other music related items.

Worldwide Internet Music Resources, "The Commercial World of Music," http://www.music.indiana.edu/music_resources/industry.html.

Resources for Music Technology Careerists

A. BOOKS

Burgess, Richard James. *The Art of Record Production.* New York: Omnibus Press, 1997.

Souter, Gerry. *Buying and Selling Multimedia Services.* Boston: Focal Press, 1997.

Hill, Brad. *Going Digital: A Musician's Guide to Technology.* New York: Schirmer Books, 1998.

Music Producers: Conversations With Today's Top Record Makers. Editors of Mix Magazine. Emeryville, CA: Mix Bookshelf, 1992.

Drews, Mark. *New Ears: The Audio Career & Education Handbook*, Second edition. Syracuse, NY: New Ears Productions, 1993.

Mandell, Jim. *The Studio Business Book.* Second edition. Emeryville, CA: Cardinal Business Media, 1996.

Wadhams, Wayne. *Sound Advice: The Musician's Guide to the Recording Studio.* New York, Schirmer Books, 1990.

Eargle, John. *Handbook of Recording Engineering.* Third edition. Hingham, MA: Chapman & Hall, 1996.

Peter, Mclan and Larry Wichman. *The Musician's Guide to Home Recording,* Revised edition. Los Angeles: Music Sales Corp., 1994.

Trubitt, David, ed. *Concert Sound: Tours, Techniques & Technology,* Lewiston, NY: Music Book Plus, 1993.

Hunter Stark, Scott. *Live Sound Reinforcement.* Lewiston, NY: Music Book Plus, 1996.

Pohlmann, Ken C. *Principles of Digital Audio,* Third edition. McGraw-Hill, 1995.

Peterson, George and Steve Oppenheimer. *Tech Terms: A Practical Dictionary for Audio & Music Production.* Milwaukee: Hal Leonard Publishing Corp., 1993.

Josephson, Hal and Trisha Gorman. *Careers in Multimedia: Roles and Resources.* Pacific Grove, CA: Brooks/Cole Publishing, 1996.

B. MAGAZINES AND JOURNALS

Computer Music Journal, MIT Press, P.O. Box 14043, Santa Barbara, CA 93107; http://www-mitpress.mit.edu/Computer-Music-Journal.

Electronic Musician, Cardinal Business Media, 6400 Hollis Street, Suite 12, Emeryville, CA 94608.

Recording, 7318 Topanga Canyon Blvd. Canoga Park, CA 91303.

ProSound News, 2 Park Avenue, Suite 1820, New York, NY 10016-9301.

Mix Magazine, 6400 Hollis Street, Suite 12, Emeryville, CA 94608.

Producer Report, 115 S. Topanga Canyon Blvd., Suite 114, Topanga, CA 90290-3141; http://www.mojavemusic.com/.

Wired, 520 3rd Street, 4th Floor, San Francisco, CA 94107-1815. Documenting the Digital Revolution from all angles.

C. ORGANIZATIONS

AES (Audio Engineering Society), 60 E 42nd Street #2520, New York, NY 10165; 212-661-8528; http://www.aes.org/. Promotes research and commercial interests of designers, manufacturers, buyers, and users of professional and semiprofessional audio equipment. Two annual AES trade shows (United States/Europe) display most current makes and models of audio equipment.

CEG (Consumer Electronics Group), 2001 I Street NW, Washington, DC 20006; 202-457-4919.

EIA (Electronic Industries Association), 1901 Pennsylvania Avenue, NW, Washington, DC 20006; 202-457-8700.

HRRC (Home Recording Rights Coalition), 1145 19th Street NW, Box 33576, Washington, DC 20033; 800-282-TAPE.

IDSA (Interactive Digital Software Association), 1130 Connecticut Avenue, NW, Suite 710, Washington, DC 20036; 202-833-4372.

International Computer Music Association, 2040 Polk Street Suite 330, San Francisco, CA, 94109. An international affiliation of individuals and institutions involved in the technical, creative and performance aspects of music. It serves composers, computer software and hardware developers, researchers and musicians who are interested in the integration of music and technology. Publication: *Array* (Quarterly)

ITA (International Tape/Disc Association), 505 8th Avenue, Flr 12-A, New York, NY 10018; 212-643-0620.

IICS (International Interactive Communications Society), 2120 Steiner Street, San Francisco, CA 94115; 415-922-0214.

International MIDI Association, 5316 West 57th Street, Los Angeles, CA, 90056; 213-649-6434. Promotes and spreads information about electronically produced music. Provides technical support for hardware and software users of MIDI.

MIDI Manufacturers Association, 2265 Westwood Blvd. #2223, Los Angeles, CA 90064; 213-649-MIDI.

SPARS (Society of Professional Audio Recording Studios), 4300 10th Avenue N, Suite 2, Lake Worth, FL 33461-2313. SPARS is a non-profit professional trade organization that unites the manufacturers of audio recording equipment and services with users. SPARS membership includes prominent recording studios, individual engineers and producers, production houses, post production facilities, manufacturers of professional audio recording equipment, schools, colleges, studio designers, leasing companies, and persons who serve the audio recording industry.

D. ON-LINE RESOURCES (CAUTION: subject to change at the blink of an eye!)
4-Track FAQ, http://www.winternet.com/~dfrankow/4trakfaq.txt.

Digital Sound Page, http://www.xs4all.nl/~rexbo/index.htm.

Harmony Central, http://www.harmony-central.com/. A great music jump site with a leaning toward music technology and gear.

Home Recording Rights Coalition, http://www.hrrc.org/. The HRRC is a coalition of consumers, consumer groups, trade associations, retailers and consumer electronics manufacturers, dedicated to preserving your right to purchase and use home audio and video recording products for noncommercial purposes.

The MIDI Farm Internet, http://www.midifarm.com/. Another jump site to MIDI and Digital Audio sites on the Net.

Music & Audio Connection, http://maac.com/music. File libraries, classifieds, event schedules, career info, and discussion forums.

Music Machines, http://www.hyperreal.com/music/machines. A site dedicated to music-making machines (like synths, drum machines, etc.).

237

On-Site Entertainment Meta Index, http://www.ose.com/ose/meta.html.

Pro Audio Network, http://proaudio.net/. A site for pro audio, including job listings, classifieds, and links. Many portions seem to be under construction as of April '97.

Producer Report, http://www.mojavemusic.com/; E-mail: mojave@sprynet.com. The only global producer newsletter plus access to industry and producer-related resources.

Sites and Sound Links, http://www.servtech.com/public/koberlan. Another great music tech-oriented jump site.

The World Wide Web Virtual Library: Audio, http://www.comlab.ox.ac.uk /archive/audio.html. A site containing general repositories of music samples, newsgroups, on-line radio, software as well as other relevant information and items.

Resources for Music Educators & Music Therapists

A. BOOKS

Hylton, J. B. *Comprehensive Choral Music Education.* Englewood Cliffs, NJ: Prentice-Hall, 1993.

Bruner, J. *The Culture of Education.* Cambridge, MA: Harvard University Press, 1996.

Newsam, Barbara and David Newsam. *Making Money Teaching Music.* Cincinnati: Writers Digest Books, 1995.

Haitun, Rosalie A. *Music Teacher's Survival Guide: Practical Techniques & Materials for the Elementary Music Classroom.* West Nyack, NY: Parker Publishing Co., 1994.

Bunt, Leslie. *Music Therapy.* New York: Routledge, 1994.

Alvin, Juliette. *Music Therapy for the Autistic Child*. New York: Oxford University Press, 1992.

Campbell, P. S., et. al. *Roots and Branches: A Legacy of Multicultural Music for Children*. Danbury, CT: World Music Press, 1994.

Bond, J. *Share the Music*. New York: MacMillan/McGraw-Hill School Publishing, 1995.

Gardner, Kay. *Sounding the Inner Landscape: Music As Medicine*. New York: Element Books, 1997.

Leonhard, C. *Status of Arts Education in American Public Schools: Report on a Survey Conducted by the National Arts Education Research Center at the University of Illinois*. Urbana, IL: Council for Research in Music Education, 1991.

Brown, Joseph D. *Strategic Marketing for Music Educators*. Gemeinhardt Co., 1985. A bit academic but full of useful insights.

Ortiz, John M. *The Tao of Music: Sound Psychology*. York Beach, ME: Samuel Weiser, 1997.

B. MAGAZINES AND JOURNALS

American Music Teacher, 617 Vine Street, Suite 1432, Cincinnati, OH 45202; 513-421-1420.

Bulletin of the Council for Research in Music Education, School of Music, University of Illinois, 1114 W Nevada, Urbana, IL 61801; 217-333-1027.

Journal of Music Therapy, 845 Colesville Road, Suite 930, Silver Springs, MD 20910.

Music Educators Journal, 1806 Robert Fulton Drive, Reston, VA 22091-4348; 703-860-4000.

School Music News, 151 Sweetwater Hills Drive, Hendersonville, NC 28739.

C. ORGANIZATIONS

American School Band Directors Association, P.O. Box 146, Otsego, MI 49078; 616-694-2092. Members: 1.3 million. Hold annual meetings in June.

Association of Concert Bands, 2533 South Maple Avenue, Suite 102, Tempe, AZ 85282; 800-726-8720. Members: 750. Dedicated to the advancement of community and concert bands.

Canadian Music Educators Association, 16 Royaleigh Avenue, Etobicoke, Ontario, Canada M9P 2J5; 416-244-3745. News, reviews, classroom techniques for the music educator. Developments in music education, national, provincial and from the International Society for Music Education.

The College Music Society, 202 W. Spruce Street, Missoula, MT 59802; 406-721-9616. This organization provides a forum for the exchange of ideas within the academic music profession. Its most important publication is the Directory of Music Faculties in Colleges and Universities.

American Association for Music Therapy, P.O. Box 80012, Valley Forge, PA 19484; 215-265-4006. Certified music therapists and schools offering music courses are represented.

Music Alliance, 1180 6th Avenue, New York, NY 10036; 212-730-9626. Encourages and promotes classical music to elementary schools.

Music Educators National Conference, 1902 Association Drive, Reston, VA 22091; 703-860-4000; http://www.menc.org/. Facilitates communication between Music Educators National Conference and the industry.

Music Teachers National Association, 617 Vine Street, Suite 1432, Cincinnati, OH 45202; 513-421-1420. Professional society of music teachers. Bestows awards and sponsors competitions.

National Band Association, P.O. Box 121292, Nashville, TN 37212; 615-343-4775. Sponsors clinics and other educational functions for band directors.

D. ON-LINE RESOURCES (CAUTION: subject to change at the blink of an eye!)

American Music Therapy Association, http://www.musictherapy.org/. AMTA was founded in 1998, its purpose is the progressive development of the therapeutic use of music in rehabilitation, special education, and community settings. AMTA is committed to the advancement of education, training, professional standards, credentials, and research in support of the music therapy profession.

Carney, Sandoe & Associates (CSA), http://www.csa-teach.com/. CSA is an educational consulting firm recruiting teachers and administrators for placement in private, independent schools across the United States and abroad. Schools look to them to help them find top teachers and administrators for their position openings. Schools, never candidates, pay the fee for their services.

Internet Resources for Music Teachers, http://www.isd77.k12.mn.us/resources/staffpages/shirk/music.html. Valuable jump site for music educators and students of all areas and educational levels

Music Education Resources @ Kelleyworld, http://www.hcca.ohio.gov/kelleysworld/index2.htm. Links to hundreds of sites of interest to music educators.

Music Therapy Info Link, http://members.aol.com/kathysl/index.html. Designed to be a place to gather information, help open the lines of communication and networking, and educate the public about the field of music therapy.

Private lessons.com, http://www.privatelessons.com/. Find a teacher, post/update a resume.

Virtual Music Classroom, http://cnet.unb.ca/achn/kodaly/koteach. Oriented to music instruction for kids, with tips for effective teaching.

Want Some Free Music Career Juice?

Visit the Music Business Solutions Web site at **www.mbsolutions.com** for updates to the Musician's Resource Directory as well as informative articles, a free subscription to the newsletter "Music Biz Insight," and MORE!

Here's what others around the world are saying:

Your site put relevant business information into a tangible form that makes it useful for business music professionals.

Eternal success, JaWar, Recording Artist/CEO

As a regular reader of your Music Biz page, I must thank you for creating such an informative newsletter. I am a percussionist, a manager of Western Australian acoustic acts and a music management lecturer at the WA School of Art Design and Media Music Industry Skills course. When I commence classes, I will be directing my students to your page as well as your book titles.

All the best,

Scott Adam, Perth, Western Australia

This has got to be the most interesting and informative electronic magazine that I have seen on the music business. Keep up the good work.

Regards,

Richard Bassett, Bermuda

I just found your Web site and wanted to give you heaps of praise. It's excellent! Very informative while presenting issues in a clear, focused language. I cannot thank you enough for providing all of us prospective music business managers with this information. Again, thanks for the site, the good work, and I'm sure you are receiving very good karma for this service.

Tom Garretson, Oslo, Norway

You have a very valuable site for the working musician.

Thanks,

Peter & Ellen Allard

PETER SPELLMAN

Peter Spellman is Director of the Career Development Center at Berklee College of Music and the author of several handbooks on the music business. He has over twenty years' experience as a performing and recording musician and is also founder of Music Business Solutions (**www.mbsolutions.com**), a business and marketing consultancy for independent musicians and music businesses. In addition, Peter teaches courses on entrepreneurship and the recording industry at both Northeastern University and the University of Massachusetts-Lowell.

a2b (AT&T), 194
ABC, 180
Abdul, Paula, 16
accountants, 12–13
Ace of Base, 11
Act! software, 88, 95, 132
advertising, co-op, 105
advertising agencies, 100
advertising industry resources, 220–26
Aerosmith, 11
AFM. See American Federation of Musicians
agents, booking, 78, 103–105, 126, 129
alcohol, legislation on, 93–94, 103
Alligator Records, 62, 63
alternative music, 62
ambient music, 11
America Online (AOL), 184, 195, 205
American Federation of Musicians (AFM), 111
American Society of Composers, Authors and
    Publishers. See ASCAP
American Symphony Orchestra League, 10
Anderson, Laurie, 169
answering machines, 56
AOL. See America Online
AOR (album-oriented rock) stations, 149
Apple IIe, 162
AppleWorks, 55
apprenticeships, 42
A&R (Artists and Repertoire)
    departments, 7, 78
    sending demos to, 127
Arbitron, 147, 149, 159
Armed Forces Radio, 17
arts management, 127
ASCAP (American Society of Composers, Authors
    and Publishers), 223–24
Assignment Editor, 134–35
associations
    joining, 73
    lists of, 214–15, 218–19, 223–25, 231–33,
    236–38, 240
    multimedia, 177
    researching, 95, 97, 132
attitude, positive, 87
audience
    defining, 29, 131–32, 139
    fan lists, 88, 120, 190, 191
    for interviews, 142–43
    radio, 148, 149
    repertoire and, 126–27
    surveys, 99

audio books, 11

"baby-boomers," 93
background music, 11
Bacon's Publicity Checker, 134
band meetings, 50
BandHost, 196
banners, 119
"barter calls," 188
Beat, The, 132
Beatles, the, 11, 66, 174
benefits, playing, 89–90
Bernstein, Elmer, 171
Bertlesman Group. See BMG
Better Business Bureau, 114
Billboard charts, 11, 61–62
billboards, 133
bios (biographies), 80, 140, 155
Black Flag, 169
Black Top Records, 63
"block bookings," 101
blues, 63
BMG (Bertlesman Group), 3, 17
BMI (Broadcast Music
    Incorporated), 224
booking research worksheet, 95, 96
Borders Books & Music, 90
Broadcast Music Incorporated. See BMI
Broadcast.com, 159
Broadcasting Yearbook, 118
Brooks, Garth, 11
Brooks, Joseph, 66
Brown, Bobby, 16
bulk-mailing permit, 119
business cards, 73, 80, 94, 100, 120, 135, 204
business communications, courses on, 13
business events, 97
business letters, 43, 94
business planning and organization, 21–46
    components of, 24–26
    professional help for, 37–41
    readiness assessment, 42
    for record labels, 65–67
    resources for, 34–36, 42, 44–46
business structures, 26–27
Buziak, Bob, 7–8

cable television, 10
calendars, year-at-a-glance, 50, 132, 139–40

"call hours," 157

Capitol-EMI Music, 3

Carey, Mariah, 12

Casablanca Records, 61

Cassette House, 128

cassette tapes. See also demo tapes
    packaging and preparing, 79, 128–29,
      136
    selling at gigs, 120
    sending to radio stations, 153

caterers, 100

CBS, 17

CD-I, 16

CD-R (recordable compact discs), 14

CD-ROMs, 167, 192
    soundtracking for, 170
    voice-overs in, 172

CDs. See compact discs

CEMA/UNI Distribution, 3

censorship issues, 18

Chancellor Media, 147, 149

Chess Records, 61

Chumbawamba, 150

classical music, 10

club owners, 78, 109, 126, 148

clubs
    anti-drinking legislation and, 93–94, 103
    booking dates in, 103–107, 126
    changing scene, 93
    contests in, 105
    guest lists for, 105, 141
    liability insurance for, 93–94

CMJ Music Marathon, 72

Coda, 132

college work, 100–101, 109–10

CommerceNet, 182

commercials, 10, 128

communication skills, 50, 67, 94

compact discs (CDs), 13, 136
    selling at gigs, 120
    sending to radio stations, 153, 155

competition profiles, 29

composers, multimedia, 169–70, 171, 173

composers' resources, 218–19

compression/decompression schemes, 168, 186

"comps," 84

CompuServe, 184, 195

Computer Game Developer's Conference, 174

computers. See also Internet; software culture of,
    168
    desktop technologies, 179–80

filing tips on, 53
interactivity and, 16, 169
as management tools, 51–53, 55,132,
    154
multimedia, 162
peripherals for, 55–56
training on, 13
web page design on, 195

Computers Simplified, 55

Connick, Harry, Jr., 90

consumption, musical, 9–11

contact information, 127–28, 129,
    136, 137, 202

contacts, 50–51, 71–74. See also networking
    following up, 120, 141–42
    log of, 74
    as recipients of press kits, 78, 132

"contract face," 111

contracts, 94, 95, 104, 109–15, 131
    advantages of, 109
    checklist for, 110
    legal disputes, 111
    with major labels, 8–9
    riders for, 111
    sample, 113

conventions
    attending, 72–73, 174, 177–78
    playing, 97–98, 101

"convergence," 164–66, 168, 179–80

CoolEdit software, 197

copyright, 18

corporate videos, 11

corporations
    standard or C, 27
    subchapter S, 27

country clubs, playing, 98

country music, 11, 61, 62

"courtesy signing," 8

cover letters, 79–80, 94, 153, 155

"covers," 125, 126

Cowles/Simba Information, 193

Cramps, The, 131

creativity, 100, 127

cruise lines, 98, 100

Cruise Lines International Association (CLIA), 98

cumulative trauma disorders (CTDs), 58

CUSeeMee, 192

customer service policy, 30, 32

cybercafés, 192, 202

DATs. See digital audio tapes

Davis, Miles, 187

DCCs. See digital compact cassettes

demo tapes, 94, 135
    customizing, 125–29
    for multimedia, 172–73, 174
    preparing, 79, 127–29, 136
    where to send, 126–28

demographics, 93, 147, 159

deRose, Gene, 179

desktop publishing, 14, 82–83, 94, 129

digital audio tapes (DATs), 13, 153

digital compact cassettes (DCCs), 13

digital compression, 10

"digital revolution," 179–80

digital tools, 14–15

digital transmission of music, 64, 167–68

Dion, Celine, 187

direct marketing, 63, 133

Dirty Linen, 158

Discmakers, 79, 128

disco, 61

Disney, 180

distribution, music, 3–4, 14, 28, 147, 149, 180
    alternatives to record stores, 63–64
    consolidation of, 63–64
    independent, 18, 194
    methods of, 30

DJs (disc jockeys), 88, 147, 149, 150
    playlists of, 188
    response cards for, 81

do-it-yourself recording, 14–15, 61–68

Dolby, Thomas, 169

domain names, 195–96

Downbeat, 132

dress, stage, 120

dressing room, 117, 120

duplication, tape, 79, 128

Earthlink, 195, 204

eclecticism, 18

editorial calendars, 134, 142

education
    adult and continuing, 13, 73
    multimedia in, 162, 173

educational videos, 11

Edward Lowe Foundation, 45

Electronic Entertainment Expo (E3), 174

Elfman, Danny, 171

e-mail, 137, 187–88, 192

EMI, 66

Emmis Communications, 149

"emotional bushwhacking," 24

Encyclopedia of Associations, 95

entrepreneurship, 23, 27, 45–46.
    See also business planning and
    organization

Epic Records, 7

Epstein, Brian, 66

equipment, 32, 64
    insurance for, 32, 110

ergonomics, 58

Events Planners, 98

Everything (band), 192

facilities, 32, 58, 64

Fairfield Research, 193

FAQ messages, 201

fax machines, 55–56, 58, 137

Feistmant, Eric, 55

Fiesta, 12

FileMaker Pro software, 95

filing systems, 52–53, 132

film, music in, 10, 171

film resources, 220–26

financial information and projections, 33–34

"flames," 201

flyers, 118, 119, 135, 140–41, 204

folk music, 62, 63

follow-up, 73, 120, 141–42, 155

Ford Foundation, 22

Fractal Painter software, 174

Friend Planet, 16, 173

Frith, Simon, 179

furniture, office, 58

"fuzak," 63

Gabriel, Peter, 169

Gale's Directory of Publications and Broadcast
    Media, 118, 134

Geocities, 196

Getting Noticed: A Musician's Guide to Publicity and
    Self-Promotion, 144

Gibson, James, 144

gigs
    booking, 103–107, 120
    finding, 93–102
    maximizing, 117–21
    schedules, 80, 119, 188, 202

giveaways, 158

globalization, 3–4, 12, 17–20

goals
setting, 22, 140
writing down, 22–23
Goldmine software, 88
golf courses, 98
"grace and favor deal," 8
Graham, Ian, 196
Grammy awards, 63
grant opportunities, 65, 173
"graphic ambassadors," 77, 89, 135, 140, 155
graphic artists, 83–84
Green Day, 11
Green Linnet, 63
greeting cards, 11
Grove, Andy, 184
growth and expansion plans, 32
grunge, 11
guest lists, 105, 141

Harvard Business School, 41
Heartbeat Records, 132
heavy metal, 11
Heflick, David, 101
HiJaak Pro software, 195
hip-hop, 11
home studios, 14–15, 18
HomePage software, 197
homogenization of music, 17
Hot Bot, 186
hotels, 100
How to Get a Job with a Cruise Line, 100
How to Make Money Performing in Public Schools, 101
HTML Sourcebook, 196

Iglauer, Bruce, 62
iMac, 15
Imagine Radio, 159
"immersive media," 166
income flow in record industry, 19
independent labels, 3, 13, 194.
See also record companies
starting your own, 61–68
industrial dance, 63
Industrial Revolution, 170
information
controlling, 192
interviewing for, 42
revolution in, 42, 51–52

technology, 180
insurance
equipment, 32, 110–11
liability, 93–94, 110
Intel, 184
IntelliQuest, 199
Intermedia, 174
Internal Revenue Service, 27
Internet, 179–209
advantages of, 182–84
bulletin-board posting, 187, 190
censorship issues, 18
chat rooms, 187
commercial on-line services, 184, 205
copyright issues, 18
cultures on, 186, 187
domain names on, 195–96
downloadable sound files, 197
e-commerce, 182–84, 189–91
e-mail, 187–88, 192
FTP function, 197
getting started on, 202–205
HTML (hypertext markup language), 194, 195, 196–97, 199, 203
impact of, 179–82
increasing traffic and hits on, 203–204
mailing lists, 187–88, 201
marketing and promotion on, 133, 186–94, 200, 202–204
maximizing on-line presence, 204
music services on, 18
myths about, 184, 186
"netiquette" on, 186, 201
networking on, 73, 173
newsgroups, 187, 191, 201
on-line music delivery, 194
presence providers on, 203
radio, 149, 158–59, 194
record sales on, 193–94
resources, 206–209, 215–16, 219–20, 226–28, 233–34, 237–38, 241
search tools, 186
service providers (ISPs), 187, 192, 195–96, 203, 204–205
site hosts, 196, 203–204
statistics of, 182–84
web page design, 194–99, 203
World Wide Web, 14–15, 133, 182,185, 188
Internet Advertising Bureau, 182
Internet Café (London), 192
Internet Explorer, 195
internships, 42
interviews, 136, 140, 142–43
invitations, 140
Irving/Almo Music Publishers, 127
Island Records, 64

I-Tribe, 192
IUMA (Internet Underground Music Archive), 197, 203

Jackson, Janet, 16
Jackson, Lucious, 90
Jackson, Michael, 11
Jane's Addiction, 150
Japan, music consumption in, 10
jazz, 10, 132
Jazz World Database, 132
Jazziz, 132
Jewel, 187
jingle houses, 128
John, Elton, 187
Jupiter Communications, 179, 193

Kaleidospace, 203
Kelly, Mark, 192
Kinko's, 80
Koch Germany, 12
Korn (band), 192
Kwatinetz, Jeff, 192

Lant, Jeffrey, 144
lawyers, 12–13, 112, 114–15
    entertainment, 127
Lemay, Laura, 196
letter writing for business, 43
libraries, buy-out, 172
libraries, public, 88, 95, 97, 118, 134, 153
licensing, music, 11
lighting, office, 58
Liquid Audio, 194, 197
logos, 79, 135, 155
Lowe, Edward, 45
LucasArts, 174
Lugosi, Bela, 131
lyric sheets, 127–28

M Street Radio Directory, The, 134
Macey Lipman Marketing, 193
Macromedia Director software, 174
Madison, John, 149
Madison Project (IBM), 194
Madonna, 16, 169
magazines, 133, 134
    lists of, 214, 217–18, 222–23, 230–31,

235–236, 239
mailing envelopes, 78, 94, 135
mailing lists, 87–89
    fan lists, 88, 140, 190, 191
    industry list, 88–89
    Internet, 187–88, 201
    media list, 87–88, 132, 139, 153
management
    artist/band, 48–49, 127–28
    keys to success in, 57
    self-, 47–59
    skills for, 48–51
    time, 54
    tools for, 51–56
management consultants, 37–46
management description, 26
managers, 104
Mango, 132
Maran, Richard, 55
Marcelo Productions, 98
Marillion (band), 192–93
marketing
    courses on, 13
    direct-mail, 63, 133
    Internet, 186–94, 200, 202–204
    mix, 30, 202–203
    niche, 12, 29, 63, 139, 189
    plan, 28–32
    research, 28–29, 103, 153
    target, 126–27, 129, 150, 153, 200
    time/money marketing continuum, 31
Marketing departments, 7
Maximum Rock N Roll, 158
MCA Records, 4
McLuhan, Marshall, 161
MDs. See mini-discs
media, choices in, 132–35
Media Lab, 164
"media mix," 30, 202–203
media technology, 180
Meeting Professionals International Directory, 98
merchandising, 120
Metallica, 11
"Microcosmos," 173
Microsoft, 180
Microsoft Works software, 55
MIDI software, 11, 188
Midnight Oil, 150
Miller, Mary Fallon, 100
Milli Vanilli, 16
miniaturization of music-making, 13–15
mini-discs (MDs), 13

modems, 52, 56, 195

Moore, Peter, 7

Morricone, Ennio, 171

Moskowitz, Robert, 48

Mouse Up Productions, 192

MP-3 format, 13, 186, 196, 197

MPCs. See multimedia personal computers

MTV, 15–16, 17, 134–35

multimedia, 161–78
    breaking into, 172–74
    business markets, 128, 162, 164, 180
    career opportunities in, 169–72
    challenges in, 167–69
    computers and, 52–53
    convergence in, 164–66
    developers, 173
    home market, 162, 164
    industry segments, 162, 164
    interactive, 16, 161, 169
    meaning of, 161
    resources for, 176–77
    school market, 162, 164
    top producers of, 175
    video game producers, 162, 163, 175

multimedia personal computers (MPCs), 162

Municipal Executive Directory, The, 98

Music Boulevard, 193

Music Business Solutions, 38, 242–43

music business trends, 3–20

Music Director (radio), 78, 149, 150

music educator resources, 228–34

music industry career resources, 234–38

music technology career resources, 234–38

music therapy resources, 238–41

music videos, 15–16, 81

musical theater, 128

Musicland, 90

music-making. See also performing
    globalization of, 17–20
    increasing demand for, 9–11
    increasing diversity of, 11–12
    miniaturization of, 13–15
    professionalization of, 12–13
    sensualization of, 15–16, 120

Naisbett, John, 66

National Association of Collegiate Activities (NACA), 100–101

National Science Foundation, 173

Negroponte, Nicholas, 164

NEMO (New England Music Organization), 72

Netcom, 195, 204

"netiquette," 186, 201

Netscape, 195

Netshow, 197

Nettwerk, 63

networking, 11, 42, 71–75, 87, 100, 120, 157, 173–74

"networking," 50

new age music, 63

new economy, the, 42

New Power Generation Records, 193

newspapers, 133, 134

"newsworthy," 136

niche markets. See marketing

Nielsen Media Research, 182

nightclubs. See clubs

Nintendo, 162

Nirvana, 11

non-profit organizations, 97

novelties, promotional. See promotional novelties

Office Depot, 58, 139

office supplies, 58, 64, 78–79

opera, 10

operations plan, 32

O-Positive (band), 7

Option, 158

oral agreements, 109

organization, 48, 132

organizations. See associations

oversight, 48, 50

Page Spinner software, 197

PageMaker software, 94

PageMill software, 197

Paper Direct, 78, 82

Pardekooper, Kelly, 21

park programs, playing, 98

partnerships
    general, 27
    guidelines for creating and maintaining, 67
    limited, 27

party organizers, 78, 100

"payola," 147, 149

Pearl Jam, 11

Pelletier, Jeff, 192

performance critique worksheet, 99

performers, multimedia, 171

performing

critique of, 99
finding gigs, 93–102
stage presence, 118, 129

performing musician resources, 216–20

performing rights, 10, 225–28

peripherals, computer, 55–56

perseverance, 66, 141, 174

photos, 79, 94, 118–19, 135–36, 140, 155

Photoshop software, 174

Pink Floyd, 81

point-of-sale systems, 62

"political signing," 8

pop music, 11

"positioning," 29

postcards, 118, 140

posters, 89, 118, 135, 140–41

Powell, Tony, 4

Premier software, 174

Presley, Elvis, 11

press (promo) kits, 77–84, 89, 94, 202
components of, 78–81
designing, 82–84, 135
preparing, 136–37
where to send, 78

press releases, 80–81, 135, 136–37, 140
on Internet, 188, 190

pricing philosophy, 30

Prince, Artist Formerly Known as, 193–94

printers and printing, 55, 82–83.
See also desktop publishing

Priority Records, 63

private parties, 100, 126

Prodigy, 184

professionalism, 12–13, 94–95

"profit-centers," 23

Program Director (radio), 150

program guides, radio, 134

project description, 26, 28

project management, 48–51

project time line, 33

promotion. See also press kits; publicity
Internet, 186–94
radio, 158
resources on, 213–16
setting goals for, 84, 140

promotional novelties, 81, 89, 135, 155

ProShip Entertainment, 98

"public relations exercise," 8

public relations firms, 100, 105

public service announcements (PSAs), 135

publicists, 144–45

publicity
creating waves of, 139–41
determining targets for, 131–35
exchanges, 157
hooks, 136
organizing a schedule for, 139–40
planning, 104, 118–19, 131–46
resources for, 143–45
tools for, 135–36, 139

Publicity Builder software, 144

Publish It! software, 94

publishing, electronic, 166

publishing, music, 10, 28
sending songs to, 127–28

QuickTime3 software, 197

Quill Office Supply, 78

Quinn, Mark, 39

radio
business structure of, 147, 149, 151
college, 90, 104, 137, 147–59
DJ response cards, 81, 155, 156
DJs, 88, 147, 149, 150, 188
formats in, 148, 152
giveaways on, 158
in-station performances, 90, 157
Internet, 149, 158–59, 194
mail-outs for, 153, 155
maximizing airplay on, 155, 157–59
phone logs for, 153, 154
promoters for, 158
promotion on, 104–105, 119, 133, 134, 140, 158
publicity exchanges, 157
reporting stations, 153
satellite, 149
song requests on, 120, 157
trades, 159–60
trends in, 147–49

"radius clause," 110

rap, 11, 61, 62, 63

RCA, 7–8, 17

RealAudio, 194, 196, 197

record companies and industry. See also
independent labels
globalization of, 3–4
growth in sales for, 9
income flow in, 19
inner dynamics of, 4–8, 28
multinational makeup of, 4–5
repositioning of, 14, 15, 61–62
sending demos to, 127

record stores, performing in, 90

recordable compact discs. See CD-R

recording artist resources, 214–18

Recording Industry Association of America (RIAA), 9, 10

Recording Industry Sourcebook, The, 89, 132, 153, 158

Redmond, John, 127

reggae, 61, 97, 132

Reggae Ambassadors Worldwide, 132

Reggae Quarterly, The, 132

Reggae Report, 132

rehearsals, 118

REM, 150

repertoire, 126

"reporting stations," 153

"repurposing," 23

"request schedule," 157

reviews, 80–81, 136, 141–42, 155

Rhymes, Busta, 187

Rhythm Music, 158

RIAA. See Recording Industry Association of America

risk assessment, 32

rock, 11, 62

rock 'n' roll, 61, 63

Rolling Stone Radio Network, 159

Rollins, Henry, 169

Rollins Band, The, 169

Rolodex cards, 80, 132

royalties, 193

Ruffhouse Records, 63

Rundgren, Tod, 169

Sam Goody stores, 90

SBA. See Small Business Administration

SBDCs. See Small Business Development Centers

SBIs. See Small Business Institutes

"schlager" folk music, 12

schools
    multimedia in, 162, 173
    playing in, 100–101

SCORE. See Service Corps of Retired Executives

Sega, 162, 169, 174

segmentation, market, 11–12, 62–63

self-management, 47–59

Service Corps of Retired Executives (SCORE), 25, 35, 39

SESAC (Society of European Stage Authors and Composers), 224

Shanachie Records, 132

Shapiro, Jake, 41

"shotgunning" tapes, 87, 129

Sigerson, Davitt, 64

signature files, 201

Simba, 184

Small Business Administration (SBA), 25, 37–38, 47, 65

Small Business Development Centers (SBDCs), 25, 28, 35, 38, 55

Small Business Institutes (SBIs), 39–40
    publications of, 40–41

small business resources, 37–46

small claims court, 111

"small office, home office" (SOHO) trend, 37

Smashing Pumpkins, 150

Smith, Joe, 3

Snoop Doggy Dog, 11

societies. See associations

Society of European Stage Authors and Composers. See SESAC

software
    contact management, 88, 95, 132, 154
    desktop publishing, 94
    graphics, 14, 195, 197
    integrated programs, 55
    MIDI, 11
    multimedia, 174
    publicity, 144
    video games, 11, 162, 163, 175
    Web authoring, 195, 196–97
    Web browsers, 195

sole proprietorships, 27

song lists, 81

Songwriter's Market Guide to Song & Demo Submission Formats, The, 128

songwriters' resources, 220–21

Sonic the Hedgehog, 169

Sony Music Entertainment, 3, 5, 12, 17

Sound Forge XP software, 197

sound producers, 170–71

Soundata, 193

sound-effects specialists, 171

SoundScan, 62

South-by-Southwest music conference, 72

"spamming," 201

Spinner.com, 159

Springsteen, Bruce, 11

Staples, 58, 139

stationery. See office supplies

storage, digital, 167–68

streaming audio, 158–59, 186, 188, 194, 196–97

student activities directors, 78, 101

studio sessions, 126–27

"success," definitions of, 22

summary statement, 26

Sun Records, 61

"sweat equity," 32

symphony orchestras, 10

table tents, 89, 119

Tahiti, 18

target marketing. See marketing

"taste cultures," 10

taxes, 26, 27

Teach Yourself Web Publishing with HTML in a
    Week, 196

technology, 14–15, 180. See also specific tools
    resources, 232–36
    speed of change in, 181

Telecommunications Act of 1996, 147

telephone
    cold-calling techniques, 103–105
    contact logs, 153, 154
    systems, 56, 58

television
    interactive, 162
    music in, 10, 171
    on-air promotion, 133, 134–35
    resources, 220–26

Tetris, 169

Thailand, 18

thank-you letters, 120, 141, 157

Thorn-EMI, 17

time management, 54

Touch 'n' Go, 63

Touchbase Pro software, 132

touring, 18, 188

tourism, 18

Tower Records, 90

trade shows, 101, 174, 177–78

trademark search, 115

Tragically Hip (band), 193

T-shirts, 120, 135

Two Ton Shoe (band), 41

U2, 150

Unabashed Self-Promoter's Guide, The, 144

"uniqueness," 127

Universal Music Group (UMG), 3, 17

urban music, 62

Usenet, 187, 201

UUNet, 195, 204

Vega, Suzanne, 90

verbal agreements, 104

versatility, 125–27

Viacom Corp., 17

video games, 11, 162, 163, 175

videoconferencing, 166, 192

videos, music. See music videos

vinyl records, 153

Virtual Promote, 202

virtual reality, 16

voice artists, 170, 172

voice-overs, 172

Volunteer Lawyers for the Arts (VLA), 112

Warner Communications, 15, 16, 193

Warner-Elektra-Atlantic (WEA), 3, 17

Wax Trax Records, 63

WebTV, 180

weddings, playing, 125, 126

Williams, John, 171

Williams, Lucinda, 7–8

word processor services, 79–80

"working the crowd," 120

world music, 17–18, 62, 63

World Wide Web. See Internet

Yahoo, 186, 196

Yellow Pages, 79, 81, 83, 88, 89, 97, 98

Yellow Pages of Rock, The, 81, 89, 132, 134, 153, 158

Yes (band), 187

"You Light Up My Life," 66

zydeco, 11

THE BEST OF BERKLEE PRESS

GUITAR

Guitar Books by William Leavitt

Berklee Basic Guitar - Phase 1
0-634-01333-5 Book $7.95

Berklee Basic Guitar - Phase 2
0-7935-5526-4 Book $7.95

Classical Studies for Pick-Style Guitar
0-634-01339-4 Book $9.95

A Modern Method for Guitar

Volume 1: Beginner
0-87639-013-0 Book/CD $22.95
0-87639-014-9 Book $14.95

Volume 2: Intermediate
0-87639-016-5 Book/CD $22.95
0-87639-015-7 Book $14.95

Volume 3: Advanced
0-87639-017-3 Book $14.95

1-2-3 Complete
0-87639-011-4 Book $29.95

Melodic Rhythms for Guitar
0-634-01332-7 Book $14.95

Reading Studies for Guitar
0-634-01335-1 Book $14.95

Advanced Reading Studies for Guitar
0-634-01337-8 Book $14.95

Jim Kelly Guitar Workshop Series

Jim Kelly's Guitar Workshop
0-7935-8572-4 Book/CD $14.95
0-634-00865-X DVD $29.95

More Guitar Workshop
0-7935-9454-4 Book/CD $14.95
0-634-00648-7 VHS $19.95

Voice Leading for Guitar: Moving Through the Changes by John Thomas
0-634-01655-5 Book/CD $24.95

The Guitarist's Guide to Composing and Improvising by Jon Damian
0-634-01635-0 Book/CD $24.95

BASS

The Bass Player's Handbook by Greg Mooter
0-634-02300-4 Book $24.95

Chord Studies for Electric Bass by Rich Appleman
0-634-01646-6 Book $14.95

Reading Contemporary Electric Bass by Rich Appleman
0-634-01338-6 Book $14.95

Rock Bass Lines by Joe Santerre
0-634-01432-3 Book/CD $19.95

Slap Bass Lines by Joe Santerre
0-634-02144-3 Book/CD $19.95

KEYBOARD

Solo Jazz Piano by Neil Olmstead
0-634-00761-0 Book/CD $39.95

Hammond Organ Complete by Dave Limina
0-634-01433-1 Book/CD $24.95

A Modern Method for Keyboard by James Progris
0-634-01329-7 Vol. 1: Beginner
0-634-01330-0 Vol. 2: Intermediate
0-634-01830-2 Vol. 3: Advanced
Book $14.95 (each)

DRUMS AND PERCUSSION

Beyond the Backbeat by Larry Finn
0-634-00701-7 Book/CD $19.95

Brazilian Rhythms for Drum Set and Percussion by Alberto Netto
0-634-02143-5 Book/CD $29.95

Drum Set Warm-Ups by Rod Morgenstein
0-634-00965-6 Book $12.95

Mastering the Art of Brushes by Jon Hazilla
0-634-00962-1 Book/CD $19.95

The Reading Drummer by Dave Vose
0-634-00961-3 Book $9.95

Rudiment Grooves for Drum Set by Rick Considine
0-87639-009-2 Book/CD $19.95

SAXOPHONE

Books by Joseph Viola

Creative Reading Studies for Saxophone
0-634-01334-3 Book $14.95

Technique of the Saxophone
0-7935-5409-8 Volume 1: Scale Studies
0-7935-5412-8 Volume 2: Chord Studies
0-7935-5428-4 Volume 3: Rhythm Studies
Book $14.95 (each)

TOOLS FOR DJs

Turntable Technique: The Art of the DJ by Stephen Webber
0-87639-010-6 Book/2-Record Set $34.95
0-87639-038-6 DVD $24.95
0-87639-039-4 VHS $24.95

Turntable Basics by Stephen Webber
0-634-02612-7 Book $9.95

WWW.BERKLEEPRESS.COM   866-BERKLEE